Contents

Introduction

"Truth be known, that's one of the reasons I'm getting out. It's all too PC.
I came in to be in an organization with a clear mission policy and a focus on
individual and unit efficiency (although at the time, I didn't know that).
Now, the focus is what you say, how you say it, and to whom do you say it.
Whatever happened to simply training Marines? And how in the hell did we
ever get stuck in this mire?"
—S.Sgt. Charlotte Crouch, USMC, age thirty, April 1998, Okinawa, Japan

Five or ten years from now, if we find ourselves in an air and ground war with Iraq or North Korea or somebody else we haven't noticed yet, and we get utterly whipped, you can blame Presidents George Bush and Bill Clinton, Secretaries of Defense Richard Cheney, Les Aspin, and William Cohen, the Congresses who wrote and passed the bills they signed, and the Pentagon leadership who just grinned nervously and sat on their hands while all of this was going on.

For the last ten or so years the legislative and executive branches have cynically, knowingly used the armed forces mainly as a political symbol to shuffle around the globe in a show of "readiness" and "force," as if the people making up those forces were toy soldiers without bodies and lives and minds. With a few exceptions, the big boys (and a few big girls) expressed their disinterest in the hearts and minds of soldiers, sailors, Marines, and airmen in various ways during the last half of the nineties: by sending a force cut by nearly half since the eighties to carry out missions that have increased 300 percent in frequency over the last decade; by asking soldiers to act, as one senator put it, like "international social workers giving rabies shots to dogs in Bosnia and picking up garbage in Haiti," then expecting them at the flick of a switch to morph right back into full Sergeant Fury warrior mode.

They allowed military pay to slip 14 percent behind civilian pay (at a time of greatly increased op-tempo and high civilian employment), cut pension benefits, and spent money that could have gone to nuts-and-bolts stuff on weapons and bases that even the Pentagon says it does not need.* They tolerated a surreal level of bureaucratic bloat while people on the ground couldn't find parts for their trucks and planes, and they set down Draconian social policies without showing any interest in—and in many cases actively suppressing—good-faith information about how those policies were playing out at ground level.

What all of this feckless policy signaled to the rank and file was that they were, in effect, leaderless; drifting toward war—already occupied with quasi-wars, wanna-be wars, scattered around the globe—with leaders whose attention was . . . elsewhere . . . anywhere, everywhere, else but on their troops and their welfare and readiness.

One of the projects mesmerizing the brass throughout the nineties was the integration of women. If they'd thought about this and kept their eyes on the readiness, war-fighting ball, things might have worked out OK. Instead, the nineties were a decade in which the brass handed over their soldiers to social planners in love with an unworkable (and in many senses undesirable) vision of a politically correct utopia, one in which men and women toil side by side, equally good at the same tasks, interchangeable, and, of course, utterly undistracted by sexual interest.

Certainly, women have been in the forces since . . . well . . . forever, and certainly, their numbers and options have been growing steadily, too. But something new happened in the nineties in respect to the way the military handled "women's issues." For reasons this book will explore, their goals changed from making good use of the relatively small numbers of women the military had been attracting over the years, to achieving what President Clinton and Secretary of the Army Togo West have called "a force that looks like America." Certainly, there has always been a political subtext around anything to do with women and the military, but in the nineties it took precedence. To bring in more women the services doubled recruiting budgets and retooled advertising campaigns. In 1991 the Marine slogan "We're

---

*As of this writing, the defense appropriations bill for 2000 contains provisions to hike pay and undo the pension rate cuts. The president supports these provisions, so it looks like some relief is on its way—but only after midlevel leaders were finally able to persuade Congress and DOD that their men and equipment were coming apart at the seams.

looking for a few good men" was replaced by "The Few, the Brave, the Marines." The big drive has brought the percentage of female recruits from 12 percent a decade ago to about 22 percent today; in a decade the female percentage of the forces has gone from 11 percent to about 15 percent. In 1994, laws and policies were changed so that in each of the services today, only a few job categories are still closed to women.

Recruiting "goals"—or, to use the Army's term, *a recognition of gender* in selection decisions—in search of "proportional representation" for women operated in the seventies and eighties, but for reasons I will discuss later, the military brass's interest in numbers became an obsession, a kind of madness. In the midnineties, a young Marine officer named C. J. Chivers, who left the corps after eight years and is now a reporter for the *New York Times*, found that recruiting nineties style was about "chasing the slide":

> We had to get numbers; if you didn't, you were in professional trouble. Basically it was a sales culture: "If you don't meet this minimum—I'm not going to use the word *quota*—but if you don't meet this minimum number of recruits, then we're going to mark up your career." . . . Invariably we would fill up the white male quotas almost immediately, usually by Christmas, because there were so many college students who wanted to be pilots or Marines. Then we'd work for the next five or six months filling the other positions. In the meantime people stacked up wanting to get one of those white male slots. I'd have twenty to thirty people for the one remaining job on a waiting list.
>
> So it became any woman who came in there that met the minimums, we gotta hire. What that did was take all the subjectivity out of it. I couldn't say, "I got a bad vibe." The subjective part of the evaluation is normally enormous. If I went to them and said, "Hey, yank this guy's application. I don't trust him," without question they'd dump his application.
>
> Basically, the attitude [about female applicants] was "Get 'em on the plane." If there were any problems, boot camp could sort it out. My boss would go through my schedule and say, "What are you doing to hire a junior female?" and then he would basically say, "Get her no matter what!" The mentality became "Smooth out the snags."

With more women coming in and moving up, the last all-male bastion had to make a decision. Assuming they were now committed to creating a force that looked like America, would they ask women to change themselves to fit into military culture and infrastructure, or would the institution change itself to ensure that women came and stayed? The significant fact about the nineties is that after decades of operating on the first premise, the institution became convinced it had to adopt the latter. For one senior Army officer who's served since the early eighties, the old attitude was something like "Let's just treat 'em the same; you gotta join us, these are the requirements: You gotta run, you gotta jump, you gotta fight; you shoot, move, and communicate. . . ." In the nineties, he says, that has shifted to "What can we do so we can join you?"

In other words, the "Old Military" said, "Here's the way we do things; we do things this way because we think they are morally right and because centuries of experience have told us they work. You can come with us, but you may have to change yourself to do things the way we do." Whereas now the official line is something like "We want you to join us; we want you to stay with us. Tell us what you don't feel 'comfortable' with so we can change it."

In decades past, without the hard-sell recruiting drive we have now, women joined the military because they loved its values, its traditions, its bloody triumphs, and the try-again quality it has always shown in defeat. They loved its guns and ships and tanks and men and its no-bullshit, shut-up-and-do-it culture. In general, they didn't join to be political symbols. Sometimes money was a factor, but amazingly often they really did join "to serve [their] country." There are still many women like this serving, and they are as appalled as the men by the changed values of what is often called the "New Military."

For reasons to be discussed later, the brass were so frantic for "numbers," and photo ops featuring women with stars on their sleeves, that they actually began to undercut the pillars—trust, fairness, stoicism, and a concern for "the unit" over oneself—on which a successful military stands. The thinking seemed to be "If the warrior culture frightened away women, then the warrior culture had to be changed," and over the decade, in hundreds of ways little and big, it was. The new policies big and small "have rendered a ready room atmosphere so different now that it is nearly unrecognizable," according to former F-18 pilot Robert Stumpf. "The emphasis has shifted dramatically from how to administer death and destruction to the enemy, to how to 'get along,' and how to prevent killing each other in the air. Pilots are hampered in their ability to train as warriors by the policies of their senior leaders."

It is a common lamentation. The author of a poignant essay entitled "We Came Here to Be Soldiers, Sir" grieves that he has lived to see "war-fighting marginalized" in his "beloved Army."

In the chase for women and to cajole them along once they managed to bag a few, the obsequious services (less so the Marines) allowed double standards (de facto, de jure) to influence everything from recruiting, to basic training graduation, to moral conduct, to promotion qualifications. Women were allowed to come into basic training at dramatically lower fitness levels and then to climb lower walls, throw shorter distances, and carry lighter packs when they got there.

In the Gulf War, physical disparities were often glaring: Men in many units took over tearing down tents or loading boxes because most of the women simply couldn't or wouldn't do these chores as fast. Moral standards were double-tracked, too, with women being able to do things that would (and did) get men court-martialed.

One of the worst examples of a military working desperately to be "female friendly" appears in an Army War College monograph by Lt. Col. Donald E. Fowler II. He describes arriving in Saudi Arabia as part of Desert Shield/Storm, finding that some of his female troops were sent home because they were pregnant, and discovering later that they "were allowed to wear a combat patch on their right sleeve and were awarded the Southwest Asia Service Medal, even though they had avoided combat and served in Saudi Arabia for a few weeks."

Perhaps the worst thing was what former Army Spec. Catherine Aspy called "the 1984 feeling, the totalitarian feel, the doublethink, how one's leaders seemed able to tell you two contradictory things and then, if they were called on it, deny the contradiction, like when they represented women as weak and exploited victims on the one hand, and as an all-powerful mighty force on the other, and then say it's an 'insult to imply that women aren't identical to men.'"

This de facto gag rule was worse around the subject of gender integration. Everyone knew someone who'd been fired or penalized in some way for saying something incorrect about the way the integration project was going. Women had become "the third rail"; not wanting to risk saying "the wrong thing," commanders who were having troubles with their new mixed-sex units simply shut their mouths or used approved language with extraordinary care.

The really sad thing, of course, is that it never had to be like this. If we had had sensible, plainspoken, morally courageous leaders, we could have had a force that continued to be appreciative of the women who are currently serving and the women who qualify to serve, without alienating (and in too many cases actively persecuting) the men who make up—and will always make up—the majority of the armed forces. We could have opened new positions for women when it was sensible to do so and discouraged overt antifemale hostility (in the pockets where it can be found) without imposing a kind of totalitarian blackout on reasonable criticism of gender-integration policies, without practicing a kind of doublethink that said, "Everything's great," when often, sometimes right in front of a CO's eyes, it was not.

I never expected to find myself writing about the military, but the politically driven "reformation" of the American military during the last decade is one of those stories that just stand there blocking your path until you have done their bidding, which means attempting to tell the story as fully and honestly as you can, given constraints of time (the story had to be told *soon*) and the often secretive, disingenuous, dissembling ways of the people who control access to troops, bases, and military records.

I remember the day I got an inkling that something strange was going on in our armed forces. It was 1995—embarrassingly late in the day to be getting this inkling, but there it is. I'd just called Army public relations to check a fact in an article I was writing. When I told the officer (most public relations people in the services are military officers) that I was doing a story on "sexual integration in the military," there was an awkward silence and then a strained laugh. "The term we use now," the Pentagon flack finally said primly, "is *gender integration*."

It was a small moment—as telling moments often are—but I suddenly felt I had drawn aside a curtain and come face-to-face with what is often called the "New Army."

As a magazine and newspaper journalist, I'd been writing a lot about various species of political correctness through the late eighties and early nineties, but I'd always thought of the U.S. military as unassailable, off the radar screen of politically correct–dom's most hawk-eyed enforcers, insulated in a cocoon of bureaucracy and tradition from the clamor outside its gates.

Well, actually, it's more accurate to say I'd hardly ever stopped to think about folks in uniform. I spent my elementary school years in a college town where nobody went off to the Vietnam War. The armed forces were just cardboard characters who made occasional appearances in grade-school history or civics textbooks.

The last relative I knew of who'd had any connection to the U.S. military had been my grandfather, who'd driven an ambulance in World War I. When World War II rolled around, my dad, then too young and nearsighted for U.S. Navy ships, became an oiler in the U.S. Merchant Marine, which was usually convoyed by the U.S. Navy in the war years. Most of his war stories, however, were about what he did after he left the Merchant Marine to sail with the nascent Israeli Navy, on the ships owned by the Haganah, an underground movement that, in violation of a Royal Navy blockade, ferried European Jews to the tiny strip of desert land that would become Israel.

Until I worked on my first gender-integration-in-the-military story, I'd never even knowingly met a real American soldier. (I had the typical condescending view I once saw in a guest at a dinner party, who dismissed a bright young Army lieutenant by saying, disdainfully after he'd left, "Yes, he was surprisingly thoughtful and articulate for someone from *West Point*." West Point, which had, that year, a lower acceptance rate than Harvard! West Point, a school where the students actually collect a salary while they attend!

During the Vietnam years the only soldier-age men in my hometown of Ann Arbor, Michigan—then a cauldron of leftist politics—were college boys who were trying to dodge the draft assisted by girlfriend aides-de-camp, who pitched in with marches and leaflets and occasionally—like my baby-sitter, who, unbeknownst to my mother, had joined the Weatherman Underground—homemade bombs.

Dismantling the war machine was the most exhilarating action around in a college town like Ann Arbor. "The Movement," as it was called, was the local version of the beach, the place to meet and mingle. Drawn by the heat, fecklessly and ignorantly, in the way of recruits since time immemorial, I enlisted in the antiwar army's preteen brigade. My "service" basically featured a lot of marching—stowing away on a D.C.-bound bus to add my body to the crowds milling around the Washington Monument, or skipping sixth-grade classes to clump along with the rest of the barefooted brigade, chanting, "Ho Ho Ho Chi Minh! NLF is gonna win!"

Who the hell was this dude Ho? I didn't have a clue, but the chant had a good rhythm; you could march to it.

The point I am trying to make is that by the midseventies one of the ugliest trends of our time—the split between "elite" civilians and their military and the consequent onset of what Phillip Gold, an essayist and former Marine, called "military illiteracy"—was firmly in place, made even worse by the availability of student draft deferments that exacerbated the cultural chasm and turned whole cities (like Ann Arbor) into "military-free zones."

The war that interested people in Ann Arbor was the one supposedly perpetrated by men against women. People in Ann Arbor actually believed that sex differences were a conspiracy driven by something called the Patriarchy, and that our town was the Brave New World where everyone would (if they knew what was good for them) become interchangeable, androgynous—which generally meant that men were supposed to get out of the way so that women could run pretty much everything.

When I finally got out of Ann Arbor, I felt impelled to spend a big part of the next two decades (in between attempting to make a living) writing about the strange—and often very funny—sexual politics mutations that were moving from cities like Ann Arbor into the national bloodstream. Accusations of something called "date rape" were dividing campuses. Antioch College in Ohio had gone ahead and, in all seriousness, published a how-to-have-sex-"correctly" policy for their students. Lawyers had been promoting a new legal concept called "hostile environment" sexual harassment, and litigation over this vaguely worded charge was beginning to appear.

Naturally my antennae began to quiver in 1991 when the news stories about the 1991 Tailhook Association annual symposium started coming out. For the dedicated student of sexual politics, this story—even though it was located in that distant continent called the military—gave off many of the same vibes as the sexual politics stories I'd done before.

It was lurid enough, but I didn't think it would come to much. I was sure the imbroglio would stay self-contained, that it was an aberration the powerful military immune system could neutralize.

Yeah, right. It soon became clear that the whole service was, in fact, in a rictus of political correctness, that it was going through an anguished self-examination, particularly over the issue of "gender"— an antiseptic word popular because it is more sexless, less dangerous, than the word *sex*. It seemed the American military had begun a huge project of transformation, and renunciation and absolution for past "gender" sins. That project was to be accomplished with the stepped-up integration and promotion of women, and the new influx was quietly affecting every area of military life—from the design of uniforms, to the weight and configuration of rucksacks, to the manuals written to define tasks and procedure, to the way recruits were trained at boot camp. And not just material aspects, the immaterial, too—like the ongoing revision, apology for, and eschewal of what is called "the warrior culture" in favor of a new value system that worshiped "sensitivity."

The concept of a huge established institution remaking itself to accommodate women (while simultaneously announcing that *nothing* had changed) was fascinating enough, but the story became even sexier when you realized that, for political and budgetary reasons, the actual logistical details were mostly hidden from the public at large. The official version of gender integration was something like "Yep, we're just kind of slotting them in and everything's going great."

It didn't work like that, of course. It was not a seamless meshing at all. All over the place, below the serene assurances of the brass, at ground level, there were armies of beleaguered middle managers (noncommissioned officers, junior commissioned officers) slogging away trying to "make it work"—and attempting to cope with the often messy consequences of the directives for a "gender free" force.

Even though everyone knew women are pretty much just like men, there were so many details to take care of, details that no one had ever predicted. Who would have guessed, for example, when they imagined flanks and flanks of men and women marching together in lockstep, that a significant number of women would develop urinary tract infections on long desert marches because they were embarrassed about taking a pee in view of their male comrades? Or that because many women were turning up pregnant while on deployment in third-world countries like Haiti and Somalia, someone would have to test routine inoculations to see if they would harm a fetus? Or that you'd have to adjust the thrust of ejector seat mechanisms so they didn't kill the lighter-boned female aviator as they punched her out of the aircraft?

Besides the medical research, there was a welter of activity on the physical infrastructure side: The living areas of aircraft carriers had to be retooled if women were going to have some privacy when they undressed for bed or brushed their teeth in the morning. And then there was the sprawl of the all-male culture that had been left mostly undisturbed for a century or so. To the women in Congress who were now calling the shots, it was rather like opening the doors to Animal House. Because the brass believed—not without the evidence of early "hostile environment" suits and such—that many women would be made uncomfortable by the way men live without the civilizing influence of women, the brooms and mops went to work. Raunchier "jodies" (the singsong rhyming chants used to set the pace when a unit marches) were banned, sailors were told to take down that locker photo of Heather Thomas and the Valvoline girl, carrying on at officers' clubs was discouraged, and all kinds of innocuous military jargon—from "cockpit" to "leg" to "box"—were examined for "sexist" potential.

At least one riddle had been explained—why the brass had officially decided to use the word *gender* instead of the word *sex*. *Gender*, a trendy, academic word, has been used to mean behavior and self-image learned from one's society, a society determined to keep women "in their place." The word *sex*, on the other hand, suggests sex differences that are hardwired, basic, primal, dictated by chemistry and hormones, as stubborn as the tides.

Given the military's new project, it's very important that the folks in charge remain wedded to the idea that sex differences are just a societal construct, erasable with a few strong lectures and a bit of "sensitivity training." Achieving a force that recruits, assigns, and promotes in a "gender neutral" way means believing that (after the requisite amount of sensitivity training, of course) men and women can eat, sleep, tent, march, and haul loads together like a merry band of brothers without the fireworks and histrionics that have characterized sexual . . . er, gender . . . relations throughout human history.

And this would be, in historical terms, quite an achievement. As anthropologist Olivia Vlahos puts it:

> There is no question that women have valor. No question that they are as intelligent, capable, and brave as men. And yet I know of no society which has routinely treated men and women as interchangeable and equivalent units in war—the policy now being pursued by the American military.
>
> Humankind has been around long enough to have tried everything at least once. If females belong in foxholes, we should find evidence of it in previous experiments that have worked. Alas, annals of the past offer no examples of formal, sexually integrated military forces, and only one of a formal but sexually segregated fighting unit.

In other words, we are in the middle of a huge social experiment. The returns are beginning to come in—and I will elaborate on them in later chapters—yet the real test is sometime in the future, maybe sooner and more suddenly than we think, when we find ourselves in full-scale war, not just an air war as in Kosovo, and something longer, on a larger scale, and against soldiers a little more resolved and well-armed (and well-fed!) than the average Iraqi infantryman of Desert Storm.

What the experiment will tell us is whether men and women—primarily young, as 60 percent of the force is under thirty—can live and work together quite intimately in conditions of high stress and still turn out the performance we need. By extension, though, the experiment will give us even deeper, more profound, information about sex roles.

Fighting a war—or even doling out supplies in the territory close to the front line of a war—is different from working in a corporation. Executives at Fortune 500 corporations like to pretend that they march into battle each day—duking it out cell phone to cell phone—but we know they don't really face matters of life and death. The stress of war and its primal, elemental, physical nature have a way of stripping away the veneer of civilization, and the physical, unforgiving, either-you-do-it-or-you-don't nature of much military work flushes out what is most elemental about ourselves. What we will know, then, in a way that thirty years of women-in-the-workplace has not really answered, is which parts of ourselves are malleable, which are unmalleable, what is fixed, what is not fixed. The experiment, in other words, is a test of the central assumption of the last thirty years of feminist doctrine.

What we will know are answers to such questions as: Does the presence of large numbers of women necessarily "feminize" the culture of the armed services? How much can one change (or "feminize") the military without turning it into something that is not-the-military? Can the sexes ever be truly "equal"—in the feminist sense, which equates equality with sameness and interchangeability? Is war an intrinsically "male" endeavor or can it be sanitized by technology? Is the kind of aggression unleashed and required by war an intrinsic male quality? What do the experiences in the military tell us about society's ability to regulate sex? A bit of data on this was provided by one ex-Marine writing on an Internet bulletin board about the Aberdeen Proving Grounds sex imbroglio in which the Army discovered that everybody was, in effect, sleeping with everybody else (and sometimes trading off):

> All the oversight programs were in place. Everyone had been through sexual harassment training. Everyone had been sensitized to EEO issues. Everyone had probably received several "warnings" about sexual misconduct and its consequences in their careers. Everyone knew what the consequences would be if they got caught. Some normal, healthy people just saw an opportunity and took it.

Well, answers to these questions will have to wait. Right now, as I write this in 1999, the military is in crisis. "The Army is broke like it's never been broke before," says a highly placed Army officer; he is part of a chorus one hears servicewide down the ranks. Morale among service people is at rock bottom. The services have just completed what military newspapers have called the "worst recruiting year in memory," and the Army's six thousand recruiters have been averaging about one recruitment a month. To counteract the pullouts, the different branches have begun offering huge new incentives to get in and stay in, yet attrition is way too high. In 1998, 79 percent of Air Force pilots declined to extend their service when the time came, even as the Air Force was offering, for one example, an additional $22,000 per year if you committed for another five years.

The services (except the Marines) are meeting recruitment goals by the skin of their teeth, if at all, even though they have been digging deeper and deeper in the potential recruit pool and offering "recruits everything but a new car," as one soldier put it. At the end of the fiscal year that ended in September 1999, the Air Force reported that it is losing 1,136 pilots, whose training has cost an estimated $6.6 billion. According to *Defense Week*, another 430 Air Force pilots have "vowed to leave" in the next fiscal year. In 1999, the Navy's ships put out to sea with what the *Detroit News* called "an astounding 22,000 berths unfilled." Attrition is a problem everywhere, even though the brass are throwing out money (in the form of bonuses, not raises) as if it were confetti. Attrition is a particular problem in the Navy, where the most experienced people (especially the aviators, who cost millions to produce) are leaving the service in droves.

The brass have many explanations, some of which are actually true—explanations involving a "hot" civilian economy, too much work for too few people, et cetera. But people like former F-14 pilot John Gadzinski, now flying for a commercial airline, say there is another "no-kidding, core reason," and it is one the brass haven't wanted to hear. "It's about the command climate, stupid," says one officer, paraphrasing Bill Clinton.

It is the reason that dare not speak its name. One learns that there is one iron rule governing military reporting these days: People on active duty do not tell reporters the truth if the truth is something they know their COs will not want them to say. Many, many service people have ruined or lost their careers testing this rule. "We live," one soldier commented, "in a politically correct fishbowl."

"It's becoming like Mao's cultural revolution," says ex-Army officer John Hillen. "Everybody knows it's a system built on a thousand little lies, but everybody's waiting for someone that's high-ranking who's not a complete moral coward to come out and say so." "I can't voice this the way I want to because you know what would happen," said one serviceman in an on-line bulletin board where much samizdat is exchanged. "I would get fragged from the top." When the press came to talk to service people on the more "sensitive" issues (the resignation of Air Force pilot Kelly Flynn, for example), whole units received strict instructions about how to answer reporters' questions, including "useful" phrases to use. Reporters visiting bases or ships usually must be "escorted" by a military public affairs officer (PAO) when they interview soldiers or sailors, and the PAO usually assumes that he will listen in so he can timely offer "corrections." Male handlers don't follow female reporters into the bathroom—thus I learned to have chats and collect phone numbers there—but I have had flacks who waited for me directly outside the door. The *New York Times*'s Steve Myers once spent a lovely evening in Bosnia in a laundry room watching his clothing go round and round with his assigned PAO sitting at his side. Sometimes reporters are able to slip their traces if they find one less diligent about his reporter-minding duties. Sometimes reporters just beg, wheedle, and threaten enough to be left alone some of the time, but often, especially if they are on daily deadline, reporters end up just recycling the same stock "quotes"—thus the stale *Pravda*-like tone of much military news coverage in the major news media.

Attention reporters at major news outlets! Read speeches, memos, press releases. If Joe Enlisted Man or Jane Junior Officer responds to your questions with lines from the last address given by the deputy secretary of defense, you're getting reportorial garbage. The only service people who will speak "for attribution"—that is, with their words attached to their names—are those who've retired or resigned, those on the brink of "getting out," those who've just joined and haven't figured things out yet, and, for some reason, drill sergeants, particularly the southern ones with that rebel look in their eyes. As a result, there are more unnamed sources than I would like in this book. Still, the majority of those unnamed sources are people I have come to know personally, people I've talked to on the job, people who've been cleared by other reliable sources. Some spoke for name attribution because they had filed resignation papers and assumed they would be out in a matter of months, but were then called back to active duty to serve in the Kosovo conflict of spring 1999, and had to retract their agreement with me.

But we have to work harder to get around the Potemkin villages they have erected. In times of protracted peace, citizens grow fat and lazy and careless. One day during London's blitz, George Orwell sat down at his desk and wrote: "At this very moment, highly civilized beings are overhead trying to kill me."

Many Americans have forgotten what a sense of threat from other-civilized-beings-who-don't-know-you-but-would-kill-you-anyway *feels* like. We forget that serious fighting always involves triage—sometimes of simple decencies, sometimes of First Amendment rights, certainly of luxuries like the thought of giving everybody equal opportunity to do everything and having everybody feel just okeydokey about their treatment. We are particularly lulled because the last war, our first "coed war," seemed so easy—at least from the TV screen. You push a few buttons on a plane and, bam, they're on the run! Proponents of putting women in infantry and artillery with men (i.e., "in combat") have spent the last decade saying serenely that "technology will level the playing field." Anybody can push buttons, right?

But our recent engagements in Iraq (limited by Saddam Hussein's mobility) and in Kosovo (where bombers had to wait for clouds to clear) showed we're decades and decades from a bloodless, push-button war. If we want women to be in direct combat this year or next, we will have to square our consciences and our desire to win with the prospect of putting them up against enemy soldiers like the hulking Serbian farm boys we saw on TV throughout the 1999 air war. There is some high-tech stuff, but it's mostly just in the hopeful planning stage right now; whether we will have the money to develop it is uncertain, and even if we really had it, it will be ages before everybody who needs to knows how to use it—and knows how to fix it when it inevitably breaks down. As Arizona senator John McCain said in October 1998, " '[B]etting on things to come' trades readiness we have on hand for technology that is still in the bush. Historically, we have never deployed such systems on time, at the estimated cost, or, often, with the anticipated effectiveness."

In times of affluence and peace, with technology that always seems to arrive like a deus ex machina to solve any problem, it becomes easy to believe that life is perfectible. But life always involves choices. Everything has its price. The pursuit of "gender equity" is exacting a huge price in dollars and morale. The brass claim we are wedded to finding ways to integrate women because we can't find sufficient numbers of qualified men and/or because integrating women is just like integrating black men: Whatever the cost, they say, it's the right thing to do.

Maybe. I didn't intend to write "the last word." This is not "Resolved: The Military Should Do Such and Such and Not Do This and That." What I wanted to do is write a "first word" for some future scorched-earth-honest discussion in which the silenced are allowed to speak.

We can start here, with *me* giving *you* a look at what I saw when I went out to look at the "New Military"—on the ground, in the late nineties, while it was tortuously attempting to become kinder and gentler, to tame the great beast of sexual attraction, to reform "the warrior culture" and become thoroughly gender integrated but sex free.

Postcard from Fort Jackson, an Army Base, Columbia, South Carolina, March 1998

"Cry Havoc! And let slip the Dogs of War!"
—*Julius Caesar*, William Shakespeare, circa 1600

"This is not your father's army anymore!"
—Claudia Kennedy, first female U.S. three-star general,
addressing cadets, West Point, 1997

The sun is just beginning to rise as Fort Jackson's "War Dogs" Platoon—part of Delta Company, 1st Battalion, 61st Infantry Regiment—is herded into formation beneath the Victory Tower, a hulking edifice of wood planks, ladders, nets, and ropes surrounded by a pen of sawdust and big squishy vinyl-covered air mattresses, like the kind one sees children bounding around on at amusement parks. The young people, average age nineteen and over half female,* have come from cities and towns all around the country to join the Army. This is the second week of basic training, and taking on the Victory Tower—this Lincoln Logs arrangement silhouetted against the rising sun—is a key step in what is called the "soldierization" process.

The first step is to get these soldiers (*soldiers* is now the mandated term instead of *recruit* or simply *private*) comfortable around the structure. Psychological comfort is a big priority in the Army of the nineties, and it is assumed that the kids haven't used their bodies much.

---

*For some reason—"Ask the recruiters," I was told—there were more women in this cycle than usual. Companies of new recruits were then tending to run about 25 percent female.

"We get them from Burger King and Nintendo," Delta Company's commander, Capt. Joe Gross, explains, driving over to the field. "When we ask the drill sergeants how a new class is looking, they'll say, 'They have very strong thumbs.'"

The Victory Tower would be a great place to shoot a recruiting film. There's a rope suspended over a very short crevice over which the trainee will have to do a Tarzan-like swing (you'd shoot from below, move the camera a lot, and run a rock music track underneath); there's one of those shaky jungle-movie rope bridges; and then the pièce de résistance, the "rappelling wall," a forty-foot slab of weathered boards.

When important visitors ask to observe basic training, they are usually steered to the Victory Tower. It is, of course, one of the most visually interesting exercises, and something about the sight of all those kids in their camouflage uniforms swinging around on ropes and climbing up walls must send a message something along the lines of "Your tax dollars at work!" or possibly "The Army of the nineties is ready!"

And there has been a steady procession of VIPs visiting Fort Jackson lately. The debate over "gender-integrated basic training" (the practical, politicized, and, for some, moral question of whether the services should continue to mix the sexes during basic training or segregate them as they did up till 1993) keeps reappearing in various forms on legislative dockets. Senators have to have some idea of which way to vote on the innumerable bills that keep coming down the pike and must be ready with a supply of sage comments for the Sunday morning news shows. Fort Jackson is always ready to host these forays. Because it processes about 70 percent of the women entering the Army, it is an ideal place to observe gender-integrated training in action, and senators, lobbyists, and sociologists tend to end up here to "study the situation" so that they can "report back" to committee or Senate or constituents or the press. Most of the men and women training at Jackson will go on to the Army's less sexy jobs—as office clerks or as "supply specialists" in supply warehouses—but since the camp delivers the still-novel sight of boys and girls in identical uniforms marching, chanting, even hefting rifles, the Army public relations corps likes to steer camera crews and print press here as well.

Today is no exception on the VIP watch. Senator Chuck Robb, the Democrat representing Virginia, is slated to make a stop as part of *his* "gender-integrated training fact-finding tour." There are the requisite flurry of false alarms announcing an important person's imminent arrival, and suddenly he is among us. While staff and recruits have been engaged in other things, a tall, lean, impeccably groomed man wearing a very crisp navy blue suit and a very deep, even tan materializes near the rappelling wall flanked by two dark-suited female aides who peer around at the sunny field suspiciously. If Central Casting had been required to provide a "senator and aides," they couldn't have done any better.

The senator spends a few minutes beaming indulgently at the acrobatics around him, then collects himself for some serious fact collection. First off, of course, one needs women. The company's only female drill sergeants at the time are summoned and Drill Sgt. Fatemba Kyler and Drill Sgt. Ruth Smith stand at attention against a chain-link fence facing the senator and a rapt audience of bystanders. Reporters are not allowed nearby because, as one of the aides hisses, "this is a fact-finding tour; the senator is trying to have an honest, blunt, informal talk—the kind of thing we can't do if we call witnesses to committee," but the reporter in the crowd manages to sidle up to the senator anyway.

"Is there anything you want to tell us, anything that would make your lives here better?" intones Robb to the women who stand before him. There is a long silence while their eyes dart here and there, perhaps looking for an escape. A difficult job faces them. On one hand, current protocol—almost the new etiquette—calls for some general statement about the need for greater equality among the men and women in the services, but good sense dictates that the complaint must be mild enough and routine enough so that Delta Company's commander, Captain Gross, their boss, standing a few feet away beaming in a proprietary way, will not get genuinely angry or embarrassed in front of *his* bosses, the lieutenant colonels who have somehow gotten wind of all this and drifted over. Finally one of the drill sergeants seems to recall a bit of editorial page boilerplate: "Well, I guess we could have more female drill sergeants," she mutters. (This has been an official recommendation in report after report, news story after news story, memo after memo.)

Senator Robb beams. With an air of mission accomplished, he strides over to a group of kids waiting to do an exercise and does a brisk receiving line, shaking each by the hand. Looking deeply into the eyes of a few of them, he asks, "And why did you join the Army, private!" eliciting a snappy "Because I wanted to serve my country, sir." Then he is in his van and barreling away. Elapsed time about twenty-five minutes. Two days later he will appear on a Sunday morning news talk show in a segment on foreign policy and start his disquisition with the statement: "You know, Wolf, I've just been down at Fort Jackson with our troops . . ."

The Victory Tower compound may make a satisfyingly dramatic backdrop for visitors seeking a look at "our military in action," but a closer look shows that the danger element is largely Disneyland-grade. There is something vaguely "set"-like. As is so much about the "New Army," the exercise seems carefully calibrated to instill "an experience" (soldier-flavored) without risk to the participants. The "crevice" is only about four feet wide. The rope bridge is actually just above a huge springy cargo net a mere ten feet below, and deep cushiony sawdust surrounds the rappelling wall. As one of the drill sergeants puts it, "There's not much that's gonna be life-threatening here, unless you climb up to the top of the tower and nosedive off of it."

Since there's no real physical challenge and little separating the wheat from the chaff in terms of danger, the point of the exercise, according to camp officials, is to "build confidence."

"It lets them overcome their fear of heights, brings them closer together as a unit," explains one of the sergeants as if reciting from a lesson book. "Let's face it, it's not that difficult physically; it's mainly mentally difficult—fear of heights and that."

The all-volunteer Army has to sell itself. One selling point, obviously, is money for college (then at $40,000 via the Montgomery GI bill). There's also the potential to learn one's way around high-tech equipment, and the chance to have some rock-'em-sock-'em adventure (thus the music video–style ads with shots of planes shooting off runways, guys talking into headsets, tanks).

But the "New Army" also works the personal empowerment angle—"Be all that you can be," as the advertising slogan puts it. One recruiting ad on TV in the summer of 1998 featured a young, blond woman soldier going through "jump school"—parachute training— with a song in the background, something about doing "it for your parents, your country" and, in the last frame, with her triumphant face filling the screen, *"for you."* And the young women in boot camp seemed to have been reached with this message. To the question "So, how d'ya like it?" I'll often hear answers like the one from Shawna Sumner: "In the weeks I've been here I can honestly say I've become more self-confident. I don't mouth off. I'm better at taking direction. I've become a better person." Another, married, a former bank teller, says: "It's really good for me; I'm feeling good about myself. I feel I can do anything I try to do."

For Delta Company, however, parachute jumps will have to come later. Right now that damn rappelling wall waits.

The two platoons from Delta Company are herded over to the grassy embankment that faces the rappelling wall. The drill sergeant hollers, "Be seat-ted," and the ninety or so recruits hunker down on a bank covered with still-dewy grass facing the forty-foot slab.

On top of the Victory Tower two more DSs (drill sergeants)—a total of ten are assigned to Delta Company—get ready to do a rappelling demonstration. The drill sergeants are hunky guys in their twenties and thirties who have "rotated in" (most of the time many involuntarily assigned) from other military specialties—infantry, Special Operations, whatever—to do a two-year tour as instructors. Honed warriors with Chippendale dancer–grade physiques, they are all immensely overqualified for the work they do and they sneak in ways of making this demo, which they've done for incoming class after incoming class, slightly more interesting for themselves. For most, this is the first time the Army has asked them to be "a mentor and role model," in quite this way, but like all good soldiers they will follow orders.

"Anybody scared of heights?" bellows Drill Sergeant Dillon to the kids on the ground. Several girls raise their hands. Taking on a much more commiserating tone, he says, "It's okay to be afraid of heights. . . . Just approach this as doing your job and you'll be okay," he yells genially. One of the brawny young instructors has been suited up with a "Swiss seat," the vaguely bondage-chic rope-and-ring contraption you see mountain climbers wear. All those ropes and hooks threading through your legs make you waddle like a duck when you try to walk normally on the ground, and the nylon ropes encircle and squeeze the genital area and butt cheeks into shameless orangutan-in-heat protuberances. Still, as well as connecting a climber to safety lines, the harness saves the upper body significant strain, since ropes and knots catch and distribute body weight that would otherwise have to be supported by one's arms and shoulders.

Back up on their platform in the air, Drill Sergeant LeFavre is the designated rappellee in the demonstration. In his role as Private Clueless he lurches to the edge of the platform, "loses his balance," and . . . falls . . . right . . . off. It's okay, though! He hangs in the air, calmly dangling from his safety line in a very civilized, upright seated position. Then before you know it the damn fool has disregarded the drill sergeant's instructions and flipped himself over so he's hanging upside down, waggling his legs around like a mentally impaired spider. The recruits on the ground titter and applaud happily and, as designed, their tension begins to dissipate. It's obvious you'd have to work real hard to get killed on the rappelling exercise. Dusting himself off, LeFavre calls out, "Any questions?" "Are there any medical personnel on hand?" asks one girl, trying to add to the joke and laughing at herself nervously.

Finally, after a suit-up process that takes the group nearly another hour (each private has to grasp how to put on the harness and then have the fit checked and rechecked), they're ready for some actual rappelling: a practice run on a fifteen-foot wall, a very miniature version of the summit they will eventually ascend. Most of this goes smoothly except for one plump girl who stands about five feet two. She freezes just as she's supposed to step onto the wall and begins to tremble and cry. It doesn't seem to be an act. She truly seems to be on the verge of hysteria. The two female drill sergeants who are handling this exercise try to coax her into it, giving her a pep talk, touching her gently on the arm—without success. Finally, she is helped off the wall and sometime later she can be seen walking back slowly from the Porta-John with her rappelling gear off and a stony, preoccupied expression on her face. Since the Swiss seat took a long time to fit, and since several drill sergeants had to check it for tightness, it's apparent that she's through for the day—at least on this exercise. Something else is wrong with this picture: She's alone. Army Regulation 350-6 of Training and Doctrine Command dictates that recruits of either sex may not go anywhere without a "battle buddy" of the same sex.

"You can't go *anywhere*, not to get a drink, not to the laundry room, not even fifty feet to the latrine," explains one female trainee, "and especially not to talk to a drill sergeant. Drill sergeants won't talk to you unless you're accompanied by another girl." Your battle buddy is usually also your bunk mate, she says, but if she's not around, the battle buddy is "whoever is the closest female." By the third week, trainees seem to have thoroughly assimilated this rule. During a break from rifle drill, out on a large grassy field, when the company is allowed to take a fifteen-minute rest, a female recruit spies a male and female recruit talking together and begins screeching, *We need a battle buddy. We need a male buddy here!*" until another boy saunters over to save the day.

So maybe Miss Rappelling Wall is a washout in the making, but perhaps not. "Washing out" simply doesn't happen very often if the Army can help it, especially for girls, who are prized for their statistical value as a measure to be used (in sessions of Congress, for example) to demonstrate that the military is bringing women in at a satisfactory pace. Anyway, after a while at Jackson, the sight of a recruit just kind of hanging out while the rest of the company is elsewhere doesn't seem so unusual. The frequency of lower body injuries (hip, knee, and back sprains, broken ankles, and the like) among the female recruits is one of Jackson's biggest dilemmas, and the corridors and grounds around the low industrial barracks buildings are dotted with young women doing desk duty or on crutches limping around the base deep in conversation with a battle buddy acting as chaperone. They cheerfully explain that they are injured or that they are on a "profile," which means they have gone to the base doctor and been given a note that says they shouldn't do a particular exercise—no PT (physical training) at all, for instance, or maybe just no running.

Back at the main action, the recruits are lining up to climb the slatted, ladderlike sides of the Victory Tower. When they get to the broad platform forty feet in the air, they drop onto hands and knees and scuttle over to Drill Sergeant Dillon, who clips their seat harness onto a safety line, hands them a rappelling line, and tells them what to do once they get on the wall. Here, it seems, is an opportunity to unfurl some of that classic drill sergeant/trainee interaction, and the drill sergeants listlessly go through the motions: "Are you scared, Private?" demands Drill Sergeant Dillon as if reading from an ancient playbook. "Not really, sir, can I go now?" says the tall, wiry boy in a bored but polite voice. After listening to the laundry list of dos and don'ts the lanky boy is finally allowed to launch his body into the sunny air, and he rappels down the wall with the energy of a colt let out of the stable, crashing into the wall with his feet and sending himself whooshing into space again with his thighs. The next boy up, a more muscular Hispanic, listens impatiently while the drill sergeant drones on about the use of the brake hand—the hand you keep fisted up behind your body to control your descent—then, when he's allowed to rappel, he lets go of his brake hand and waves it in the air, impishly showing off his control and daring. "Put that hand back," snaps the drill sergeant. "Yes, sir," he calls back soberly.

One tries not to notice, but a pattern is undeniable. In general, the boys attempt the exercise calmly, a bit bemusedly. One or two are awkward, but overall they are self-assured—to the point of mild boredom and disengagement. A sweet-faced black recruit of about eighteen is taking his turn on the swaying rope bridge; he stops halfway as if he just has to savor the feeling of being high in the air on a brilliant sunny day using muscles he hasn't used since he was a kid and hollers, "This is great; just like a big jungle gym!" It is a bit of a disconnect after listening to Captain Gross's somber pronouncements about "overcoming fear" on the way over to the practice field.

I find myself thinking that the harder the Army works to downplay sex differences—the whole point of training the sexes together—the more sharply they seem to stand out. When you put big blocks of kids roughly the same age, in identical clothing, doing the same task, together, sex difference *becomes* the thing one sees. With no other major differences between recruits, one begins to notice how the women, on the whole, are about a foot shorter and have a different shape—overall it is a pear compared to a stalk of bamboo. And so it is with the rappelling exercise, where obvious sets of group norms begin to appear. "The boys train a lot more physically, less mentally; the girls, the reverse," is the way Sandy Molyneaux sums it up. Owner of a local company called Videorama, she has been making commemorative tapes for recruits to buy as a souvenir of boot camp and has seen the training of cycle after cycle for the last ten years.

Roughly half of the girls are fine going through the various paces on the Victory Tower. They are game, matter-of-fact. They are generally not showy on the ropes, but like the well-behaved students they generally are in school, they listen intently to the drill sergeants and approach the task seriously and methodically and it gets the job done. It's hard to ignore, though, that most of the boys don't even bother listening to the drill sergeants. The process seems to be more instinctive. They make a show of listening politely, then seem to shrug off the directions and take on the rappelling like they've got energy to spare. There's also the embarrassing spectacle of a whole other half of the female contingent who are having fits (maybe because public schools no longer require daily gym class).

One is nearly catatonic as she approaches the lip of the platform and the waiting drill sergeant. Her brown face is streaked with tears, and her mouth is quivering. In the old days—we all know the script—the recruit who freezes up would have been humiliated shamelessly for showing fear. A drill sergeant would have "gotten in the kid's face" and snarled about his loathing for little mama's boys and little wusses, et cetera. The sergeant of the nineties, on the other hand, is under strict instructions not to "abuse the recruits." Though his degree of nonabuse is supposed to be "gender neutral," in practice, everyone says, it always works out that the drill sergeants (terrified of sexual harassment charges, sex discrimination charges, or general trainee-abuse charges, which they believe are more likely to come from women) "are softer" on the girls—as is this drill sergeant, who murmurs "You can do it"'s to the girl until she shakily steps off the supporting platform and makes a jerky and tearful descent.

Some of this comes out because of the difference in the way the sexes interact with the drill sergeants, and here again, despite the Army's constant declarations that "soldiers are just soldiers," there is a subtle but persistent difference. The girls tend to confide in the drill sergeants, and to flirt. They tend to hang their fear out on the line without shame—or even as part of the flirtation—while the guys tend to hold fear inside, becoming tighter and more closed as they approach a challenging exercise.

The girls tend to enlist the drill sergeants in the problem of their completion of the exercise, they talk a lot, ask questions a lot, ask for help a lot; and moved by the fresh young pretty faces and the curious or frightened voices, the drill sergeants turn indulgent and paternal. It seems to be hardwired in their "decent guy" code. The new military may require gender-neutral training, but another code, an older code, a code that is wired into the viscera, says that a strong man helps a woman if she is in need. "Will you catch me?" pleads a girl to the drill sergeant who is telling her to swing across a gap in the platform on a rope. "I'm here," he says. He's clearly exasperated—at her, at the rather shamefully unmilitary situation he's been put in ("mentoring" girls instead of the manly pursuit of bellowing at boys), but his feet seem rooted. Something older and stronger than logic or ideology makes him unable to leave the shaky voice and the soft, young, worried face. Another girl, a small athletic-looking blonde who looks like she could have just stepped off a tennis court in Evanston, Illinois, begins to sob when the drill sergeant begins to give her rappelling directions at the top of the Victory Tower.

Her skin has turned very pink and she flinches and cries out a little every time the structure jiggles. "What's the matter, Private?" the drill sergeant asks a little tauntingly. "Drill Sergeant," she says between gasps for breath, "the platform is shaking, Drill Sergeant, and I'm very high off the ground." "Okay, c'mon. This is not hard," he says. Finally he is able to get her through it, and when she hits the ground, she jumps up and down and whoops ecstatically. "How you feeling now, Private?" says the drill sergeant, gruffly trying out his new role as "facilitator." "Great, Drill Sergeant!" she howls back. Another self-esteem safely raised.

The self-esteems of the privates may be growing by leaps and bounds, but the little cluster of drill sergeants huddled on the platform at the top of the Victory Tower are Discontent Central. Each is attached to a short piece of rope that is, in turn, attached to a plug in the center of the platform—in case they take it upon themselves to fall off the platform or in case a hurricane-grade wind suddenly blows up. "It's for safety," they will explain sourly, but their tethering seems like a metaphor for the restrictions of their role in the "New Military."

On their little perch high in the air, far away, for the time being, from their COs, who are generally too fat and/or too lazy to climb up, the rage they feel at their forced sojourn in what they call "Camp Jackson" is bubbling to the surface. "In the old days we used to throw them off the tower," Dillon says disgustedly. Another begins hopping around so the platform begins to sway and he smiles devilishly and says in a high-pitched effeminate voice, "Oooooh, it's an earthquake! The platform's shaking!"

Sgt. Robert Saunders, a handsome black man of thirty-four, is sitting silently, slightly away from the others, staring at his black boots with his Smokey Bear hat pulled very low on his forehead. Finally a clue to what has been bothering him bursts out. "It's too easy," he mutters to no one in particular. "Sometimes it's harder to be easy than to be hard," snaps Dillon, as if he is repeating something he's heard many times before. Sergeant Saunders broods some more for a while, but then it all overflows again:

"This is boring," he says in a much louder voice as if in defiance of Dillon. "This is too easy. I'm leaving. 'Kinder, gentler military'! I'm leaving! I want my kids to train as they fight. I'm leaving. I'm sick of this."

Sergeant Saunders did his basic training at Fort Benning, Georgia, which has always trained infantryman and accordingly has always been all-male. The training, he recalls, was much, much harder. When a company did PT, the guys didn't use gym mats to cover the cold, dewy 5 A.M. ground like they do in nineties boot camps, and when they came back from PT, the boys peeled off their regular clothes in a big mob, Spartan-style, and then, without a break for a shower like they get at Fort Jackson, changed into their regular uniforms and stayed in them for the rest of the day. If a recruit—and they were called recruits then, not given the honorary title of "soldier"—misbehaved, he was told, "Drop down and give me twenty." Here, one sergeant says, "you can't make them do more than ten push-ups in thirty seconds because it's called 'abusing the private.'"

And the rappelling was much harder and faster. "We went one right after the other, just like that . . . and we went off from a D-ring; we didn't have this," Saunders says, pointing with disgust at the extra ring, which takes more of the rappeller's body weight and distributes it into the harness, channeling the strain of the descent off the rappeller's shoulders. "They have to slow everything down when they add women. I want to go back to Benning. I want to train all men again. It's so much more intense. When I went through basic in 1987, I was trained by strong men, Vietnam vets. I can't repeat some of the things they used to call me," he says wistfully. "I had an uncle who used to call me 'knucklehead.' I call my boy 'knucklehead.' I'm not allowed to call [the recruits] 'Knucklehead.'"

"What's wrong with *knucklehead*?" I murmur. The ranking sergeant, the one who'd reminded us all it's harder to be easy than to be hard, singsongs, "Because saying that is degrading to the recruit and when we degrade, we lower self-esteem. Supposedly," he adds with a sniff and a glum expression.

There is something hospital-like, laboratory-like, old-ladyish, about the atmosphere of squeamishness, of caution, even hypochondria, at Fort Jackson. This is not, as one drill sergeant puts it, "a throw 'em in and see if they can swim kind of place; it's more 'how easy can we make this for you.'" The outside wall of the drill sergeants' shack beside the Victory Tower, the place the sergeants decamp to drink coffee and bitch, is plastered over with a six-page memo detailing a Risk Assessment Analysis of the Victory Tower exercise—all the ways recruits could conceivably hurt themselves clambering around the chutes and ladders. There is the Risk Assessment Matrix and a Risk Management five-step process: "identify hazard," "assess hazard," "make risk assessment," "implement control," "supervise."

As one sergeant puts it, "Here, everything is hold their hand, walk them through it, tell them A B C D, 'Now you do it, Private.' . . . We're not allowed to push them at all because that is called abuse."

The new philosophy starts at the top, from the Army's highest echelons. This same sergeant, who describes himself as "just a Georgia farm boy," tells a story in his southern drawl:

"I was talking to a major once, a female. We were standing around shooting the breeze; I was mentioning that we were too easy on the privates, 'This is Camp Jackson,' that kind of thing, and she said I was 'extreme in my ideas about training.' I said, 'Well, ma'am, I'm an infantry soldier. Our job is to kill people and blow things up, and it's hard, and people try to kill us while we're doing that and nobody feels sorry for ya, and you don't do your soldiers any favors by bein' easy or soft on 'em. When it comes to trainin', ya hurt 'em in the long run'. . . and she said, in this matter-of-fact way, 'You're a fanatic.'

"So I kinda wandered off to talk to somebody else. . . . That's when I realized there're two separate armies out there."

All of this worrying, all this baby-stepping, tends to create a kind of cognitive dissonance in the company men, the guys going "career military," the guys like Captain Gross, Delta Company's commander. Men like this want to be loyal to the institution that taught them discipline and courage and turned them from boys to men—even though that institution is in the middle of radical change, change that, in many ways, impunes their notions about the way values like discipline and courage are expressed. Gross enlisted as an infantryman at age seventeen, and, like most guys who grew up in the South, he did rough, infantryman's basic training at Fort Benning. He is tall and lean, with an open, friendly face, a quick smile, and a determined gait; he is ambitious, very bright, diligent, conscientious, energetic, personable, and he has always loved the Army. Obviously, this enlistee from Sulphur, Louisiana (population 25,000), was officer material, and eventually he earned a commission, which puts him right up there, officially at least, with the generals' sons who went to West Point. Everything about him says he's determined to go further.

But it is a "New Army," and rising in the ranks in today's Army puts a former infantryman in conflict with what was always the infantryman's code: For one thing, it means signing on to new agendas and they are very far away from the old one that was so simple to remember, the one that said your job was to "kill people and blow things up."

The new agendas, for instance, dictate that the future force must be "gender-integrated" and "gender-neutral" and "gender-blind." These are nice abstract labels, but on the ground, for someone charged with directing basic training, the new mandate means accepting the idea that one will be surrounded by lots of very young women, which, in practice—most clearly in the Army—has meant that one has to deal with an entire stratum who will, as Fort Jackson's experience shows, rack up lower body injuries (shinsplints, broken ankles, strained backs, and worse) if they train as hard as the men.

What do you do if, like Captain Gross, you are in a position to influence the pace and style of training? How do you satisfy the Army's competing demands to turn out war-fighters—or support people who can be converted at a moment's notice to war-fighters—*and* fill the ranks with women, who in Captain Gross's experience are proving harder to convert to war-fighters for the simple reason that they have smaller frames and weaker muscles?

Do you speed things up to the boys' pace and risk injuring or discouraging the girls? Or do you slow things down to suit them—a tactic that tends to make the boys feel restless and cheated while impuning one's cherished instincts about the military way? Or do you try to do both at once—which usually means you're not doing either very well. And how do you handle these conflicting demands mentally? Some upper-level-management folks, who don't have to actually deal with real soldiers, learn to exercise doublethink—as George Orwell put it, "the act of . . . keeping two contradictory thoughts in your head at the same time." A legal officer for the Army, for instance, was once quoted as saying: "The military is training young men to be aggressive in combat and face life-threatening situations, yet they also have to realize that in dealings with female counterparts they have to switch gears." A network news show asked the question "How do we protect our female soldiers [from sexual harassment] while they learn to protect us?" Like so many others, Gross could retreat into denial—that is, simply not see the problems, deny they are going on—but he is too bright to deceive himself for long, so apparently he copes by attacking the conflict with great bouts of positive thinking.

Listening to him, one can hear the various sides wrestling with each other. First the infantryman in Gross: "We had to march most places at Benning, like to our exercise fields," he says with annoyance, watching a truck filled with seated recruits arrive at a practice field. "When I first came here, it kinda bothered me that they truck 'em around here so much."

Then the attentive manager takes over: "We constantly talk about how we can add rigor to the program but without getting more injuries, because we're dealing with very different physical capabilities—like in the morning runs where we have a lot of women who tend to fall to the back."

He sits in the car drumming his fingers. A shadow has crossed his face, but then the sun comes up. "But that," he says, regaining his usual peppiness and his mental certitude, "is why we have Ability Groups!"

The Ability Group concept was added to basic training in the early nineties. In the Army of 1998, if you can't keep up with your platoon when they run in formation, it doesn't mean you're a weakling . . . a wus . . . a lazy bastard, or any of the taunting, shaming names drill sergeants used on recruits in the past. (In fact, recruits aren't allowed to call each other "wus," even jokingly; that would be considered "trainee-on-trainee abuse.") And falling out of morning run isn't taken as a sign that you should, maybe, find a quiet spot on the base and spend some extra time on your own trying to build up your legs. Falling out simply means the Army needs to find you a different Ability Group.

But you can see why the COs are nervous: Even with all this caution, when the truck comes to take the equipment and the officers back, three girls limp toward the truck, casualties of the day. And when we get back to barracks, there are two girls and one boy from Delta Company waiting to leave the camp. Both girls say they have no plans to come back. (The boy says he will return once he gets treated for his asthma.) One girl is going home because she passed out after the running part of PT—the doctors say it's the resurgence of childhood asthma; the other, who is twenty-four, is going home because she's "developed child care conflicts." Her husband, who is a construction worker, just got transferred to work farther away from home, so he won't be able to take care of the kids. "I wanted to be a soldier, but my family always comes first," she says.

The eight weeks of basic training aren't all about swinging around on ropes, of course; the "New Army" believes it has plenty of work to do on the recruits' souls, so along with the sexual harassment sensitivity training there is values training, which has been added, as Pvt. Steve Gugliameti solemnly explains, "so we can learn values because we aren't getting them at home."

Today, two platoons, the War Dogs and the Terminators, approximately a hundred kids, sit on the floor of a classroom while a heavily built, slightly older black drill sergeant delivers a lecture about courage, one of the core values the Army wants to implant during the eight weeks. At first, recruits who have a question for the sergeant stand at parade rest with their hands clasped behind their backs until the trainer grants leave to speak, but quickly this convention falls by the wayside and the lecture/discussion begins to look more like your standard "rap session" in any would-be progressive high school across the land, with kids calling out whatever is on their minds, whispering, tittering, interrupting each other, even interrupting the sergeant.

To start the discussion the drill sergeant asks the group, "What's the thing in your life that you did that required the most courage?" "Coming here," one kid calls out. Another says it was leaving home for the first time and getting a job in a new city. "I had two children," one young woman volunteers. The seasoned infantryman leading the group nods sagely to each of these. But the sergeant's job here is to talk from his own experience and eventually bring the lecture around to the subject of courage, so he launches into a long anecdote about a deployment in Somalia, the gist being, once again, that "it's okay to be scared"—a mantra he repeats many times without closing the equation to make the point that courage is doing what you have to do despite being afraid. "If they want to send you over there, do you have to go?" calls out one girl, but her question is lost in the general rhubarbing.

Many aren't listening to the general discussion by this point anyway. Away for a few hours from chow lines and formations and yelling and drilling, this herd of colts has a chance to look around and let the realization sink in that they are away from Mom and Dad and Grandma and Dubuque, in a large room full of people their own age, virtually prisoners together for the next five weeks, half of them men and half women, as cute as any group selected with some attention to physical and mental standards. A boy and a girl have plunked down next to each other on the floor. As the drill sergeant drones on, their eyes connect once or twice. She looks like she has Polynesian blood, with lovely caramel-colored skin, smooth as polished teak, and shiny black hair pulled back in a bun. (Girls at Fort Jackson are allowed a range of hairstyles, while boys, per the ancient tradition, are still shorn down to the skull with an electric razor during the "reception" period.) He is black and lanky and handsome, approximately her age, and shifting restlessly as the drill sergeant rambles.

As the sergeant continues to improvise on the general (and it is now quite general) subject of courage, they begin to whisper together, and after a while she grabs the boy's palm so that she can trace a diagram as illustration of a point. He grabs her hand back and draws another map and then they look into each other's eyes and smile and then look straight ahead a little too rigidly and shift a little self-consciously, perhaps suddenly aware of each other as fine young specimens of the opposite sex, not just "fellow soldiers." Later, as the drill sergeant makes his way to the door over the seated bodies of the chattering privates, the same girl pipes up from the floor, not even bothering to stand up to address him.

"Drill Sergeant!"

"Yes?" he says, his face lighting up, clearly a little startled at the sweetness of the face that has materialized in the middle of the mob.

"I want to ask you . . ." she says, but trails off as she looks at all the people still in the room.

"I'll ask you later," she says coquettishly, like someone who is quite confident she'll have his attention later.

"Fine!" says the drill sergeant, his face still glowing.

Watching this scene, I take the whole cast of characters and transport them to Saudi Arabia, where I plop them down in a desert encampment a ways back from the front lines of some future war or operation other than war. I imagine the drill sergeant, whose age and rank make him a plausible platoon sergeant for the girl in the field, ordering the girl to do a job that may put her in harm's way. In the Gulf War, there were times when a dangerous job could have been anything from unloading a truck to stringing concertina wire. The front had a way of shifting suddenly. Thirteen people in a supply unit way to the supposed rear were killed, for instance, when their barracks was hit by a Scud. At the core of their being, men like this are loyal to two codes: (1) that good soldiers obey orders and show courage, and (2) that an honorable man does not let a woman get hurt while he sits in safety. Period. Only a coward would send a woman out to do a very dangerous job when he is there to help her.

I think of my sergeant with his job that needs doing, looking for some soldier to do it. Would he send Miss Skin-as-smooth-as-polished-teak? And even if he remembered the new mandates and decided to obey them, would his attentions be divided? Would he watch her nervously, his muscles aching to help her (and finish the job faster) while some other unit task went unfinished? The characters of this fantasy—the Army's fantasy—wait for us, on stop-action hold in the desert, until the next war gives us an end to the story.

The Kinder, Gentler Boot Camp

"[T]he training, the discipline, the daily humiliations, the privileges of 'brutish' sergeants, the living en masse like schools of fish are all directed toward breaking down the sense of sanctity of the physical person, and toward hardening the awareness that a soldier is the chattel (hopefully the proud chattel but a chattel all the same) of the society he serves."
—"The Evolution of a Soldier," James Jones, circa 1940

"Basic training is a safe and intensely supervised experience."
—Gen. Claudia Kennedy, December 1998

"I'm going to refer to it as the crying tape . . . there's a piece of this tape whereby a recent female graduate comes on and it shows some individuals crying [and she tells them], 'It's strenuous and it can get hard, but it's okay to cry.'"
—Representative Steve Buyer (R-Ind), before House Armed Services Committee (subcommittee on personnel) hearing describing orientation video he'd seen at Great Lakes Naval Training Base, fall 1997

U p until about the middle of the nineteenth century, the Sioux Indians of the American plains states practiced a rite of passage they called the Vision Quest. The tribal elders would send a teenaged boy out onto the land without provisions or protection from the elements save a loincloth and moccasins. The boy was to stay there, sleeping under what cover he could find, foraging for any sort of food or water, until he was contacted by the gods. (This usually happened on the fourth day, given the body's reaction to these kinds of deprivations.) If the candidate was lucky, his vision would include an introduction to his Totem Animal (the Great Thunderbird, perhaps, or the Great

"Vision Quest"

Lynx—in any case, a kind of permanently assigned personal spiritual trainer), who would hunker down with the boy out on the barren plain to impart wisdom of the how-to-live-a-good-life variety. The boy could then return to his tribe to sit before a council of elders who would probe and dispute the account of the Vision Quest. If the description of the Totem Animal and the advice he had imparted seemed genuine, the boy was deemed fit to join the company of men. He had lost some of the freedoms of childhood. His life was now ordered by the rules of his tribe's Totem Animal Lodge, but, in the mixed bag that is adulthood, he now shared in, was amplified by, the power of the institution. He was thus embedded in the universe. He had brothers, seniors, a tradition, and a share in collective plans for the future.

All societies have their coming-of-age rituals: across time and in every sort of culture making up our Family of Man, from the so-called primitive to the Marines of 1997 who pounded wing pins into the chests of newly qualified paratroopers. The ceremonies share a few core ingredients: They're always a trial of some sort, often one involving physical pain accompanied by a healthy wallop of humiliation, for at their core, stripped to their most elementary symbolic level, they are nearly always "about" celebrating and hastening the death of the child in the supplicant so that he may be reborn into the tribe of men (thus the pain, thus the rather infantile postures the supplicant is often forced to adopt, thus the recurring references to death—as in one fraternity initiation in which initiates were shut into coffins).

In "primitive" cultures, and until fairly recently in our own ever-so-advanced one, the society of men was recognized as a special and distinct place, distinct from (not necessarily above) the world of women and certainly not replaceable by "the society of humans" or the "society of adults." Even among the "educated classes" there was a quantity called "a good man," and becoming one was recognized as an achievement one had to actually strive for, as this state didn't necessarily accrue just because you were born with the right chromosomes. "Good men" and "good women" shared some qualities, of course, but because they ensured the "tribe's" survival through different means, aspirants faced different training and different tests.

Until the midnineties, boot camp was just this sort of rite of passage for millions of men—a sort of secondary benefit of sustaining armies and promoting national security. The experience has been so important in the lives of so many men (we have all seen the picture of young men slogging through the mud urged on by the bellowing fellow in the Smokey Bear hat so many times) that even the term *boot camp* and its synonym *basic training* have become lodged in our vocabulary, signifying an experience that pushes the candidate to his limit, separates the wheat from the chaff. One still hears that the now-defunct *Chicago News Bureau* was a "boot camp" for the cub reporter, or that New York University's film school, in which one half of the student body is dismissed after the first year, is a "boot camp" for filmmakers.

Certainly the first armies never set out to design a rite of passage for men. We were much more utilitarian then, less concerned with whether people felt good about themselves, just whether they did the job. The job of boot camp, as ex-Marine lieutenant Adam Mesereau wrote recently, was "to simulate the stresses and strains of war." And old-fashioned boot camp, with its loud noises, sleep deprivation, scarcity of food, and the indifference of others, "simulated" just about as well as one could without killing the trainee. Since it was assumed that, even with evolving weaponry, the core experience, the climate, the human dynamics of war, wouldn't change much, the training formula stayed more or less the same decade after decade. As recently as the late eighties, for example, basic training still looked very much like the coaching scenes portrayed in, say, the movie *Sands of Iwo Jima*, in which John Wayne, as "Sergeant Stryker," looks at his motley group of men and snarls, "I'm gonna keep atcha until you act and think as one person." Journalist C. J. Chivers, who went through entry-level officer training in the Marine Corps in 1987, remembers officer candidate school through "a blur of sleep deprivation. Every day someone was shouting at me. Throwing a garbage can next to my bed to wake me up. Making me crawl around in the mud just to prove that I could do it."

At Fort Benning in 1981, when Brian Roou went through, "the drill sergeants screamed at you, got in your face, were very, very brutal to you—like the movies show. The whole idea of it, of course, was to tear you down and build you up as a unit, working together." (In the seventies, the Marines even had a recruiting slogan along those lines: "The Marines build men—body, mind, spirit.")

"They'd wake you up at all hours of the night and have you do calisthenics outside or clean the barracks or whatever. You were tired all the time. Physical training to me was not all that difficult because I'd gone into it in really good shape, but for most of the guys it was pretty demanding. They had to push themselves. A lot of them came in there in not particularly good shape, and after twelve weeks of that I saw a lot of guys lose a lot of weight and get into good shape."

In the name of the "noble chatteldom" described by James Jones, you started boot camp stripped of your name and identity, reduced to a kind of blank slate: They called you "Private," or by the last name that was stenciled on the front of your uniform. Your hair, that little flag of individual expression, was shaved off, and your "real clothes" packed away. But after spending the next couple of months living "en masse like schools of fish," you emerged supplied with a new identity and a place in a hierarchy of special people: men who had earned the description "soldier" and the right to be identified as such (with all its attendant glories) by wearing the uniform. The only difference between hazing ceremonies—which the Army and the Navy have banned—and what they did in "the old boot camp" is that one was authorized and the other was not. (In 1997, Marine commandant Gen. Charles Krulak disseminated a new order that permits a tradition "that celebrates milestones and professional achievements . . . [as long as they are] properly organized and supervised.") Hazing is perhaps more violent—carried out in secret, it can be. In 1997, for instance, home videos, shot surreptitiously by a participant, were released showing members of the Marine equivalent of the Army's Green Berets pounding the "wings," metal wing-shaped pins, that signify official status as Marine parachutists into the chests of those newly qualified. When the grainy video of this ritual (called "blood pinning" for obvious reasons) hit the evening news shows, there was a cacophony of hand-wringing and a new round (it is a perennial topic) of questions about the violent tendencies of young men. (How did they get this way? Is it our fault? Is it the fault of their violence-filled military training?)

Sociologist Lionel Tiger, author of *Men in Groups* and *The Imperial Animal*, which examine sex differences in regards to aggression and the importance of male bonding to society, assures us that "initiation spans the world's cultures" and that male initiation rituals "are nearly always more violent than their female counterparts." While adults tend to shudder at initiation rituals, "the young men who perform [them] often make [them] worse. They increase the pain, complicate the task, prolong the endurance. . . . In a word, they're testing each other, in military camps (Lejeune as surely as Sparta), on college campuses, in street gangs, to prepare themselves to be warriors . . . to earn the respect and potentially useful friendship of their peers."

In other words, ya gotta know if the guy you're gonna trust to cover your back has "the Right Stuff," and you also have to differentiate yourself from everybody else—the old, the weak, and especially the female. Since boot camps are now full of women, and since society itself has fewer testing grounds where men may be birthed by other men, I predict that the "old" hazing rituals will not seem to suffice, and that new hazing ceremonies, harder, bloodier, will be invented.

Some soldiers have found that life after boot camp is harder physically (usually men who go on to elite units like the Army's 101st Airborne Division), most say that it has been easier, but the important thing is: *Nobody treats you quite that badly again.* As C. J. Chivers, who served for six years and then went to Columbia University's graduate school of journalism, put it, "Once you'd walked the pot across the coals you were in the club." And once you got bored, there were new clubs, new tests to separate the men-who-had from the men-who-hadn't: earning your "wings," first "kill" or downing of an enemy plane, first "cruise," first equator crossing, first carrier landing, first night carrier landing, first jump, first night jump, Airborne school, SEAL training, and on and on because men can never stop inventing new tests for themselves and ways to one-up each other.

In its eighty-year life span, Fort Benning, in Columbus, Georgia, has put thousands of men through basic training. "The Home of the Infantry," the place that was a temporary home for men like George Patton and Omar Bradley, is on a sprawling piece of land once occupied by a huge plantation, and one feels the ghosts of its past simply by driving on red clay roads flanked by great oaks that look a century old, then following a road as it winds round the base past the handsome officers' homes with their shady, wraparound porches, past dusty training fields, and finally up into windy hills full of tall pines.

The "Old Army" still lives here and it is still the home of basic training that retains some resemblance to the training of past decades. Jump School is here. Open to people of all services, all ranks, all MOSs (military occupational specialties), and all genders who want to try for the badge that certifies that they are ready, if needed, to jump out of a plane. The Ranger regiment is stationed here, and since most of the training is for all-male units like this and the all-male infantry, its character is more old military.

"Benning's really tough," basic training trainees at other bases tell each other. To prepare men to be "ground-pounders"—men who shoot at other men without the protection of the metal shell of a plane or a tank—it has to be. It was only fair to the men. As Col. David Hackworth (Ret.), a much-decorated combat veteran and author, puts it, "The more sweat on the training field, the less blood on the battlefield."

Even Fort Jackson, where most of the recruits go on to jobs in combat support—which can mean anything from unit veterinarian to parachute-rigger to the registered dietician in a base cafeteria—trained recruits Benning-style. Then, Benning-style was just plain Army-style. The assumption at all Army boot camps up until the midnineties was that even if a guy never saw combat, *he was a soldier,* a known quantity. Just like a McDonald's hamburger, anywhere you find it, the package would be expected to contain certain predictable elements (within a range, of course).

The idea was that a general standing over one of those topographical table maps with the little flags and the pushpins could say, "We'll send the 187th Armor over here," and be fairly confident that he didn't have to think too much about human variables—just variables like weather, equipment, and terrain.

Given good selection *for* type, given adequate training *to* type, and given the assumption that the soldier would follow reasonable (and, to a certain extent, even seemingly unreasonable) orders, a certain level of field performance could be predicted, could, so to speak, be "ordered up."

Given the fluidity of war (remember, for instance, the battle to take Omaha Beach, where enlisted men suddenly found themselves acting as officers, where radio operators found themselves acting as infantrymen, where infantrymen suddenly found themselves acting as tank drivers, and clerks found themselves drafted as battlefield medics), one simply couldn't field infantry divisions if the men within them had radically different abilities.

If part of military training was intended to impose some kind of physical standard and ideal, the other part was for the mind, for indoctrination, inculcation of values. The point of instilling a military ethos was that it could make up for, overarch, *any remaining differences of ability and background,* fill in the chinks like a kind of spiritual spackling. The ethos—about duty, bravery, loyalty, the dishonor of cowardice, and so on—would be shared by everyone whether he was a cook or a tank driver because it was always understood that a cook might have to become a tank driver, or a soldier with the skill and mind-set of an infantryman. Most important, the ethos would be there, to be ignited if needed, as a kind of spark plug—the thing that could propel an ordinary man into the realm of extraordinary, highly unnatural behavior. Something had to push the man (ready in all other respects) into the series of unnatural acts that is combat, and ethos (combined with constant simulation of those unnatural acts—i.e., training) could make the difference.

Stepping out of a plane into . . . air . . . is highly unnatural. Every nerve in your body will scream this. Even if you remind yourself you have a parachute—*and* a backup 'chute—the body, a species survival and propagation machine, perfected by centuries of Darwinian selection, sometimes overrules the mind, and troopers find themselves "refusing." That moment, when your veins seem to fill with concrete, feels as involuntary as a fever or an epileptic fit. "Since you are clearly not thinking straight," the body seems to say, "I'll take charge here."

The acts of jumping out of a plane (even if it is just into cheerful sunlit air and not blackness or air illuminated by tracer rounds) and of charging toward people who want to kill you have to be taught and practiced. They require an immense amount of will or that pure "Hooooaaah," hang-it-all-out-there lust for adventure that young men tend to be full of. But these extraordinary acts are made easier by the backup of a national and military culture giving assurance that this kind of risk is worth it, that the option of cowardice is unthinkable, and that there will be ample reward for these risks or sacrifices—ticker-tape parades, the adoration of women, medal ceremonies, glowing smiles, goggling kids, whatever. Today, from our safe perch we look back at Omaha Beach and marvel at the near-foreign culture and training that produced thousands of men (many plucked right out of civilian life) who got off relatively safe landing craft (well, in a lot of cases they were dumped or pushed off) and strode forward—out of the enveloping, caressing, gently rocking cradle of the sea—onto naked shingle, circled by bluffs full of enemy riflemen crouched in concrete pillboxes.

The battle for Omaha Beach, the most famous clash in the story of the Allied invasion of Normandy, doesn't work as a perfect model of what future battles will look like. (One certainly hopes twenty-first-century technology will prevent a *few* of the screwups that ultimately caused that bloody morning.) But that battle, re-created so brilliantly in Steven Spielberg's film *Saving Private Ryan*, illustrates what military philosopher Gen. Carl von Clausewitz called "the fog of war" and "friction," phenomena that seasoned soldiers predict will always be with us. The infantrymen of World War II often found themselves in that state and pronounced the situation FUBAR: "fucked up beyond all recognition." Whatever he calls it, every combat veteran has experienced a FUBAR moment: those periodic breakouts, despite the best people and the best equipment, of sheer, howling, What-the-*hell*-is-going-on-here? surrealism, chaos, and confusion.

"Everything about war is simple," Clausewitz advised, "but the simplest thing is difficult. Countless minor incidents—the kind you can never foresee—combine to lower the general level of performance so that one always falls far short of the intended goal. . . . The military machine—the army and everything related to it—is basically very simple and therefore seems easy to manage, but we should keep in mind that none of its components is of one piece. Each part is composed of individuals . . . the least important of whom may chance to delay things or somehow make them go wrong."

From the technical side, Omaha Beach would seem to be a classic illustration of FUBAR—as well, of course, as an illustration of the most heartrending courage in the face of technical failures. Many of the men on Omaha Beach had had to shed equipment and backpacks to keep from drowning because they were as heavily loaded as pack mules and their landing craft dumped them off in water too deep to stand in. Many companies crawled onto parts of the beach that had not been "prepared" by advance bombing because their boats were pulled off course by heavy tides. If we could have restaged Omaha Beach with some of the technology we have now, wouldn't our communication equipment at the very least have prevented these deadly mistakes? Lt. Col. Robert Carrington, a forty-one-year-old West Point graduate and commander of several infantry companies, mulled this question over for about fifteen seconds, shrugged, and said matter-of-factly, "Something else would go wrong."

We see a wonderful illustration of the necessity of "all-purpose" interchangeable soldiers in Stephen E. Ambrose's book *D-Day: June 6, 1944.* A senior officer lands on the beach, fresh and full of vigor. Striding around to find some (any!) troops to direct, he comes upon a group of shell-shocked men standing dazedly near a driverless tank and roars, "Can anybody drive this thing?!!" Ambrose doesn't say what happened next, but you can figure somebody learned to drive it pretty quickly.

Modern warfare, with its light, compact, take-'em-with-you weapons, is even more fluid and unpredictable. In the famous Mogadishu battle where eighteen American fighters died, raggedy Somali men who looked nothing like soldiers suddenly produced portable missile launchers—called RPGs (for rocket-propelled grenades). Men who had been flying in mighty Black Hawk helicopters (with rotor wake strong enough to peel babies from the arms of their mothers) suddenly found themselves on the ground, fighting for their lives at close range with townspeople. This, most military planners think, is a sketch of "360-degree wars" in years to come—wars fought in dense cities, full of civilians, full of very portable, hideable weapons, and certainly with nothing like a front line.

Military experts often cite the Gulf War as an example of a war where "there was no front" or where "the front did not stay the front." Scud missiles, for instance, hit support encampments in what was supposed to be the rear a number of times while American troops were in Saudi Arabia.

In a "360-degree war everybody has to be able to do anything" is the way Marine brigadier general Jim Mattis puts it. That means we're back at the soldier-as-interchangeable-unit, everybody-up-to-the-same-battle-ready-standard concept. That means support troops have to be as tough as the guys on the front line.

"Disrupting distribution of supplies is a legitimate historical tactic," Capt. Joe Gross of Fort Jackson points out, "so if you have people who can't protect themselves, they couldn't repel a threat and the enemy could take advantage of a break in the line. For instance, cooking tents are usually in the rear. If someone comes around and busts through there, the guy who's going to be repelling them is going to be your guy at the stove there. I wouldn't want to go to war with a fat untrained cook."

The going-for-the-"weakness"-in-the-line scenario actually happened to Jim Mattis, then a lieutenant colonel, while he was leading a battalion of Marines through Kuwait, ultimately to liberate it from the Iraqis.

We were moving north on the right flank of Task Force Ripper. In front of us a quarried area showed up, so we had to slide slightly to our left. We checked out the quarried area [for enemy troops hiding for an ambush]. Some Cobra Gunships flew over it; some men went up and looked into it from their vehicles, but they couldn't see much because of the humps of ground in front of them that extended for quite some distance. So we skirted it to the left, and as we came around it and got into our normal position on the right of Third Tank Battalion, Iraqis to the north and northeast opened fire on us at quite some distance—mostly tank-gun fire. At about this time my combat train (this is your corpsman, the cooks who are providing security for the corpsman, stretcher bearers, the mechanics, the supply people, ammunition resupply people, administrative people—that sort of thing—who ride in Humvees and trucks) were coming around the quarried area. Suddenly the enemy came out of it in armored personnel carriers of Soviet manufacture. So, while we were confronting an enemy to the north and northeast, behind me our support troops were being attacked by Iraqi combat troops that we'd overlooked. At that point I turned over the fight in the rear to my XO [executive officer] and he took the reserve company back. But in the interim, before they got there, the support Marines had dismounted and opened fire on the bad guys. I remember one mechanic in particular, Lance Corporal Castleman, who just sat there firing, furiously defending the combat train. A lot of Marines in the combat train were firing—and two lieutenants, one the battalion motor transport officer, the other the battalion maintenance officer [both were in MOSs that are now open to women], ran across open ground under fire with shoulder-launched rockets and knocked out two of the enemy armored personnel carriers. The fighting continued, but that took a lot of the steam out of the Iraqis' aggressiveness; they lost their will at that point. By the time the reserve company got back there, there was not a whole lot of fighting left. Up front I was allowed to stay focused on my job because I had a lot of real tough guys who happened to be in combat service support MOSs back there doing their job [in addition to] doing what becomes their job at a time like this: to find an enemy and kill 'em. They may be involved at other points in resupplying us with fuel or water or ammunition or whatever, but wars don't go real neat.

A drill sergeant, naturally, has the shortest, most vivid answer to the question of whether the Army's clerks should have to be able to heft 70-pound backpacks, and drag 190-pound men out of an area quickly. "Who's defending your airfield? Your support weenies!" he crows.

Understanding the unpredictable, often irrational, random nature of war was what enabled many men to endure boot camp with stoicism and occasional bemusement, but there were other men who found a special significance in basic training. Something about the structure and challenge fed a spot in their souls that had been empty and hungry.

For boys who were drifting, who were trying to find a purpose in life, for boys whose fathers had been distant, or ridiculing, or weak, or simply not there, boot camp opened a portal to a world of strong and worthy fathers. For men from the big cities, particularly from communities where households run by single mothers (and grandmothers) abound, and where many of the most spirited, entrepreneurial men turn to crime as an alternative to the drudgery of a job at, say, the local Wendy's, boot camp offered a model of "the good man" and the path *to become him*. Finally one could face danger, work out the kinks, be aggressive, do things women couldn't do, feel like a man, get out from under the thumb of women, and schoolteachers, and feminized social service bureaucracies, without risking life in jail.

Military boot camp is not the only place where young men have found this experience, of course. In between adding color commentary to TV coverage of the 1997 NBA championship play-offs, ex-basketball star Isiah Thomas talked about coaches he'd had on the way up. One of his favorites used to keep the starters on the court even if they were hopelessly behind so his stars "could feel the pain" of losing. Thomas wasn't crying abuse—as is so often the case when someone faces TV cameras these days. On the contrary, he choked up as he remembered the "beautiful man." "We matured under him," Thomas said reverently. "We grew up."

The point is that many young men come to the military—and its portal basic training—seeking the experience they know from the movies, hoping to match the experience of their fathers, hoping to earn and find a worthy direction and a new and better self, hoping to rise above their peers by earning something *difficult* to earn. When journalist Susan Faludi spent a month in the summer of 1997 at a Marine recruiting post in an area of southern California "beset with . . . gang fights, with Southeast Asian refugees overwhelmed by culture shock and poverty, and a school system that relies more on barbed-wire fences and truancy patrols than on quality education to retain its teenagers," one of the recruiters told her, "It's sort of a weird thing. They want to be disciplined. We're seeing that a lot more. A lot of them will actually say, 'I'm looking to be disciplined.' Not at first. First they'll say they want to get away from their dads, but then when you really get down to what's bothering them, they'll say, 'My dad doesn't discipline me enough.' They'll say their dad disciplines them just when he sees them for five minutes. Most of them don't think highly of their fathers. It's like they are looking for a father figure who tells them what to do all the time."

"All cycle long they hate you," says Sgt. Rick Ayala, who tries to be tough on recruits whenever he can get away with it, "but they come up later and thank you for being harsh and demanding on 'em 'cause they learn. One female private came up and said, 'You're the first positive male role model I've ever had.'"

On the other side of the continent, also in the summer of 1997, a summer in which the hunger for discipline seemed to hang in the air, a lieutenant colonel who is still on active duty and thus didn't want to be named was noticing the same thing in the young people coming into his Army unit: "They are looking for discipline," he said. "When you treat 'em the worst, they respect you more. . . . They seem to want to be made into men by a strong father figure." Boot camp often fulfilled this, of course, but apparently not these days: The complaint this colonel says he hears "over and over again from new soldiers coming into [his unit and their first duty station] is that [their basic training] was not tough enough."

"Not tough enough" is an understatement. As Mark Thompson, *Time* magazine's military correspondent, wrote in 1997, "no one who went through boot camp in the 1950s or '60s would recognize the place today."

Looking for Discipline !!!

Certainly a group of middle-aged noncommissioned officers seemed a bit unsettled in 1996 when they went back to their old boot camp, Great Lakes Naval Training Base, for a tour.

As *Soundings*, a Norfolk, Virginia, Navy-flavored community weekly, tells it, the first thing these middle-manager types are confronted with at their alma mater is the new base commander, one Capt. Cornelia de Groot Whitehead, who uses her opening briefing to inform the visitors that "40 percent of new recruits have at some time been victims of serious physical or sexual abuse, while 26 percent have contemplated suicide." Accordingly, Whitehead, who referred to critics as "Old Navy dinosaurs" and recruits as "the youngsters in our care," says, "We've decided we needed to do something different."

One big change is the infamous "obstacle course." It's been renamed the "confidence course" and moved indoors to comprise "an indoor labyrinth of pipes to crawl through, monkey bars to swing from, ladders to climb up and balance beams to sidestep over." (No more crawling through the mud on your belly.) At one point one of the geezers (for in military terms these midfortyish men and women are senior citizens) grumbles, "It sounds like we're starting to bend over backward for them," then apparently remembering his "New Navy" catechism, he follows the faux pas with "Some of us have got to leave our old ways. It's a new Navy."

According to Secretary of Defense William Cohen, Great Lakes is a jewel of the "New Navy." He pronounced the base "a role model" during a visit in September 1997.

Cohen might have been alluding to the base's all-out assault on the problem of recruit stress. In 1998 the campaign to soothe the recruits starts on the bus that carries them from O'Hare Airport to the sprawling base on the shores of Lake Michigan, some forty miles from Chicago's most northwestern edge. Just off planes from everywhere in the country, boys and girls, in standard American mall kid uniform of baggy pants and a T-shirt, pile onto buses. The first thing on the orientation agenda is a video. The part about "it's okay to cry" has been excised since Representative Buyer needled the brass about it, but the format is the same: Real-life recruits or recent graduates look into the camera and tell the newcomers what to expect. "Cherish your letters from home," one girl advises. "The hardest thing is the loneliness, but you can overcome that and make friends." The "confidence course can be a great stress reliever," says another brightly, offering the assurance that "physically, anyone can get through boot camp."

"I hated getting screamed at, but I realized it's nothing personal," a female recruit says. "The hardest part was being away from my family and my baby." And don't get too sad, other trainees tell us, "Mom and Pop Night," the night before graduation, is really fun.

After the video, the recruit division commander (RDC—the Navy's term for what is, in effect, a drill sergeant) takes questions. Two girls' hands immediately pop up. "Will we be allowed to keep journals as a stress reliever?" asks one. "Can I keep photos of my father and my son [near my bed]?" asks the other. There are no more questions after that.

At reception, the new recruit is handed a kind of survival kit, a "Recruits Bill of Rights," a rundown on sexual harassment policy, and a trainee guide, about a quarter of its pages given over to a chapter entitled "Rape and Sexual Assault Awareness." "Remember," it counsels, "if the victim says 'No' and the assailant continues to pursue sex to its conclusion, the assailant is a rapist . . . 87 percent of rapists know their victims," and "everyday images in the media present women as weak, indecisive, and ineffective." Sexual harassment, the guide says, "includes a preconceived belief associated with gender."

The good news is that "CARE counselors are available to talk over traumatic incidents pertaining to this incident. . . . The CARE counselor will assist you with generating the internal motivation you need to make it through boot camp."

Until the fall of 1998 the recruit also got a pocket-sized blue card with the message: "In the dumps? Thinking about giving up? Thinking about running away? Help is less painful. Remember, we do care about you!" The recruit was supposed to be able to hold it up in the middle of an activity to indicate to the instructors that he needed a break, and it was also supposed to be a handy pocket reference for locating base support resources like the chaplain's office, a mental health counselor, and such. The Navy eventually withdrew the "stress card"—or the "blues card," as some wags called it—after it was ridiculed in the civilian press and after a congressional committee* charged to investigate boot camp training recommended that it go. Recruits are still able to avail themselves of something called a "train-

---

*Kassebaum-Baker, headed by Nancy Kassebaum, a former Republican senator from Kansas.

ing time-out": much the same, except instead of holding up your card, you raise your hand to get the attention of the RDC.

Great Lakes, now the Navy's only training base, is saturated with the jargon of therapy. A visitor to the office of Rear Adm. Kevin Green, who commanded the base in the late nineties, is sent on his way with stacks of Navy-commissioned studies supposedly documenting the base's assertion that today's recruits are more fragile than ever before, that they are victims of broken homes and domestic violence.

Special handling was virtually unknown in the "Old Navy," but as Paul Richter reported in the *Los Angeles Times* in 1997, when a Great Lakes CO decided that a trainee named Travis Bullard lacked motivation, "[h]e was packed off to a 'personal applied skills' class, where he was offered emotional support, instructed on deep breathing and stress reduction and given a chance to explore his feelings by pasting cutout magazine photos on a piece of cardboard. 'These instructors, it turns out they're really nice guys,' said Bullard," who Richter described as "a gentle, gangling 20-year-old from tiny Hackett, Ark."

In general, most of what the new drill instructor is called upon to do these days is to be "a nice guy" or gal.

"Not long ago," Richter wrote, "the recruit asking why he had been ordered to perform some task would be told, fortissimo: 'Because I said so!' Now instructors are to explain the rationale behind each order so recruits learn to think and understand and carry on willingly. 'They've always got a question,' sighed Chief Petty Officer 1st Class Garry McClure. 'Whatever it is, they want to discuss it and discuss it some more.'"

According to Richter, "The RDC of the '90s serves as counselor as much as disciplinarian—talking to recruits about military issues, careers and matters of the heart. Navy boot camp instructors say they spend hours each day dispensing advice to the curious, confused, homesick and lovelorn. Requests to chat are always heaviest after dinner, says McClure, a thirteen-year veteran from Roxbury, Massachusetts, 'because that's when they get the letters from home—and they want somebody to talk to.'"

Recruits no longer drill with rifles; all training in the winter months is held inside, and they do PT every other day—instead of every day. By contrast, recruits spend more than forty hours some weeks in lecture-hall settings, and many more hours in hands-on training in such areas as fire fighting and basic nautical skills.

In the fall of 1998, the base tweaked the recruit division commanders' job description again. Each division—the Navy's equivalent of a platoon—now gets one more RDC, so that divisions are now staffed with three RDCs. Furthermore, the Navy ended the practice, used in all the services during basic training, of allowing instructors to "deputize" one of their more responsible recruits as a temporary supervisor and drillmaster. It's always been a way to reward particularly motivated recruits and groom him or her for a leadership position. It's also a way to instill independence and responsibility in the platoon as a whole. (Along the lines of "Class, teacher's going to leave the room now and I expect you to . . .") Now, however, Navy policy dictates that divisions will be supervised by at least one RDC from 4 A.M. until around 10 P.M.,when the kids crawl into their barracks-style bunk beds. Capt. Craig Hanson, commander of Recruit Training Command, says the new policy gives the RDC more time to set an example, and that "the more interaction there is [between staff and recruit], the better recruit we're going to be turning out in the end." RDC Linda Murrah told the *Navy Times* that she saw it as "baby-sitting." "When they hit the decks," she told the paper, "they won't have anyone to lead them around." Another staffer at Great Lakes, a former RDC, told the *Navy Times* he thought the new policy was really instituted because of gender integration and the danger that, "if left to their own devices, male [recruits] and female [recruits] will find ways to sneak off, and, well, you know."

On my first whole day at Great Lakes I got to take a look at a fire-fighting drill. "Learn or burn!" says the public affairs escort cheerfully as we drive over to the training hall. The military is good at simulations, and I expect smoke, maybe a few flames, maybe some kind of simulated roaring sound, but when we enter the hall, there is not much going on. Several lines of recruits stand holding fire hoses. Each hose is supported by about thirty kids, boys and girls, standing very still, all very evenly spaced, with about eight inches between them, as if the body configuration had taken some time to arrange and as if they are now afraid to do anything that would mess it up. Everybody continues to stand motionless while the instructors bustle around purposefully.

By way of conversation during what is seemingly a lull, I ask the young male officer standing next to me, a fire specialist, if one actually has the luxury of so many hands for one hose in a real shipboard fire. Probably not, he admits, but on the other hand, you don't really need so many people. Actually, a full hose could be handled by one or two. Once again, the point seems to be to learn to work as a team and to avoid the awkward subject of strength differences among recruits. After all, if twenty people can't control an active fire hose, who can? This thought seems to set him off because he begins quite spontaneously and openly (considering that a public affairs rep is standing nearby) to vent about the lack of realism in this training: "This is nothing like a ship fire," he says. "It's not hot, it's not dark, there's no smoke; the fires I was in scared the hell out of me."

While the kids continue to stand there dutifully holding their few inches of hose, Petty Officer Denise Gillespie wanders over and joins the carping session: "When I got here in 1984, we started off running. For three days all we did was run. And we carried an eighteen-pound rifle everywhere. We had limits, but they were higher limits so you ended up with that indomitable spirit of 'I won't give up.' You knew that you had accomplished something. The females that come in now are treated very differently—not like sailors, sort of like softer sailors."

On another day, two mixed-gender divisions are herded over to "the confidence course." Before recruits are let loose on this collection of balance beams and climbing walls, they have to watch a safety video that carefully goes over the technique to be employed on every element ("Grasp the rope firmly") and each element's possible dangers ("You could get rope burn if you grasp too firmly"). A trainer wearing a cap that reads "I think safety!" gives a lecture about the spirit with which this is to be attempted: "I don't care how fast you go or how slow. This is just to have a good time," he says. "Go at your own pace. At least give it a try. This is mostly an exercise in teamwork. That playground over there," he says, gesturing at the confidence course, "is a stress reliever."

"The pull-up," he says, pointing to some stainless-steel bars, "is an exercise where some of your teammates are gonna need some help. If you see them hanging there and they can't pull themselves up, don't just walk by. Grab 'em by the legs and push 'em up. But I don't wanta see any hands on butts, on thighs. You can grab the calves, the knee."

When the group starts the course, most of the girls immediately fall behind the boys or get hung up on some element—a pull-up bar, for instance—where they can't do all the required reps and then can't move on. The boys, seeing teammates hanging from bars or scrabbling at the bottom of the climbing pole, immediately help their teammates. Inevitably a second boy comes by and gets in on the teamwork action to help—since this is the point of the exercise. After a few minutes the huge swatch of exercise area is filled with what looks like a modern dance performance: Boys have grasped girls' legs and are furiously pumping the girls up and down; in some cases, there's a boy on each leg. Meanwhile the RDCs (two men and one woman), standing off to the side, make bitter jokes about the "unmotivated" and "apathetic" company they'd been given to train.

But maybe a "softer sailor" isn't a problem. Wars of the future (everybody is vague about when the future starts) will call for "warrior technicians" rather than pure Sergeant Fury–style warriors, say service chiefs and congressmen and most D.C.-based officers. In a hearing called by the House Armed Services Committee's (HASC) subcommittee on personnel to investigate the efficacy of gender-integrated training, Representative Jane Harman (D-Cal) painted a shining picture of "future wars [which] will be more technological and information-based than past wars."

"Women and men will be asked to perform key combat missions that are far from the battlefield," she said, and "[i]nstead of relying solely or primarily on ground forces, future wars will increasingly involve platforms operating in the air or at sea, electronic information interception, and smart weapons. Women and men will operate those platforms from consoles far back from or above the front lines."

This bloodless, sanitized *Star Trek*ian future of "platforms" and "consoles" and "digitized soldiers" seems very far off for the Army, which is still having to make do with tanks from World War II, but not as far-fetched for the Navy, whose primary combat ships are aircraft carriers, those "giant floating factories," as the *Navy Times* once put it. The Navy says that strength training and the macho endurance stuff were relevant when about 40 percent of the tasks on ships were manual and labor-intensive, but this is true of only about 10 percent of normal carrier tasks today.

The modern aircraft carrier can indeed feel as stable and unmilitary as, say, a Ramada Inn motel—with interior decor that is about as thrilling. Seamen still have to slog up and down narrow, metal, clanging, open-air stairways to get from level to level, but the heavy, expensive stuff gets toted around by elevator. The bombs travel by elevator from lower levels up to the flight deck, where they are secured on the fighter planes. At each end of the trip, ordnance handlers have a minute or two of hard hefting to get the bombs into or off the cart they travel on, but the elevators have certainly reduced the amount of strength one needs—periodic hefts are a lot less challenging than a job that requires constant lifting and carrying. The Great Lakes base commander makes the point that "twenty-eight years ago a Sumner-class destroyer had three gun mounts shooting five-inch shells and it took twenty-seven people to man each. Now two can man those guns from a communications center."

That's all very well, argue "the dinosaurs," but many carrier jobs—even those improved by machinery—call for more endurance than the average civilian is used to or capable of. Think of flight-deck crews who have to be on their feet for a twelve-hour day,* often, as in the Mideast, exposed to blistering sun, in air made even hotter by exhaust from revving jet engines. And you can't slack off on this twelve-hour shift. A plane is launched every forty-five seconds during most of the shift and nearly as often a returning jet shoots toward the deck at around 120 mph. If any of the flight-deck crew messes up a tiny detail—leaves a hand-tool on a runway, tells an incoming plane that the deck is clear for landing when in fact another plane hasn't finished taxiing off—there will probably be a crash and the loss of a multimillion-dollar plane and several million-dollar aviators, as well as any of the deck crew nearby.

Furthermore, argue the dinosaurs, a carrier quickly stops being a floating Ramada Inn when something actually warlike happens. Maybe the ship is hit with a missile, maybe it hits a mine, maybe a plane crashes on the flight deck and starts a fire. Abruptly, wires in all those marvelous pieces of machinery melt, machines begin to mal-

---

*Sometimes, shifts for flight-deck crews stretch to eighteen hours. On those days, "green shirts," as the guys who work most directly with the planes are called, don't even bother going to their rack to sleep; they simply collapse on the floor in an area that has been dubbed "the graveyard" (*Navy Times*, 12/98).

function, hard drives crash, the "fog of war" descends, and suddenly you need people who can do everything and do it with brute force—whether the task at hand is hauling high-pressure fire hoses, or dragging unconscious pilots out of burning planes, or carrying wounded sailors up flights and flights of those spindly metal ladders—so narrow they won't accommodate two abreast. And some ships don't have the number of people that a carrier does. A minesweeper, for instance, one of the classes of ship recently gender-integrated, has a crew of about fifty and it is easy to imagine a fire engaging all fifty people working their hardest.

It's very hard to believe as fervently in the "bloodless" war of the future after our operations in Iraq and in the Balkans in the winter of 1998 and in 1999. Deployed to bomb Kosovo, superb planes like the B-2 bomber (so beautiful, so high-tech, it might have been lifted from one of George Lucas's *Star Wars* movies) were grounded by clouds. They had to sit in hangars until it stopped raining!

Manned fighter jets could have flown under the cloud cover—there was even a level at which they could have flown within strike range and escaped radar detection—but because there was a chance of losing pilots, the president didn't send them. So technology has not brought sublime confidence and a bloodless war yet.

What stands out starkly in the revised curricula of modern boot camps is ideology. Selections of actual exercises seem almost arbitrary or chosen for their symbolism. The new boot camp is a product of changed philosophy, a change in the way society values what is often called the "warrior culture," and a change in the willingness of the Army brass to defend its unique culture to civilian overseers.

This is what wags sometimes call "Boot Camp Lite," where the goal is to "develop the soldier's self-esteem, self-confidence, and positive attitude towards army service" and where recruits are routinely sent to "sensing sessions" in which an NCO asks them questions like "How's the laundry service?" "How's the food?" even "Do you think your drill sergeants have done anything wrong?"

Col. David Hackworth (Ret.), who has become something of a cult figure for his broadsides at the Pentagon's "perfumed princes," has used his widely read on-line newsletter to rail that "initial entry training has been too watered down, made too politically correct, to accommodate women and to give the recruits that warm, fuzzy Boy Scout summer camp feeling.... Too many of the kids graduating from Army basic training are walking cannon fodder."

New boot camp defenders argue that the changes are minor, that they are only being a little more "accommodating" to the recruit, that this is what you have to do to man an all-volunteer army. "It's not fair to be harsh on them," explained one boot camp CO. Many have signed up as casually as if they were "taking out a subscription to a paper," and are thus not "educated consumers." If challenged, he asserted, they'd drop out "in the blink of an eye."

There is an argument that some of the changes called "soft" and examples of creeping "demilitarization" are, in fact, just smart. The switch from Army boots to running shoes, for instance. Why, says Capt. Joe Gross, should we flirt with overuse injuries (chronic low back pain, wonky knees) that tend to crop up in a soldier's late twenties and thirties when we have the tools to prevent them and extend his career? We hang on to stuff that has no practical training value just because we're nostalgic about "the tradition," say the new boot camp proponents.

Maj. Jefferson Figuerres was XO (second in command) of a training unit at Fort Knox, Kentucky, "back in the days when men were men, women were women, and everyone else was a hairdresser," he jokes, adding quickly, "Just kidding. I'm all for that equality thing."

"Unofficially (because it was never written down anywhere), the goal was to break trainees down and build them back up into the soldiers we wanted them to be," explains Figuerres.

We are heirs to a training system inherited from Frederick the Great of Prussia and the British Army, where soldiers were taught to be more afraid of their officers and NCOs in peacetime than they were of the enemy in wartime. This style of training was appropriate up to modern times when we fought conventionally and most soldiers would fight under the supervision of their first-line leaders and for a draftee army, but it is less so now.

I agree [that] raising a soldier's self-esteem is important. The problem, in my opinion, is that the soldiers raised under the old system believe that the way they were trained is the way "real" soldiers should be trained. They don't understand, for example, the way a martial arts teacher mentors a student into becoming a warrior. . . . But either method would identify those recruits who are not suited for military duty.

The current budget-worried Army is more concerned with trainee attrition than they are with putting quality soldiers in the field. We lose money when a recruit drops out. The whole "up or out system" requires a certain "intake" (read quota) of new recruits to maintain the Army as it suffers normal losses from retirements and end of enlistments. The Army lacks flexibility (e.g., to adjust the up-or-out time limitations) to accommodate good or bad recruiting years. [In other words, in "bad" recruitment years the Army should not enforce "up or out" so rigorously.] The Army also has no way of tracking quality recruiting. Recruiting officers have to satisfy quotas based on numbers of recruits they sign up. Maybe it should hold them to the number of soldiers that successfully graduate from basic training. . . .

With the plea "Please don't get me fired," a lieutenant colonel who has commanded an all-male, infantry-bound basic training battalion defends the new climate by saying:

[The concept of tearing down in order to rebuild] doesn't have to be part of the process. If you look at what the end state is, you would like to have a soldier who feels like it's acceptable in this profession to have some initiative. We want 'em to have initiative, we don't want 'em to just be robots and blindly respond to orders—just do things because somebody told them to do things. And part of our analysis is in order to continue to foster the idea that the guy, that initiate, is valued. So you take 'em when they come in and you accept what they bring to ya, and you identify what is acceptable and what is not acceptable and you try to get rid of the stuff that's not acceptable and build on the stuff that is—and also put more stuff in their tool bag.

John Hillen came of age on the cusp of the "Old Army" and "New Army." Through a father who was an Army Ranger in the sixties and seventies, he's seen what the Army once was. As commander of a tank unit in the Gulf War when he was in his early twenties, he's seen what the Army of the nineties could do when it was working right. Now, at thirty-three, as a fellow at the Institute for Strategic and International Studies, spending his days listening to high-level brass pledging total allegiance to "New Army" policies, he is exposed to the "New Army" in full bloom. The Army, he says, is "going through a colossal identity crisis concerning its role as an institution in American society and the extent to which its values and ethos must change to accommodate changes in America herself."

To see that identity crisis in full force, perhaps the best place to watch is in the Army, the oldest, largest, and most tradition-encrusted of the four branches, and particularly in an Army boot camp. Basic training camps are visible—that is, every civilian adviser knows about them and has a vague idea of what goes on there—and they involve youth (a constant focus of public fretting). Thus they become labs for the newest vogue in training philosophy and the focus of passion over the defense of tradition. Thus the constant hurly-burly in the late nineties, in Congress, and on the TV pundit shows, over gender integration: whether it should be scrapped (thus "taking a giant step backward," as the integration proponents put it) or continued so that (in the proponents' view) we may "train as we fight." Anyway, here the Army's struggle between which set of values (civilized or warrior culture) will direct training has produced a very strange hybrid indeed: part John Wayne, part Outward Bound, part one of those weekends in which employees of big corporations are sent to a country retreat for sensitivity training.

The Army boot camp of the nineties has preserved many of the showiest, "sexiest" elements of their training tradition: Recruits still stand at attention while the drill sergeant howls, "What is the spirit of the bayonet?" (Answer: "To kill, Drill Sergeant! To kill!") In what the drill sergeant training manual has dubbed "The Gunfighter Phase" of the nine-week basic training course, recruits are issued rifles and get to march around fields with them. Recruits still learn to dismantle mines, to rappel down walls—very, very cool-looking—and the fine points of bayoneting tires that are supposed to be enemy soldiers.

But many elements of basic training camp have become amalgams of old and new: There are still hand-to-hand combat drills, but since the recruits aren't allowed to actually touch each other, they split up into pairs and simulate moves ("Knee to groin!") as the drill sergeant calls them out, which gives this group exercise a sort of dreamy, slow-motion, Tai Chi–in-the-park appearance.

Open-bay barracks—the airplane hangar–like space full of rows of metal cots—are gone (replaced by ordinary rooms with a couple of bunk beds, wall posters, comforter sets, and radios, very much like a college dorm), but recruits still have to snap to attention for quarters and dress inspection. But you can't have just anybody doing those inspections. In the name of "sexual misconduct and harassment prevention," the regulations decree that any time an NCO inspects quarters he or she must be "accompanied by personnel of [the] same gender area inspected" and that the inspector must be "assisted by two same gender enlisted soldiers" who will "maintain entrance security."

Army recruits still get up at four in the morning, but now they pull on sweat suits and running shoes instead of uniforms and stiff, leather, lace-up Army boots. They still do PT first thing (before breakfast!), but now instead of struggling along to meet one standard, instructors separate them into Ability Groups geared to very different fitness levels. Because training regulations note that "many new soldiers are not physically fit or capable of strenuous activity," they no longer do a required number of push-ups to a count, the drill sergeant exercises along with them as a sort of "role model," and they drop out when they feel like it. As Col. Byron D. Greene, the director of Plans, Training and Mobilization, told the *Army Times*, "You're not competing with the rest of the company. You are competing against yourself and your own abilities." In week two of training at Fort Jackson the members of one Ability Group were judged "not ready to run yet," so they spent that portion of the morning walking around the practice field at a leisurely stroll, sometimes breaking into twos or threes for conversation.

All of these "regs" come from a slim sheaf of paper with the very *2001: A Space Odyssey*-ish title of TRADOC 350-6, or "Initial Entry Training (IET) Policies and Administration Regulations Issued by the Training and Doctrine Command (TRADOC) of the Department of the Army"— drill sergeants just call it "The Regulation."

One of the most fundamental changes is that Army boot camp has turned away from what the Marines call a "transformative" mission. To want to transform the recruit would imply that there was something bad about him to start with and that could erode self-esteem. So rather than start the recruit at the bottom of the human totem pole and ask him to work his way up, current regs declare that "[a] soldier is a soldier from day one," and that "although the term 'trainee' may be used to describe a soldier in [initial entry training], . . . IET soldiers will be addressed as 'Soldier,' 'Private' . . . or by last name."

If the status of the recruit has changed—he is now automatically a soldier—so has the job of the drill sergeant. TRADOC 350-6 dictates that boot camp staff "will train their soldiers by building on and affirming their strengths and shoring up their weaknesses. . . . It then becomes incumbent on the cadre [all boot camp employees, including COs and drill sergeants] to coach, mentor, and assist their soldiers in meeting the standards through performance counseling and phase goal setting" because "it is essential that the cadre develop the soldier's self-esteem, self-confidence, and positive attitude towards army service."

As Gen. William W. Hartzog, the head of the U.S. Army Training and Doctrine Command, put it in the late nineties, "The drill instructors today need to understand the soldiers they deal with. . . . To do that they need to understand the culture and the mores of those soldiers. Our drill instructors today have to be role models. They have to really function in a way that the very impressionable youth hopefully will emulate."

But while kids are encouraged to look up to the drill sergeants as role models, they are also encouraged to be rather epicurean. Recruits are regularly herded, for instance, into "sensing sessions" so they can deliver "feedback" about the respect or lack thereof they have been shown by their instructors. In some ways drill sergeants are at the mercy of their trainees. At least this Fort Benning drill sergeant, writing in David Hackworth's on-line newsletter, thought so:

> A private can tell a Drill to ——— off and be told "The private's having a bad day, leave him alone." No more Article 15's (Unit punishment)—way too many in the brigade this month. If a gung ho private squares away a dirtbag [i.e., fights with or yells at another recruit who's cutting up], it's the Drill Sergeant's fault, so relieve him. My battalion Sergeant Major's favorite saying is "This is a business. We are putting out a product. Don't take too much pride in the product because the soldier's going to graduate whether you're here to train them or not."

Drill sergeants take the new dictates very seriously. They are soldiers first, so most have been bred to believe that they have to do their job—not ask why. But they also feel they have to accept regulations they mock in private because the power balance has tipped against them drastically in the last decade. Partly it was the imbroglio now known simply as "Aberdeen"—during which daily newspapers across the country portrayed drill sergeants as predatory monsters. It left them in the doghouse, they say, automatically suspect, guilty until proven innocent. (A 1995 Herblock political cartoon showed a smirking older male in a drill sergeant's hat leading a chained, dog-collared female soldier.) "Old Army" trainee culture disdained "snitching"— actually, complaining in general. (Lt. Kyle Smith says soldiers he knew had their own name for the anonymous complaint hot lines: "Dial 1-800-WAAAAAH.") But with a lot of encouragement from officials, trainees are beginning to feel differently. To be on the safe side you handle the recruit with kid gloves.

Though reg 350-6 continually reminds us that the purpose of boot camp "is to prepare soldiers to operate effectively in the extended atmosphere of combat," it gets very finicky on the issue of recruit stress. Pages and pages are devoted to the near-scientific undertaking of "managing stress": The regulation understands that "some stress in IET [initial entry training] is necessary to prepare soldiers to operate effectively in the extended atmosphere of combat." However, "[c]ommanders must manage stress in their units to reduce unnecessary stress in IET and to help trainers . . . cope with unavoidable stress." So the regulation stipulates that "leaders must help soldiers cope with unnecessary stress by . . . conducting periodic morale/feedback sessions and conducting and requiring effective counseling." The "guiding principle," it declares, "is that stress should exist between the soldier and the task to be accomplished, not between the soldier and trainer."

Being ordered to do, say, thirty sit-ups in two minutes can be very stressful, so the reg tells instructors that it's okay to use exercise as corrective action if "the number of repetitions of any exercise [is] commensurate with the soldier's physical conditioning" and "with climatic conditions." What this means, drill sergeants say, is that you don't "drop" people on rain-soaked pavement or snowy ground.

Hearing about this innovation, Lt. Kyle Smith, who served in the eighties and is now a staff writer for *People* magazine, sputtered "standards without timing are meaningless; everyone can do a hundred push-ups or run two miles *eventually*."

The brass seem as uncomfortable with physical injury as they are with psychic injury. "In order to prevent unnecessary injuries," six paragraphs in the reg detail where, when, and how much recruits can be ordered to run.

Recruits are allowed to run "only in ability groups" and only if DSs "adhere to the principle of recovery"; "unit formation runs . . . will be limited to one per cycle/class or one per month"; and runs are to be scheduled on days in which "soldiers are not required to walk for extended periods of time."

"Physical contact with soldiers for disciplinary or other reasons is prohibited"; on the other hand, "[p]hysical contact when making corrections directly related to training is permitted." This can be a gray area. Basic training is now gender integrated except in camps preparing soldiers for infantry or artillery, so sex has been added to the mix—along with the seemingly inevitable possibility of sexual harassment or discrimination charges. In an article entitled "The New Drill Sergeant," Jackie Spinner of the *Washington Post* describes a group of drill sergeants at Fort Jackson's U.S. Army Drill Sergeants School trying to hash it all out in a class on "sexual harassment and trainee abuse":

> "Suppose there's this female," someone asks, "and her uniform is out of order and you have to correct it, and suppose someone sees you and thinks you're putting the moves on her? Or suppose there's this other soldier, and she's lying on the road, and she's hurt or collapsed or something. Suppose she needs mouth-to-mouth. What if somebody sees you when you're giving her CPR and you get in trouble because they think you're kissing her?"
>
> They seem like absurd questions to an outsider, almost comical, but none of the students is laughing. Instead, they are nodding because these are precisely the questions they have been wondering about, too.
>
> [S.Sgt. Anthony Houzah] finds the [photographic] slide he's after, one of an Army regulation, and displays it on the overhead. "It says, 'You can touch a private where the safety of the soldier is

in question or when making correction directly related to train-ing,'" he recites. "That is permitted."

"But didn't you say you have to ask her permission before you can touch her?" a student says. Houzah sighs. "No. You can touch them to correct . . ." He's cut off. "But it's safer to ask?" "Yes," he concedes. "It's safer to ask."

Drill sergeant discontent seems to be especially acute in the Army because the Army drafts its drill sergeants for two-year tours and it likes to cull them from the most macho, combat-related specialties: Infantry, Artillery, Special Forces, and Airborne. What you end up with, in other words, is a guy who's spent most of his career practicing to "kill people and blow up things" now charged with "coaching, men-toring, and assisting."

"You're not being a soldier, you're being a mama," snarls one Fort Jackson noncom who used to be a drill sergeant and now observes training from a related job at the base. "Abuse is one thing," he contin-ues, "being tough and demanding is another. . . .

> We're setting them up for failure down the road. In reception recruits get a speech about dos and don'ts that the drill sergeants are allowed: "They can't do this and they can't do that." It destroys what we call our power base right there A drill sergeant can't touch you, a drill sergeant can't cuss at you, a drill sergeant can't this, that, or the other and "you have the right to do this, you have the right to do that," right on down the line. By the time they get down to the basic training company they have this huge attitude.

He doesn't like the "trainee is a soldier from day one" philosophy either: "There's no rite of passage here at all; it's a free ride. It's just given to you: 'Here take it, along with the college money, take it. What can we do for you?' That's why I'm glad I got six more years and then I'm getting the hell out—work as a security guard for a nuclear com-pany, go fishin'."

"We used to be able to push them to the limits," says Sgt. Garvin Gourie, an instructor at the Aberdeen Proving Grounds. "It's unheard of now. They call it trainee abuse. As a drill sergeant, you're always having to do a mental check. It changes your spontaneity, and in doing

[handwritten margin note: "No Rite of Passage"]

that, it changes the way you think. It's like you are protecting your own interests."

"You're either making war-fighters or you're not," grouses Fort Jackson's Sgt. Kevin Carter. "We're making peacekeepers here."

Even at Fort Benning, the infantry school, where trainees at camps like Jackson will tell you they've heard the "training is much more radical," a drill sergeant (echoed by many others) sounds much the same:

"Dignity and respect are this big thing now; you hear that over and over again in every address," he rants. "The problem is, if some private takes you on in front of the platoon, you're going to lose that platoon if you don't lean on him."

As a case study of how the military "identity crisis" manifests itself on the ground, we can take a look at how the brass have tinkered with that old classic: the grenade-throwing exercise. It is important to keep in mind that soldiers can be expected to actually use grenades for another ten years or so (unlike bayonets), especially in the kind of close, urban, Special Operations–like fighting military experts project. Once again, the Mogadishu disaster comes to mind. Grenades are valuable because they are light, easy to hide, don't require lengthy setup, and flexible—you can dump them, place them, throw them, whatever conditions demand.

The angst over the grenade exercise started around the time the military put men and women back together for basic training. Years of anecdotal evidence and formal testing conducted by the Army contends that the average female recruit has trouble throwing thirty-five meters (or safely outside of bursting range). Coincidentally, that was the distance required to pass this exercise and graduate from boot camp. According to Representative Steve Buyer, who toured basic training camps in 1997, drill sergeants at Ford Leonard Wood, Missouri, dealt with the conflict by erring on the side of safety—that is, by passing women anyway, by letting women throw shorter distances, or by letting them "waive" the test entirely.*

Fort Jackson went further: It didn't require that one threw the grenade any distance at all. According to Fort Jackson trainers, for sev-

---

*In a phone conversation, a spokesman for the camp denied that anything like this happened, but the base made no official protest when this information was published in an op-ed by the author in the *New York Times* in October 1997 or when Representative Buyer put this in his press releases and spoke about it in committee hearings.

eral years in the late nineties, all the recruit had to do to graduate boot camp was pick up a live grenade and essentially dump it over the wall of a deep cement enclosure, where it could burst to its little heart's content. "It's another confidence exercise," said a Fort Jackson drill sergeant, explaining the point of allowing people to go out into the world having "passed the grenade exercise," though they may not be able to throw a grenade far enough to avoid blowing their heads off. "They've handled a live grenade and not totally freaked out."

"All you had to do was get it out of the pit," he said. "You could graduate from basic training and have a noodle arm. I'm telling ya, I've sat in the tower and watched 'em. There are some that can throw the damn thing fifty meters and others that go in there and barely get it over the edge of the wall, and it'll explode right on the other side of the damn wall. [The exercise] probably has something to do with confidence and hell if I know [what the point is]."

In 1998, after even William S. Cohen, the secretary of defense (or SecDef), who has generally been very supportive of "New Army" changes, complained that boot camp was too easy, Fort Jackson announced that it would start requiring all recruits to run a course with a grenade in which one had to hit targets from a variety of distances. Drill sergeants, however, are skeptical that this will change the tenor of nineties-style basic training. The grenade course has been around for a long time. Recruits were encouraged to "qualify" on it—run it successfully—as a kind of extra credit. Fort Jackson liked to "see people get the badge," so drill sergeants interpreting what they thought was their COs' wishes often let recruits run the course until they got it right. Being able to hit a target once in a while is not the same as being able to hit it consistently, of course, but they expect that retesting will continue to be the unofficial policy while Fort Jackson requires the full course.

Dogged with media stories about double standards and policies like "gender norming," the reg attempted to pin its standards policy right down to the ground: "We should train [i.e., integrated] as we fight,"* it reads.

---

*Whether this slogan makes any sense or not depends on how one defines "fight." Women soldiers are currently allowed to carry and fire guns in self-defense but not "in direct ground combat" or "to actively engage the enemy"—meaning they can't go on missions expressly designed to kill other people. On the other hand, women soldiers often assist "direct ground combat," so maybe this is what the slogan-coiners meant by "fight."

"All soldiers," it continues boldly but confusingly, "regardless of gender, train to a single standard, the Army standard. Differences in performance requirements between sexes, such as Army physical fitness test scoring, are based on physiological differences and apply to the entire force."

As to the problem of "unmilitary," "undisciplined" recruits showing up for work, camps would adopt the SecDef's suggestion: add another week—a ninth week—to basic training and spend the time imparting "core military values."

All seemed to be going swimmingly in the fall and summer of 1998 as these reforms rolled out of the pipeline. Maj. Gen. John Van Alstyne, then commander of Fort Jackson's basic training program, was quoted as saying, "We've taken the last steps in ensuring that training is identical, regardless of gender. We're trying to make sure there are *no overt distinctions*" (italics added). The Army's public affairs officers (PAOs) launched a flotilla of faxes trumpeting innovations like the "Victory Forge," a sort of marathon field exercise mimicking the much-publicized Marine "Crucible," which for its snazzy visuals—a mixed-gender platoon sweating up hills, getting mud on their faces, et cetera—played well on major news shows.

In the winter of 1998, however, there was some discouraging news: Basic training attrition rates had jumped from 14 to 19 percent over the course of the year, meaning that a thousand recruits (at a General Accounting Office–estimated cost of $4,700 per head, total $4.7 million) didn't go on to join the service after all or part of training. "The Army," said *U.S. News & World Report*, "is scrambling to fix the problem," and it quoted a senior Army official who said, "Many recruits lacked the needed motivation." Also, the article went on, the old bugaboo of "pre-existing medical ailments" (the most common is asthma) not discovered in recruitment and intake physicals had continued to flare up.

Meanwhile, the top brass didn't seem to have changed their basic philosophy. A report on drill sergeant selection and training from the Army's Office of the Inspector General, which stands until a new one is issued, complained that "[t]he [program of instruction in drill sergeant school] has not maintained pace with the changing philosophy of basic training. Instruction continues to reinforce 'in your face,' aggressive leadership while this technique is no longer used in the field."

One of the components of the discredited style, one of the mightiest weapons in the drill sergeants' arsenal, is what former Marine Adam Mesereau calls "the healthy but fierce competition between platoons within each company . . . that is a significant aspect of recruit training." Drill sergeants, wrote Mesereau, "foster that competition to build platoon unity and teamwork and to inspire recruits to stretch their physical abilities." Kyle Smith agrees. "Ability Groups are a very poor motivator. When I was training, the most popular humiliation tactic was having the entire formation run together and circle back every so often to pick up stragglers, which (a) pissed off all the good runners, creating huge peer pressure, and (b) openly humiliated the [stragglers] who kept falling off the pace. When you have an organization of one leader and, say, thirty-six sheep, peer pressure is a very effective motivator."

"We used to sing a cadence," remembers Sergeant Ayala, a swarthy thirty-year-old with pumped-up, bodybuilder-like muscles: "It went, 'Which pla-toon is the best pla-toon? Our pla-toon is the best pla-toon! Which pla-toon is the worst pla-toon? Third pla-toon is the worst pla-toon.' You can't do those things anymore because you're trying to instill teamwork in everybody." In the "New Army," competition—except against oneself—is out.

Of course, you can't tamp it down entirely. It is "a spirit you can't keep out," Ayala contends. "People come here with competition already bred into them and they strive to be whatever they want to be." And lo! one damp March day, there it was, attempting to raise its boisterous head on a muddy field to which Delta Company had been trucked for a hand-to-hand combat exercise.

There are always ten or so unscripted moments in between exercises while the drill sergeants consult their training manuals, call their spouses, or whatever drill sergeants do when they can find an excuse for an all-too-rare break, and on this break the platoons were told to keep busy by jogging inside a big muddy ring. Apparently in a frisky mood, a group of six boys from the "War Dog" Platoon began running around the perimeter of the circle in a kind of flying-wedge formation. Matching their gaits, they went faster and faster chanting in time with their thumping feet, "We are the War Dogs, the mighty mighty War Dogs; we're not the Wolf Pack, the wussie, wussie Wolf Pack." Drill Sergeant Smith, standing nearby, yelled their names and shook her finger. (The word *wus* and the act of razzing another platoon are degrading to others and not allowed.) There was some puffing while the "War Dogs" attempted to think of a more suitable cadence, but by then the momentum had seeped away and the boys drifted off to join the other kids jogging halfheartedly around the muddy track.

On another day, we see a "New Army" drill sergeant attempt to get a roomful of tired, hot nineteen-year-olds to do something they really don't want to do—put on gas masks and sealed, rubber MOPP (mission-oriented protective posture) suits—without using competition as a motivator. He explains that in the event of a chemical weapon attack the MOPP suit will become their best friend. He holds up the hideous rubber thing and explains that, used correctly, the suit is almost completely airtight from its hooded top to its booteelike shoes. He explains that its inside is lined with charcoal and that while it's a great insulator, charcoal has a way of seeping into your skin and causing "blackheads all over your body."

By employing a lot of explanation and demonstration, Sergeant LeFavre gets the one-hundred-plus kids into their sauna suits. He now has to get them to "acclimatize" by keeping the costumes on for about half an hour. ("We wore them in Saudi every day," he tells them, "*over* BDU [battle dress uniform] pants and a T-shirt!") After about ten minutes, one girl's head begins to sag until she seems to have passed out (she revives quickly after some drill sergeant attention) and kids all around the room begin tearing off the visored hoods or taking "urgent" trips to the bathroom in order to sneak a breath of cool air. There's practically a mutiny under way. At another time, Sergeant LeFavre would have tried to shame them or to threaten that they'd be kicked out. Instead he says, "This is meant to be a confidence builder!" That goes over like a lead balloon, so he tries another tack: "This is an evaluation. We need to find out who . . ." but cuts off in midsentence and attempts a more beseeching tone: "You did Victory Tower right? And you felt good about that. This is just as important as first aid [another training subject]. I'm not asking you to do this for me; I'm asking you to do it 'cause the Army may someday require you to do it. We're going to try to build you up gradually. Just do the best you can."

Finally, sounding very exasperated, he lectures, "I'm cutting you a break here. I'm not asking you to wear the gloves. Some of you don't have the things on correctly—like you've got gaps."

Ridiculous - cant wear MOPP suits for 10 minutes!

"Okay, now, at a slow, conservative pace so nobody falls out, we're going to go outside and pick up trash on the lawn." The group shuffles out numbly. "Anybody spazzing out?" he calls when the line of recruits begins slogging down the hot sidewalk that encircles the D Company HQ. A couple of hands go up and one female voice calls out, "My mask doesn't have a drinking straw!" Immediately an NCO is at her side holding a cold drink with a straw in it up to the mouth opening in her gas mask. They walk along together, she slurping from the drink, he holding the cup steady like a courtier. A few paces later, someone else pipes up, "Drill Sergeant, can we sit in the shed please!" He doesn't seem to hear the comment, so they keep shuffling until they get to the lawn and the MOPP suit people start staggering across it. Potential bits of trash are ignored, but the drill sergeant doesn't say anything. Probably, with the end of the exercise in sight, he doesn't want to push his luck.

The obstacle course, especially the climbing wall the recruits are supposed to charge and rappel over, always seemed to crystallize everything about the "Old Army" that the "New Army" now eschews. Here in one measly wall everything was combined: the potential for heavy recruit stress, loss of self-esteem, and the development of inter-platoon competition. Nothing gets that competition going like hanging halfway up the wall, flapping your legs ineffectually like you're a fish on a line, hearing the other trainees baying like bloodhounds as they charge on to the finish line.

But, as in the Navy, the Army's obstacle course/climbing wall exercise has been reconfigured as an opportunity to learn to work as a team and to learn to deal with the dicey issue of touching team members of the opposite sex. Recruits now scale the wall in squads—pulling, pushing, standing on shoulders, whatever it takes to get your teammates over. According to an Associated Press reporter who watched the exercise one day, it's "designed to teach trainees trust and confidence in one another while learning where they should or shouldn't grab when helping others through the course's many obstacles."

But for drill sergeants competition is practically a religion, so as Rick Ayala puts it,

> We find ourselves encouraging it quite a bit when nobody's around. The commanders, they want to promote teamwork,

teamwork, teamwork. But the one's who are doing the best, they need to be rewarded somehow. We run in the fastest group, Drill Sergeant Carter and myself. We have eleven males at any given time running with us, so when anything comes around and we're at a range or something and they give us some crumb cake or something, we say, "OK, unless you're in A Group, you're not getting any, because they're doing their best." Anybody has the opportunity to move up anytime if they feel like they can challenge it. We're not going to get mad at anybody for falling out of that group [if they want to try running with A Group] because we do run fast, but there have to be some perks for being the best.

If we followed [350-6] to a T, there wouldn't be anyone working here, 'cause there's a lot of things you do to bypass that regulation in order to get things done. If you went strictly by the book—and some people, they claim to—you couldn't get through to everybody. . . . Whenever it benefits [a CO], they throw it at you, but they can look the other way when you need to do things the old way. . . .

Finding this delicate balance, understanding how to live with a system that he believes "is not going to go away," is the secret to drill sergeant survival and advancement, Ayala says. In the winter of 1998, after two years instructing recruits at Fort Jackson, he was on his way to Fort Jackson's Drill Sergeant School where he would become an instructor of other *drill sergeants* and, he hoped, impart the really vital stuff: like the understanding that "it's all about politics."

"I've never been a political person, but I believe in telling it like it is," he explained, "and I believe I can help NCOs coming in to be drill sergeants and let them know exactly what they're up against and what to stay away from. It's a matter of being sensitive to what's going on around you. You have to just watch yourself because your worst enemy can be yourself; if you don't know what you're doing, you can get yourself in trouble."

One of the most difficult concepts Ayala may have to explain to potential instructors is that in the "New Army" effort is considered just as good as actual achievement. It isn't exactly spelled out in the regs, but the suggestion appears in regulation sentences like "Corrective PT is to be used only for attitude deficiencies, never for lack of ability," and "If a soldier tries hard and fails, corrective PT is not appropriate."

Ayala is fairly resigned about the "best effort" philosophy. "It comes down from higher, way up. Eventually, I guess, everybody's gonna come into it because that's what they want you to feel, that's what they want you to believe. You know it's not going to go away, so you have to do what you can in order to survive."

He can play along—up to a point. One day, he says, he was approached by several female recruits who had just failed the grenade qualifying course.

"They asked me why they didn't pass, because they had tried as hard as they could. That's when I kind of laid down the law. I said: 'There are some situations in a war where your best effort doesn't matter. You either throw a grenade out of bursting range or you get yourself and your buddies killed.' They seemed kind of shocked at that."

At Sea with the "New Navy"

The USS John C. Stennis—a Case Study

There are a couple ways to get on a carrier once it is at sea. You can be helicoptered, or carried out on a small boat of some kind, or put on a fat-bodied cargo plane called a COD along with the bags of mail from home and the boxes of frozen french fries. The plane's acronymic name stands for "carrier onboard delivery," which means that this relatively bulbous craft is actually able to charge at a heaving flight deck in the middle of the sea, then swoop in close enough to hook itself onto one of the deck's arresting cables in the "controlled crash" that is a carrier landing. The COD can also leave the ship—just like its slim-bodied cousins, the fighter jets—via a catapult that drags it 350 feet down the flight deck and then hurls it into the sky.

American Airlines it isn't. The COD has hardly any windows; you're sitting facing the rear; and you're so strapped down, you can't shift around to see out of a window anyway. The gist is you can't see where you're going and can only guess at what the plane is up to by its squeaks, whines, shudders, and thumps, and so you don't experience the usual gradual acclimatization to the new place that one gets with sight of the approaching destination.

One minute you are in a dimly lit hull full of roaring noise, and in what seems like the next moment—after a bone-shaking thump (as the plane in full throttle is "arrested" by the wire) in which anything not strapped down goes flying missilelike to the front—the rear hatch is pried open, revealing brilliant white light and the faces of Martian-esque beings in goggles and radio headsets who hover around peering into the murky hold. For some reason, landing on a carrier (and going from a 120-mph approach to a shuddering standstill in about two seconds) feels sort of like waking up from anesthesia—maybe it's because you've just been in this state of limbo, of sensory deprivation and forced passivity, and then you're abruptly hatched into the middle of life at full tilt, life that has been going on without you all this time.

On the week I am CODed out to this floating city of around five thousand ("4.5 acres of sovereign American turf," as the ship's public affairs officer describes it, referring to the area of the flight deck), the *Stennis* is in the midpoint of a six-month deployment to the Persian Gulf, where it will patrol, enforce no-fly treaties, and generally "show the flag" of the United States.

About ten miles to port, through the haze that so often drapes itself on the Arabian horizon, is a grayish shape, the USS *San Jacinto*, a guided-missile cruiser there to escort the 97,000-ton *Stennis* lest anybody out there get ideas about going after this huge chunk of state-of-the-art American electronics and steel.

Flying into the Gulf and being left on a floating platform in the middle of the sea had sounded lonely, but it turns out that it's downright crowded out here. Somewhere out there on this waveless, windless, 80-degree pond is a *second* carrier battle group—the USS *Independence* and accompanying flotilla—which has been here since February 5, around the time President Clinton decided to remind Saddam what it looks like to have two carrier battle groups patrolling his coastline.

Actually, the Gulf is so full of military personnel that by noon the cloudless blue sky is buzzing with American planes as if we were putting on an air show. There are helicopters of different types, fighter jets, radar jammers, even mini-AWACS with the mushroomlike satellite dishes that they wear over their fuselages like umbrellas.

It's a show of force, all right. Though Saddam has been docile as a lamb (at least outwardly) in the last few months, the *Stennis* remains on something close to hair-trigger readiness. The ship's loudspeaker system monotonously announces upcoming battle station drills of one kind or another, and after sundown the carrier goes into a wartime condition called "darkened ship"—so it won't sit there in the night, blazing away like some kind of damn Carnival cruise flaunting American wealth and power. (After seven o'clock, the floating city becomes a more mysterious, more poetic, more romantic place. When you look out over the water, all you can see in the blackness are a few glowing orange smudges strung along the horizon—oil refineries burning natural gas. You're not allowed to take photos with a flash during darkened ship, and the lighting in the passageways changes to bloodred [dimmer than regular fluorescent]. With fewer crew striding this way and that, one becomes more aware of the huge vessel itself and its rumbling machines, and the narrow red corridors begin to seem like the ventricles of a huge creaking, humming body. The cavernous Hangar Bay, which holds about half the ship's fleet of aircraft, gets dimmed, too—to an eerie sepia, the color of really heavy Los Angeles smog, which gives the place, even at this hour filled with mechanics crawling monkeylike about the planes, a surreal feeling.)

But the biggest element of readiness, the main event, the reason these five thousand people are all here, is to keep those warplanes flying. This means that every day, seven days a week, at about 10 A.M., the floating airfield cranks up and the F-18s, EA-6B Prowlers, and E2C Hawkeyes begin their first roaring charges off the deck. From then on, for the next thirteen hours or so (as long as it takes to fulfill the day's flying quota), the flight-deck crew will be in a constant cycle of launch and trap, launch and trap.

So far there is no culture shock for visitors to the "New Navy." Here are all the reassuring and exhilarating accoutrements of war. This is a place of blazing, shimmering heat and suffocating humidity. With the Arabian sun's rays beating down, heating the ocean to 80 degrees, then bouncing off the sea and the dark surface of the flight deck with jet engines in full burn while they jockey and chivy to take off, the temperature on the flight deck usually reaches 100 degrees or more at midday. To avoid heatstroke, many of the flight-deck crew wear "camelbacks," pouches full of water strapped to their backs, which are fitted with tubes that snake around the body to hover near the mouth.

There is grease and grit and clanks and whines and satisfyingly ear-splitting bomblike blasts and a constant urgent crackle from the control tower. Every forty-five seconds there is a bone-shaking thud, when the steam-fired catapult block (the part that attaches to the plane to pull it down the deck) hits the end of its track, then an eerie air-raid-signal-like whine as the block is reeled back to its starting position. The guy with "Shooter" stenciled on his yellow jersey keeps performing that age-old Kabuki mime sequence that signals "Clear," "Clear," "Rev," "Go!" and there are genuine aviators, the Top Gun guys, like something out of Central Casting, swaggering around in their dirty flight suits with helmets tucked under their arms. Alone in the center of this expanse of shimmering tarmac sits the six-level imperious tower, bristling with antennae and radar dishes and other communications equipment. It is the location of the command bridge, the admiral's and captain's staterooms, and air traffic control—a kind of throne where the flag officers can sit, hidden behind broad panels of darkened glass, overseeing the flight deck like medieval lords observing the peasants toiling in their fields. Usually the tower emits a general audience crackle, but every once in a while, like an all-seeing eye of God, the tower issues a surprisingly personal command—as when it thunders at me, "Hey, you, Not-in-Uniform! Get off the deck—*now!!!*"

The flight deck is definitely recruiting-poster land. After just a few minutes of watching this, any sentient being has got to get a huge lump in the throat, tear up, and start humming "God Bless America."

But eventually one has to go lower, to the decks below, where the lower-ranking officers live and work, and even deeper to the "downstairs" of this "Upstairs Downstairs" catacombs, to the underground prole city, where about thirty-eight hundred enlisted men and about two hundred women, average age nineteen, live and eat and work shifts that go round the clock to keep the ship's basic systems functioning and the flight deck flying. Compared to the light and freedom, expanse and exhilaration, of the flight deck, the decks below are another realm, almost the flight deck's inverse. This is a place of narrow, low-ceilinged, fluorescent-lit corridors, segmented by huge, heavy, locking hatch doors and spartan steel boxes where the officers live. In places, the ship's interior looks like the Pentagon or any other badly lit federal office building; in other places, especially on the decks meant for the enlisteds, it looks like the break areas of a Detroit auto plant, or the food court at one of the less deluxe malls, or a high school cafeteria. At all hours there are T-shirted young men (enlisted work uniform is bell-bottom dungarees and a T-shirt) slamming pinball machines in the video game arcade or staring vacantly at the omnipresent TVs that beam a constant stream of movies like *Sister Act* and *Golden Eye*, broadcast by the ship's own TV network. Everywhere dungareed young men and women stream past as if it's change-of-shift time at a factory, or sit at the rows of Formica tables, or stand in the omnipresent lines. There are lines to have food slapped on one's partitioned plastic tray, to cash paychecks, to mail a letter, to gain entrance to the ship's store they call the 7-Eleven (only about fifteen allowed in at a time), to call the States on the AT&T "sailor phones." There are no windows here (someone like the chief of staff, with a stateroom in the tower, might have a porthole or two), and if you have certain job specialties, it would be possible to go for days without seeing the sun. While sitting in the enlisteds' mess, whose long Formica tables and vending machines could have been imported directly from my old junior high school, I meet a twenty-three-year-old enlisted man from Texas who works twelve-hour shifts near the very bottom of the ship, in the propulsion plant, overseeing the people who are overseeing one of the carrier's four nuclear-driven turbines. Technically he's deployed in the Mideast, but his skin is white as a sheet because of his molelike existence; still, he has the contented air of someone whose life is focused on just salting away those paychecks. The nuclear program is undermanned right now and paying big bonuses. Of the dozens of men and women I meet on the carrier, he is one of the very few who doesn't volunteer after a few minutes' conversation that he is "getting out" when his tour is up.

When the others leave, they will only become more evidence of the Navy's current crisis: its inability to keep sailors, especially its most valuable sailors, and its inability to get enough people—especially qualified ones—to sign up. Issues of declining recruitment and retention are plaguing all the services (except for the Marines), but the Navy is especially hard hit. Every week, in the *Navy Times*, the country's only independent Navy newspaper, there is a story about "the exodus" or the "current retention crisis" and about some new enticement proffered by Pentagon-level brass to stem it. (In 1997 to the decade's end, the powers-that-be showered reenlistment bonuses: On the recruitment side their strategy was to "dig deeper in the recruit pool"—that is, to accept more kids without high school diplomas and increase the number of foreign recruits with green cards.) The *Navy Times* is known for its sober (some might say boring), bland, exactingly politically correct tone. Still, in 1998 and 1999, uncharacteristically emotional headlines or cover stories appeared nearly every week in the good gray *Times*:

"Where Have All the Sailors Gone?" one cover line blared, then, inside, "They're Outta Here." The next week's brought screamers like "Undermanned and Under Way," " 'Please Stay!': Can the Navy Slow the Flood of Departing Officers?" "Persuading Sailors Not to Abandon Navy Career," "Attrition Rate Costly, Painful for Military," "No Relief in Sight as Services Squeak by in Recruiting Goals," "Sailor Shortage Hits 18,000: Recruiting Alone Falls 6,300 Below Fiscal 1998 Goal," "Bigger Bonuses Not Enough to Hold Pilots," "Navy Considers Retention Bonus for SEAL Officers," and "Navy Hopes Bonuses Will Lure Recruits."

In 1996, according to one statistic, only 30.8 of first-term sailors reenlisted—short of the 38 percent the Navy says it needs to maintain itself. Most discontented sailors simply wait out their tours, but if you're really chafing to get out, there are, as a letter to the *Navy Times* suggested, other strategies:

"I'm not sure anyone has looked," wrote someone signing him- or herself M. Ewing, "but overall the Navy's administrative discharge rate has risen at an incredible rate. . . . Know you're leaving the service . . . to start a civilian career? Why not gain a little weight, fail a few physical readiness tests, and presto: Uncle Sam gives you a generous check, transition benefits, and an honorable discharge! Don't like the service and want to leave? Tell your commanding officer you feel you have homosexual tendencies, and you're out (most often with an honorable discharge). I can't believe someone in the Defense Department has not put two and two together and realized that these are the reasons for the increase in administrative discharges."

Asked to explain why the number of discharges for homosexuality had actually gone up since President Clinton's implementation of "Don't Ask, Don't Tell," a policy that was supposed to give homosexuals more protection from harassment, Rudy de Leon, undersecretary of defense for personnel and readiness, said it was possible that the increase was due, in large part, to people who were using the act of "telling" (there are other ways to "tell" besides actually marching up to your supervisor and saying, "Guess what, I'm gay!") as a way to get out of a service contract.

There are a number of reasons why folks desperately want out right now, and those reasons are interconnected. Sailors, actually military people in general, don't like the humanitarian or peacekeeping missions of today's military. They grouse about being used as "policemen" in Bosnia, and about the psychological stress of being "turned on and off"—that is, being asked to switch back and forth from the mentality of a soldier (whose job is killing) to that of an Oxfam worker (whose job, say, is to hand out boxes of baby cereal).

Another reason for flight is the downsizing of the midnineties and the fact that the services are having to do more with less. Budgets have been slashed, but overseas commitments have grown. This means that the typical soldier, sailor, Marine, or airman has less time at home between overseas deployments. At the peak of the ongoing crisis, it was not unusual to spend two thirds of the year away from home. And once they get to Bosnia or Saudi or wherever, they are confronted with tool shortages and aging equipment. Mechanics in the Navy and the Air Force report that they can't get enough spare parts, that they have to play a kind of parts shell game, putting a part from Plane B, which is going to sit in the hangar, into Plane A, which is slated to fly. "The Navy cannot continue to cut, cut, cut and honestly expect to maintain operations and personnel tempos," wrote a sailor named Craig McVeay in a letter to the *Navy Times*. "On paper, sure, it will be done, but what kind of manipulation goes into the facts presented to the groups who watch such things?"

Charged with saving money, the Defense Department has tended to look for cuts in the defense budget that go directly to the rank and file instead of looking closer to home, to the Pentagon's sprawling "reservation," and at some of the paper-pushing departments tucked away along the dim halls of that byzantine "Puzzle Palace." The reluctance to cut the most pointless, redundant parts of Department of Defense bureaucracy has meant that in the last decade just as rank-and-file morale was at rock bottom, pension rates had been cut by 10 percent and military pay crept along at about 13 percent less than civilian pay for comparable jobs.

There are, of course, the age-old reasons for sailor discontent. Spending six or so months at sea, away from friends and family (in the old days away from women), has always been a challenge. All the E-mail and StairMasters and pinball machines and VCRs (fixtures in the new carriers) don't eliminate the fact that boredom is a major problem—you can't exactly jump into your car for a weekend road trip. The *Navy Times* recently ran a cover story called "Beating Boredom: 180 Days on a Ship." The illustrating photo—of a bunch of young male sailors staring glumly at a few weedy-looking fishing poles they'd propped over the side of a deck—said more about boredom than anything in the story could.

There's also the cramping factor or "the total lack of privacy, even when you are on the lavatory," as British columnist Jeremy Clarkson, who spent some time on the aircraft carrier the USS *Eisenhower* (apparently under the influence of a vile hangover), snarlingly put it. "I don't care what foul vat of sewage has been dreamt up by Lucifer," the scribe (who seemed particularly sensitive to loud noise) wrote, "because it cannot possibly be any worse than life on an American air-craft carrier." Most commissioned and noncommissioned officers share their spartan "staterooms" (the name is left over from another age; we're not talking *Titanic* here) with at least one roommate. The communal bathroom is down the hall, and since carriers are now gen-der-integrated, you can't just toddle down there for a midnight pee without taking stock of your attire—the topless-with-boxer-shorts look is not allowed, but a nice tightly sashed bathrobe will do. Junior enlisteds have even less privacy: At night, or whatever your shift des-ignates as your night (since so many operations run round the clock), enlisteds return to their "berthing areas," which look sort of like high school locker rooms (steel lockers; girls padding around in various states of undress, sleepily brushing their teeth, blow-drying their hair, et cetera; clothes draped everywhere) except for the rows and rows of concentration camp–like people shelving—banks of narrow bunks the enlisted kids call "coffin racks." Your rack may be about the size of the bunk in a train's sleeper car, but as ordnanceman Niki Smith puts it, "It's all you have to yourself." So Niki, like many of the thirty or so women in her berthing area, decorates the tiny space allotted to her on the *Stennis* with pictures from home and piles of stuffed animals.

There is also a reason particular to the *Stennis* that must be taken into account as part of the explanation for the strikingly low morale I found nearly everywhere. People on that ship were particularly dis-gruntled because the *Stennis*, at the time of its first cross-the-Atlantic deployment, the newest of the fleet's nuclear-powered Nimitz-class carriers, had been slated to do a magnificent show-the-flag, Goodwill Ambassador, around-the-world cruise, stopping for leaves at the most exciting ports of call. Instead, Saddam started saber rattling and the ship was diverted to the Gulf to be part of the "two-carrier presence." Instead of seeing the world, the crew was stuck tracing a rectangle in the Gulf; instead of Perth, Australia, and Singapore, they got repeated trips to the "same old" Gulf-adjacent ports like Jebel Ali and Bahrain, which tend to be every bit as oppressively hot as the ship's flight deck or engine rooms.

It is as if they're stalled in the Sargasso Sea. "We're in a spaceship caught in a time warp," sailors say. "We call it Ground Hog Day," says pilot Rocco Mariani, using a description I'll hear over and over. "It's always daylight inside the ship; you see the same people over and over again; you do the same job; the sun is always shining outside; the sea always looks exactly the same." For the aviators the boredom is compounded by the fact that they go out and fly the same rectangular patrol—"three left-hand turns"—over a no-fly zone that refuses to come up with anything worth reporting and a sea that stays as smooth and unruffled as the desert sand nearby.

When Congress summons the military's service chiefs to explain the recruitment and retention problems, the brass tend to favor explanations involving factors over which they have the least control. Thus, in 1997, they tended to say that they were having a hard time competing with the "booming civilian economy."

And they had a point. It's true that there are jobs galore. True, a kid just graduating from high school can wander over to the local mall and wander away with a job immediately. It's also true, as the brass keep reminding us when they want to explain why pilots and other "older," more skilled people are leaving, that the commercial airline companies have been on a hiring binge and that there are suddenly a lot of jobs in the high-tech industries for people with computer and communications skills. Still, this explanation doesn't really explain the "exodus" of the best and the brightest, people who have invested fourteen or so years, people who once joined up out of . . . yes! . . . patriotism. And the money explanation completely comes apart when you try to use it to explain an eighteen-year-old would-be recruit's lack of enthusiasm. Young people sign up to get away from small towns, to "find adventure," to "see the world," to get away from their families, even to "defend their country," as much as to get a steady paycheck. The military's never offered the highest paycheck anyway—guys who were looking for big bucks could stay at home and get a construction job if that's all they were after. In other words, if one leaves out the intangible rewards that used to be a motivation for enlistment (and occasionally still are), and if one evaluates the choice to enlist or not to enlist purely on economic terms, the services are quite competitive. In other words, if you add up the chance to "see the world" and to get away from Small Town, U.S.A., and everybody in it, and the fact that the services' package includes health insurance, room and board, technical training (if you have the aptitude), thirty days paid vacation, the GI bill, which through most of the nineties offered up to $40,000 toward college, and a wage that's only slightly lower than the one you'd get at Burger King or Radio Shack, the Navy, or any military service, should still look like a pretty good deal. Even in a "hot economy," an eighteen-year-old without a college degree or family or union connections is looking at your basic low-paying service job. Many of the young enlisteds I met had *already* spent a year or two in a kind of musical chairs at the local mall, bouncing from burger frying to sales clerking to box loading without finding anything approaching happiness.

So what's the problem?

The explanation is that there is a powerful demotivator out there that the service chiefs either don't fully see or simply, stubbornly refuse to acknowledge. It sits there like the proverbial nine-hundred-pound gorilla in the services' living room. It's a reason that tends not to show up on official data-gathering radar screens (government surveys, for instance; quotes in the articles of major news media like CBS and the *New York Times*) because it is intangible, abstract, qualitative, and (and this is a *big* "and") very politically incorrect in the very politically correct world of today's military.

Understand only one thing about the current military social climate and you will understand a lot: The social climate of the armed forces has become, as analyst and combat vet John Hillen put it, "like Mao's cultural revolution, a culture built on a thousand little lies." In an atmosphere of official avoidance, doublespeak, and euphemism, one reads management's pronouncements not for what they say but for what is conspicuously avoided—as if one were deciphering seating arrangements on a Kremlin dais.

This means that when one is searching for the truth about the motivations and core feelings of today's servicemen and -women, one has to look around the margins, between the lines, and several levels below the Potemkin village displays of happy, efficient workers that the brass set up for visiting reporters and government officials. One finds expressions of samizdat opinions, for instance, in the scores and scores of unsigned letters on the letters page of the *Navy Times*, in op-eds written under pseudonyms in Navy periodicals, on Internet bulletin boards (where people identify themselves with "screen names" instead of real ones), in memoirs written by people after they've left the services, and in interviews with active duty folks when they have begun to trust you and when they feel confident you won't use their names.

One sign that they are having morale trouble, that the masses are near revolt, is the restrictive way they handle reporters—by assigning escorts who accompany the reporter very nearly everywhere, and certainly to interviews. He's there, he tells you, "for safety reasons." Like everything about the "New Military," an aircraft carrier is considered a cauldron of maiming, killing possibilities and a magnet for liability suits—all those narrow steel ladders, you know.

Is it safety or is it a fear of reporters wandering around talking to seamen who haven't been properly briefed? David Matthews, who'd just moved from the *Air Force Times* to a spot at the *Navy Times*, had his first taste of the Navy way of handling the press, particularly when a reporter attempts a "third-rail" gender story. He was asked to do a piece commemorating the fiftieth anniversary of the assignment of women to Navy ships, a history that, like most, has been both bright and dark. Matthews showed his inexperience with the heavy hand of Navy press aides right away. He asked the PAOs to supply sources about this "New Navy" phenomenon. They did and they also dictated that a PAO would be on the line throughout the interview. Predictably, the responses he got sounded very "stock," "canned." When Matthews tried to interview a certain commander who had written openly bemoaning problems he'd had with a mixed-sex crew, first Matthews was discouraged from doing that story and then the people in the Pentagon, where the commander was now working in a prominent office, said they "couldn't locate him." They continued to insist over the course of several days that they couldn't locate a flag officer who had an office in the same building.

But whether or not PAOs actively try to censor what sailors say to journalists, the PAO's very presence, his dogged insistence on gluing himself to the reporter's side, puts a wall between the reporter and the world he is trying to understand. When one does manage to corner an Actual Sailor (with the PAO a couple of feet away, trying to appear as if he really is just suddenly concerned with the condition of his fingernails or the patch of linoleum he's found himself standing on), the sailor will stand rigidly at attention, observe the PAO out of the corner of his eye (while the PAO is watching the sailor out of the corner of his eye), and then proceed to spout a lot of boilerplate that the reporter might as well have copied off the official DOD-sponsored Navy Web page. Going "off script" in today's military is too often a career killer, and nobody's ready to take the risk of saying what they really think unless they've signed their resignation papers.

Yet another element obscuring the Navy attrition issue is the ham-handed way it's been surveyed. One way surveys often make a mistake—and thus render themselves nearly useless—is by giving respondents a choice of a few preselected categories. Usually they also offer a category called "Other" and it often becomes the dumping ground for interesting data, data the researchers would prefer to ignore because it doesn't support their thesis.

On January 19, 1998, for example, the *Navy Times* surveyed sailors who identified themselves as "planning to leave or leaning toward it," about their reasons. The survey supplied the categories "Erosion of benefits," "Loss of confidence in leadership," "Excessive time away from home," "Better opportunities as a civilian," "Job isn't fun," "Lack of promotion opportunity," "Lack of clear mission," and "Other." It sat there in the pie chart like a big, fat maddening unexplored continent, this category of "Other," the one that had been selected by 50 percent of enlisted respondents and 54 percent of officers—a higher rate than any of the other categories. Luckily, the *Navy Times* had done a smart thing: It also invited respondents to scrawl out a few lines explaining their reasons. Of course, the reasons everybody anticipated showed up—there were complaints about operations tempo (the frequency with which troops are deployed overseas in any given year), about low pay, and about having to do more with less. But given a chance to speak their minds, people also wrote about a "change in the culture," which to varying degrees alarmed them, infuriated them, alienated them. In fact, "Loss of confidence in leadership" and "Job isn't fun" combined with "change in the culture" to make up a block that simply dwarfed the economic reasons. And, for all the talk about "booming civilian economies," only 25 percent of officers, the people more likely to have the kind of technical and managerial skills that could be traded in for big bucks in the civilian sector, reported "better opportunities as a civilian" as their reason to resign. "Loss of confidence in leadership" and "Other" both received nearly double what "Better opportunities as a civilian" received.

It becomes apparent that Paul Maubert, a Marine lieutenant colonel who resigned from active duty and now serves in the reserves, was onto something when he wrote, "Warriors do not serve for bread alone. . . . When the young men and women of the United States believe its armed forces offer them more than a jobs program, they will join and stay and make the necessary sacrifices." And maybe the psychoanalyst Erik Erikson, who once said, "Deprivation by itself is not demoralizing, only deprivation without meaning," was onto something, too.

So what is the new culture, this thing often called the "New Navy"? According to Capt. Tyler Woodridge, writing in a 1998 issue of the Navy journal *Proceedings*, it's characterized by too much bureaucratic drudgery:

> Although Saddam Hussein provides interesting interludes, surface warfare [as opposed to another Navy specialty, submarine warfare] in the 1990s can be a life of drudgery. Nontraditional missions such as preserving marine life, humanitarian operations, and maritime interdiction operations and the sheer monotony of managing gender integration, plastic waste disposal, liberty behavior, and similar "hot issues" are just a few of the time consumers with which today's SWO [surface warfare officer] must contend. . . . Managing an effective plastics waste disposal program, saving turtles entangled in fishing nets, and making sure that your personnel do not engage in sexual misconduct just don't provide the same thrill—nor, more important, the same pride and sense of accomplishment—as meaningful operations at sea. We seem to take some form of perverse pride in making any task harder than it needs to be. I could write for pages just on the time and effort it takes a wardroom to write and act out the great Broadway show we call the Tactical Training Strategy.

The problem is not just what sailors often call an increasingly corporate feel. There's a new bloodlessness, a kind of wholesome dullness. In other words, if it's "not your father's army anymore," it's also definitely not your father's Navy. In fact, unless the hard-drinking, skirt-chasing old goat got lots of remedial sensitivity training, he would probably be off the boat, even penned at Leavenworth, in no time.

"We have what we call the 'Old Navy,' and we have the 'New Navy' and the 'kinder, gentler Navy,'" says firefighter Carol Rouquet. This, as one enlisted man put it, is the new, more "sensitive, more touchy-feely" Navy. It's the Navy where Capt. Douglas Roulstone of the USS *Stennis* gets on the intercom every night during a 1998 Gulf deployment to congratulate a dozen or so "Sailors of the Day" selected from what seems like every department, as if he's doling out those little star stickers you got in first grade if you turned in your homework. (Another night, he clucks to his troops, "Keep drinking water! Stay hydrated! It's hot out there," and he ends one day's "fireside chat" by saying, "Take care of each other. We don't have long to go.") It's a Navy where the supervisor of the ship's fire-fighting department (who'd filed his resignation) told me it's too hard to get underlings to work in today's Navy because you have to worry all the time "what you say to somebody."

"You might hurt their feelings. They get very emotional and take it up the chain of command."

Perhaps to cope with sensitive sailors like this, the medical team of the aircraft carrier USS *Carl Vinson* recently added a psychiatrist and a commander named Karin Lundgren, who offers a massagelike alternative medical treatment called the "healing touch."

It's an institution that has adopted Total Quality Management as its executive philosophy, that urges ship's crews to be more diligent about shipboard recycling, and that treats its personnel to sexual harassment sensitivity training "refresher courses" four times a year, consisting of "5 to 8 hours . . . of movies and lectures" capped with a video about date rape, sometimes one produced by the Coast Guard. (With all apologies to that noble service, the savior of so many fishermen and weekend boaters, I am compelled to report that some servicemen of the Army, Navy, Air Force, and Marines view the Coast Guard the way one would view a distant cousin whose Labrador-like overfamiliarity one is forced to tolerate at family reunions. Much of this stems from the fact that the "Coasties," as they call themselves, are only quasi-military, since they are governed by the wimpy, civilian Department of Transportation instead of the DOD. The CG's low status is also reflected in the ugly fact that during World War II, servicemen sometimes called the Coast

Guard "Abey's Navy" because Jews were rumored to be "hiding out" in the cutters to avoid the battlefields of Europe. Anyway, the fact that some of the date rape videos are Coast Guard–produced only adds an extra veneer of "silliness" and "hilarious[ness]," as sailors put it, to a video Navy personnel [people in their thirties, forties, and even fifties] are compelled to view four times a year.)

This is a Navy that posts "U Booze, U Cruise, U Lose" signs in the enlisted mess hall, a Navy that bans smoking except in a very few places. This is the Navy that recently "separated" (or kicked out), and subjected to psychiatric testing, a highly trained lieutenant (Lt. Patrick Callahan had a Ph.D. in chemistry and toxicology, which one would think could be of some use to the military in these days of proliferating chemical weapons) because, on a quasi-rural jogging path, early in the morning, he briefly yanked down his shorts to "moon" a bunch of cronies standing nearby. (Ironically, in the same week, a female naval flight officer, citing "matters of principle," "the First Amendment," and the need in "a male-dominated profession . . . to hold on to [her] identity and femininity," appeared in a six-page nude spread in *Playboy*, with parts of a pilot's uniform spread about as props, and received only a letter of reprimand from the Navy high command.)

The "New Navy" is intensely family-centered—mom-centered especially. In fact, the service that was once, as air wing maintenance chief Fred Sessions put it, the "last great bastion of male society" sometimes sounds as female homemaker–fixated as, say, *McCall's* magazine. An in-house TV network on the *Stennis* broadcasts a public service announcement reassuring sailors that it is possible to "keep in touch with your child on deployment." ("Do you have a copy of your child's schedule for sports events, field trips, school programs, and other special events?" the PSA asks. "This will give you something to talk about when you phone home.") Babies are everywhere in the "New Navy." In fact, sometimes, as Brenda L. Fritz, a Navy optical-man, reports, "parents take their babies to work or on watches with them" because there are not enough Navy-run child care centers. (The quote appeared in an op-ed entitled "Memo to DOD: Child Care Includes Weekends" and was answered, in the next issue, by a sailor, retired naturally, who sarcastically suggested that the Navy create a new baby-sitter job category. They could call it "Infant Maintenance Specialist Third Class.")

Meanwhile, ship-deployed new mothers and mothers-to-be chat on Military City Online's Internet bulletin boards about the pros and cons and logistics of "pumping" and sending breast milk home to newborns. Pregnant sailors routinely fly off ships for abortions on land; and though Navy policy requires women to return to shore duty when they reach their fifth month of pregnancy, infirmaries on some "New Navy" ships have several times been host to new life—when women concealed, or in one case had not known of, their condition.

Ever since 1995, when Secretary of the Navy John H. Dalton outlined a new pregnancy policy stating that "pregnancy and parenthood are compatible with a naval career" and that pregnancy should never lead commanders to a "presumption of medical incapacity," the alarm about pregnancies discovered while a ship is "under way" has subsided. The press no longer run articles cackling about "Love Boats" (as they did in 1991 when the supply ship *Acadia*, with a crew of 360, had to fly 36 pregnant crewmembers back to shore). Often male and some female officers will grouse about what they see as a shocking incongruity. As one male officer put it, "A pregnant sailor is a contradiction in terms." But a kind of normalcy is setting in about a condition that once seemed unmilitary in the extreme. (There is, in fact, a wing of the Navy's policy community that is lobbying for "overmanning" for pregnancy as a matter of course, in the same way the service routinely "overmans" for, say, the inevitable broken leg, cancer diagnosis, et cetera.)

And since current policy dictates that pregnant women serve on their ship until their fifth month (though they are often shifted into a new shipboard job to avoid heavy lifting or exposure to fetus-damaging chemicals), the "New Navy" has started designing its newest war ships with the needs of pregnant sailors in mind.

The newest class of amphibious crafts (ships that are capable of crawling up on a beach to disgorge a company of Marines), for instance, has been designed "from the ground up to accommodate mixed-gender crews," including the roughly 10 percent the Navy acknowledges will discover they are pregnant once deployed. "It's not your Grandpa's Gator—but it might be your daughter's," crowed an article in the Navy journal *Proceedings* about the new, improved class of amphibs. The article went on to report that "[p]rojections anticipate that women will make up from 10% to 25% of the crew [on these new ships, dubbed LPD-17s], but this may change. Combat Logistics Force ships already are projected to have female manning of up to 40%."

In any case, the design team studied everything that might have caused women trouble on an "Old Navy" ship. They studied the height of shelves, the height of levers, foot traffic patterns in and around berthing areas (on gender-integrated ships one suddenly has to think about the fact that the only way to get from, say, an important watch station is to walk through a berthing area), and also, of course, the weight of hatches, doors, and what have you. While the article repeatedly reminded us that "strength is not a gender issue" (lest we begin to think that women are weaker than men), it went on to explain that, as part of the ship's gender-neutral design, "watertight door and multi-dog elevator door designs are being critiqued for easier, less strenuous methods of closing." The LPD-17 designers took their task of designing a woman-friendly ship so seriously, they even organized a Mixed Genders Issues Workshop (made up of the branches of the Navy who are charged with monitoring military women's issues) to supply "vision and guidance." The workshop had originally been called the Women at Sea Workshop, but was renamed Mixed Gender by the sponsoring Bureau of Naval Personnel (BuPers) "not just to be politically correct, but to reflect more appropriately the prevailing viewpoints."

The workshop (which was kind of about women's-issues-but-not-really-because-everybody-knows-gender-differences-aren't-that-important) generated suggestions like putting more mirrors and showers in berthing areas, exercising "privacy considerations" around "all the bunks in the medical wards"—which translates to "Put up some curtains between those beds in the med!"—and addressing concerns about "the delicate nature of women's undergarments . . . in today's industrial-strength shipboard laundry facilities."

Thinking specifically about pregnant sailors, the LPD-17 team tried to identify which shipboard chemicals could hurt fetuses and looked at ways to "try to reduce heat and noise, improving the health of the entire crew while supporting standards developed to protect pregnant sailors." "Fetuses will not be the only ones to benefit from overall enhanced hazard management," the article cheerfully concluded. Just announced in late 1999: The LPD-17 amphibs will be the first class of ships to get innovations like the ability to produce more freshwater (allowing longer showers), more bathroom facilities, and the new "sit-up rack," a sleeping bunk with two more feet of head space than the Navy's standard "coffin rack."

Well, it's not going to kill anybody to lose just a bit of that "Old Navy" shipboard heat and noise—and the elastic at the waist of men's "undergarments" could probably use some relief from those "industrial strength" washers, too. No, the biggest problem with this bustling infrastructure and culture overhaul, as far as many male sailors are concerned, is that most of the energy of the Navy's redecorating effort has been focused on the "Old Navy" fixture called the "Old Navy" male. The old salt who inspired the description "as drunk as a sailor on leave" will be as out of place in the sunlit, chintz-trimmed house the Navy is building as the proverbial bull in a china shop. Of course, there will always be a place for men in the Navy—at present, women make up only about 12 percent of the service, so obviously we're still going to need a lot of men—but coming generations of men must be ready to fit into what Tailhook historian Jean Zimmerman called "a gender-neutral workplace" in its first stage of "hopeful beginnings."

We see the "Old Navy" with its ribald, scabrous ways morphing into the "gender-neutral workplace" of the "New Navy" throughout the nineties, but the transformation really accelerated in 1994. Women had been serving on hospital and supply ships since the late eighties, but, in 1993, Congress repealed the law that had kept them off combat ships.

The new policy had its first test in 1995, when four hundred women joined the crew of the aircraft carrier the USS *Eisenhower* as it left Norfolk to patrol the Persian Gulf, with the nation's press corps crowing about the first "Coed Cruise" on the "Coed Carrier." Awaiting the arrival of the fairer sex aboard their combat ships, Navy brass acted a little like party hosts anticipating the arrival of dignitaries from darkest Pago Pago. Nobody was quite sure what women wanted. Nobody was sure of what would bug them or what would please them, and the "hostile and offensive environment" wording of the current sexual harassment law certainly didn't give commanders much specific direction—except to suggest that it would be extremely dangerous to allow any speech or behavior that someone, anyone, at anytime, might find "hostile and offensive."

To be on the safe side, the Navy began to ban everything associated with the old "warrior returning from the sea" culture and anything vaguely evocative of the big frat party that was the Tailhook symposium of 1991. Alcohol went on the hit list, as well as lechery (aboard ship in the form of pictures and magazines, and in port in the form of brothels), rowdy port leaves, fistfights, and hazing.

"You remember that bumper sticker that said, 'Sailors have more fun'? Not anymore," said Fred Sessions, a fiftyish maintenance master chief from the *Stennis*'s air wing in the summer of 1998. "Things are a lot more stifling."

"This ship is so wrapped up in not failing and feeling good that in my opinion it's not a [fully] effective war-fighting ship," raged Lt. Cmdr. Graham Guiller, a twenty-five-year veteran then posted on the *Stennis*. "We have a Mommy ship. You set up a situation where no matter what you do you get an award for it. You get congratulated for it." In his opinion the interminable "Sailor of the Day" broadcasts were a key symptom.

The "Mommy ship" imagery, the image of the "New Navy" as feminized, specifically as a nurturing-to-the-point-of-infantilizing Mommy—a smothering Mommy who corrects your language, who takes away your booze, who slaps you if you gawk at a woman or tell a dirty joke, who worries overbearingly about danger and prescribes tons of tiresome safety procedures—comes up again and again from disgusted sailors.

"No smoking. No drinking. I don't want women aboard. I want what a civilian has a right to have: *Playboy, Penthouse, Hustler*," railed a ship's storekeeper quoted in the *Navy Times*. "I'm not a baby. Don't be my mother."

"This [ship] is my home and I can't even come home drunk," complained a sailor who'd just been written up for his second alcohol-related incident in five months. "That's why I left my parents' house."

As I sat in the *Stennis*'s Damage Control Shop—the area where the ship's firefighters are based—a mop-haired sailor who looked to be in his early twenties burst in yelling to nobody in particular: "Warning: You are not allowed to have a good time on the JCS!" When I asked him what he meant, he said, "I don't know, it just seems like every time

I look like I'm having a good time, they slam me down." Sometimes, the fellow said, "I wish it was the way it was when my dad was in the Navy. People weren't treated like adolescents. People were treated like people. They treat me like a three-year-old. This ship is a floating Washington, [D.C.]."

"You're old enough to die for your country but not old enough to take care of yourself," groused David Shackelford, a twenty-six-year-old enlisted man from Portland, Oregon. "In the old days nobody would have had a problem with someone getting tore up drunk [on leave]. If someone came in like that, you'd just put 'em in their rack. Now they'd take you up to medical to evaluate you for 'alcohol abuse.' The worst thing is they call someone from your division to watch you while you're in the med and that person has to write an incident report."

The ship's "females"—everyone habitually uses this cautious, formal term—don't seem as personally bothered by the restrictions, though often, like twenty-six-year-old Carol Rouquet (the only "female" on the ship's fire-fighting team and a newly appointed supervisor in that division), they empathize deeply with the frustration of "the males" they work with.

"They're not giving them the chance to act like the adults they are," Rouquet said. "When people are treated like little kids, they're gonna act like little kids." Rouquet signed up for what she called "the usual reasons": "to get out of where I was from . . . and to get money for college." The Navy had given her a foothold in life. She said she "grew up a lot and learned a lot, met a lot of people, got a chance to do a lot of stuff I wouldn't have had a chance to do as a female on the outside." (For three years she was based in Groton, Connecticut, working as a carpenter building cradles for the dry-docking of submarines.) But now, she said, she'd learned everything she wanted to learn and wanted to stay in one place for a long while; she hinted that marriage was in the very near future. "It's time to put the [college] money to use," she said, besides, she added, before a deafening *clump whine* of a cat shot drowned out the rest of the sentence, "The Navy is not a place to be right now."

If the ship is Mommy and the crew are little boys (and little girls) and we are trying to excise anything that could in any way lead into Tailhook-style temptation, booze will have to go. And not just in the old wink, wink, de-facto-but-not-de-jure way of the "Old Navy." This time they mean it, lads! Navy carriers are now as dry as an Iraqi sand dune. There is no black market. Believe me, in desperation, I looked.

Lt. Cmdr. Guiller has seen it all:

> Prior to Tailhook it was not uncommon to come on a ship and find alcohol. Course, it's been outlawed since a long time ago, since turn-of-the-century time, but it was not uncommon for officers and chiefs—because of the privacy we have over the lower ranks—to have alcohol hidden away, for example, in our rooms, whereas the younger guys, they'd have to secret it somewhere in the ship and hope nobody else found it either, so it was just harder for them to do it.
>
> Then maybe you had a bad day; you might come up and have a drink or two . . . or three . . . or you might have a ritual where every Sunday nine o'clock at night it was time for that weekly drink. I knew a pilot who was an alcoholic. He flew tactical aircraft, but he couldn't live without it, always had one three-quarter-liter bottle in his stateroom at all times, used to drink every night—never caught, never got put in a hard place—always quit drinking twelve hours before flight time but always had his nightly.
>
> If you got caught drinking in those days, the skipper would punish you, wouldn't let you fly for maybe a week, might not let you have liberty, and then if there were no further incidents, it'd be forgiven. Today it's a different Navy; it's a different social climate; there's a different political climate. If I pulled out a bottle of booze and was sitting here with you and for any reason whatsoever in walks the XO of the ship, I'm done. I'm beyond having my last promotion. Could be off the ship. Could be here but might not have liberty for the rest of the cruise. Would not get good fitness reports and that one bad fitness could end my career. We live in what we call a zero-defect world now: You have one screwup, you have one error, you have one perceived error . . . you stop, your professional growth stops. So people now won't do what they did five years ago.

It's really tough, after a grueling day in 100-degree heat, to face 6 P.M. or 10 P.M. or whatever is your personal "Miller Time" without anything that'll disconnect those ceaselessly churning worry gears (something I experienced quite acutely at 6 P.M. every day while I was on the *Stennis*). Sailors throughout the fleet talk wistfully about the British Navy, which allows its sailors three beers a day!

"They have a bar," says aviator Jeff Novacek incredulously. He had been a guest, a kind of exchange student, on a British carrier. The British flattop had remained in Novacek's brain as a shimmering Arcadian vision, a Peaceable Kingdom of gender cooperation far from the tribunals and sex scandals plaguing the U.S. Navy. "There were men and women sunbathing together in bathing suits on the fantail!" he said with a voice full of awe. "We're not allowed to go bare chested to the bathroom; we're not allowed to wear tank tops on flight deck. [The British] don't make life as hard. . . . They treat them like grown-ups." (The part about the beers is true, but as far as peace between the sexes, the Royal Navy has had its share of truly nasty scandals.)

Meanwhile, on an American carrier, if you so much as wobble when you walk up the ramp coming back from a day on leave, "that's it," an enlisted man says. "You're going to med and get written up for alcohol abuse." One of the fliers from the *Stennis*'s air wing tells a similar story: "If you went out [at port] and you're having a good time and something happened, even if you're just there, not necessarily directly involved, and you have been drinking, it's now a Major Issue, an Alcohol-Related Incident."

Aviators are the princely class of the carriers. (When you think about it, a carrier is actually an inverted pyramid: levels and levels of men and women and machines who exist to maintain that royal polo field up top.) They are the guys who risk violent death every day and think it's a gas, the guys who taxpayers have spent millions to train, the guys who love living in the sky so much that they have evolved a whole erotic language for what they do up there. And even in the chastened days of the "New Navy" they still look like they're having more fun than anyone else on the boat.

Their carefree air is partly a result of their semi-independent, guns-for-hire status. Air wings (consisting of about ten thirty-pilot squadrons, organized around types of planes—an F-18 squadron, a helicopter squadron, and so on) are shuffled from ship to ship, wherever they are needed in the fleet. Back on shore, personnel belonging to, say, Air Wing Seven, live on and around the same base so they can be assembled and shipped out quickly. Thus, when they deploy, the air wing is a self-contained, to some extent self-sufficient, entity with its own mechanics, controllers, and deckhands. "Attached" to a ship, as they say in the Navy. "Plug and play," as they say in the computer industry.

Of course, once deployed, they are under the jurisdiction of the host ship . . . but not completely, and so the irreverence and maverick nature of the pilots can be seen in the air-wing support staff as well. When I asked an Air Wing Seven mechanic his opinion of some nugget of *John C. Stennis* policy, he shrugged and said gleefully, "I dunno; they're not our bosses!"

The pilot exodus is all the more significant when one realizes just how much aviators love to fly. John Gadzinski's favorite poem, which he will recite over long-distance telephone wires if necessary to make a point about flying, is William Butler Yeats's "An Irish Airman Foresees His Death," in which, as in this verse, life in the sky seems more vivid than a gray, out-of-focus life on the ground:

> Nor law, nor duty bade me fight,
> Nor public men, nor cheering crowds,
> A lonely impulse of delight
> Led to this tumult in the clouds.

Navy aviators love their planes and love the sky . . . and when you really get off on something, the language that your tribe evolves to capture the nuances of its world gets suffused with sex. The fighter jock world is fueled by a core of libido. The burn from a jet engine, the charge of a jet down a carrier deck, a jet's razorlike trajectory in the sky, is what libido would look like if it had a physical shape. (I'm talking here about libido in the sense that Sigmund Freud meant it, as a core or current of pure energy, energy that can channel itself into creation, or violence, or sex.)

A Vietnam-era Air Force pilot named J. D. Wetterling once called jet flying "dancing the wild blue."

"We used to joke about our passionate love affair with an inanimate flying object," Wetterling wrote. "We flew F-100s and we marveled at the thought that we actually got paid to do it. We were not draftees but college graduates in Vietnam by choice, opting for the cramped confines of a jet fighter cockpit over the comfort of corporate America. In all my life I've not been so passionate about any other work. If that sounds like an exaggeration, then you've never danced the wild blue with a supersonic angel."

Aviators aren't just flying patrols, they're fucking the sky. And in the "New Navy," a "s'cuse me while I kiss the sky" attitude (à la Jimi Hendrix) will get you in trouble. Since sex got the Navy in big trouble in 1991 at Tailhook, the Navy gets very nervous at anything carrying the most faint vibration of sexuality. Thus, the nervous purge of anything "they" might find "hostile and offensive." In some parts of the Navy, you can't say *cockpit*. "It's supposed to be called a 'flight station' now," says an aviator. "It's not like there was an official memo or anything," at least as far as he knows, but "if you say 'cockpit,' someone standing there will say something like 'Uh, that's the flight station.'"

For decades people referred to a common aviation mechanics' wirecutter as a "dyke." No more. For decades fliers made a short, straight line on a landing grading chart when they wanted to indicate that a landing hadn't been graded—most likely because the landing hadn't happened, because the pilot had been "waved off" and told to come around and try again. The little mark was called a "gash." Maybe because the term reflected the wounding in the act of drawing this mark under someone's name, maybe because it reflected the inherent aggressivity and libidinousness of aviators—whatever—it's out of the vocabulary. As the same aviator puts it, "Somebody decided that 'gash' sounded too much like a part of the female anatomy." In a spirit of helpfulness and reconciliation, the brass distributed a memo suggesting that squadrons replace "gash" with "stich."

When an entire squadron of planes was able to complete a day without "wave-offs," you'd say the squadron had had a "cherry recovery"— signifying purity, a day unsullied by error. You don't do that anymore, not since the memo that came down excising "cherry." "Any other fruit would be fine," the memo from the brass said.

Banning "cherry" (as an adjective) knocked out a number of common expressions. You couldn't say, "I heard you got your cherry popped today!" to a flier who'd just completed his first cat launch and carrier landing.

Another tiresome bit of verbal political correctness aviators report is that one must always remember to say "and women," as in "We're very proud of the achievements of the men . . . and women in Iceland," or "The men . . . and women who will be deploying to Bosnia." This habit can produce some odd results—as when a student at the U.S. Naval Academy was quoted as saying that a new academy curriculum would help a student "become more of an officer and a gentleman—or lady."

All of the above leads us to the case of a lieutenant commander and EA-6B Prowler pilot whom I shall call Pilot A.* In May of 1998, he was thirty-seven, an age of utter ripeness for a jet pilot, because you combine years of experience (in his case fourteen) with reflexes and physical stamina that are still sufficiently young. Fourteen years "in" also meant that he was only six years away from locking in a military pension. (And who wouldn't like getting a regular check while you're still young enough to start a whole second career?) Pilot A was also getting within striking distance of his life's goal (or what had once been his life's goal) to become commander of a squadron. Fit, lean, with a uniform always impeccably pressed, this guy was about as "squared-away" as they get.

But when I met him on my Mideast crawl, he had just filed his resignation papers and was beginning to think about what he'd do in civilian life. He knew the airlines were hiring, so he thought he'd "check that out," but he didn't seem particularly excited about giving up high-performance jets for the big lumbering buses of the air.

And despite what the brass were saying about the commercial airline's hiring spree, ultimately, he insisted, his leaving was "not a money issue." "I joined the Navy with the intent to fly. Money wasn't a factor. I felt I made plenty of money for what I did, and I didn't stay in for so long because of the money but because I was enjoying what I did, but unfortunately I've seen the way that it's going and I'm like 'I don't want to do this!' My reasons for leaving just show the state of the Navy and why people are getting out."

The nut of what drove him out, he said, was "the overall pressure of senior leadership saying we should be politically correct. It's no fun anymore; we can't be men. We can go out and kill people, but we can't

*Originally he agreed to speak for name attribution, but as this book was going into galleys, certain factors changed and I agreed to take his name out.

look at *Playboy* in our own ready room—or even in our own stateroom technically. Last time I cruised in 1990 we weren't allowed to put centerfold pictures up on our own wall—because the stateroom cleaner who comes in might be offended. People still have *Playboy* and *Penthouse*, but they hide them in other magazines.

"The senior leaders are very scared to allow anything that could impact their career. They're trying to legislate how we think and act and trying to change something that men have done for centuries. It's going to take a long time for society to change. There's nothing wrong with trying to be a New Age Sensitive Guy. You can be that, but there're also times when you just wanta be with the boys, go out drinking and have a good time and act like pigs.

"Leaders no longer lead from the viewpoint of doing what's right from a military standpoint, they lead by what they think other people will think [and how] that will affect their career.

"In the olden days," Pilot A said (and he seemed to consider anything that happened before 1993 "the olden days"), "we had this thing called recognition training [to train aviators to identify targets twenty-five thousand feet below the plane]. A guy would stand up and he'd flash a picture of a ship and we'd sit there and go, 'OK, that's a ship or a submarine or airplane.' . . . It was very boring to go through those slides time and time again. So in order to lighten up the training, every so often guys would put a slide of a naked lady up there . . . like, 'OK, can you identify this?' It broke it up."

He didn't remember a specific directive eighty-sixing the babe shots, he just said it's accepted that "we can't do that anymore . . . if someone walked in and said there are naked ladies up there and that's wrong; it doesn't matter if you have women in your squadron; it's unacceptable with today's standards."

Well, no matter how stifling it is on ship, there're always port visits, right? Not for nothing is our popular culture laced with expressions and images of the sailor on leave: "Hey, sailor, new in town?" "What do we do with the drunken sailor (ear-li in the morning)," "spending like a sailor on leave," and so on. Not for nothing are most of the traditional port stops of the world ringed with brothels, strip clubs, and raucous anything-goes bars where you can get a watered-down, usuriously priced drink.

It will be interesting to watch in the coming years and see if those brothels and strip shows can survive on revenues from the navies of other, more liberal countries—they will certainly not get as many American clientele. "Liberty," as the *Navy Times* put it recently, "ain't what it used to be."

It's around noon on the *Stennis*. I'm in the enlisted mess sitting at one of the Formica-topped tables fiddling with the pull-off tab from my Coke can and staring desultorily at one of the six or so TVs in the room. Suddenly Whoopi Goldberg and her movie *Sister Act* are interrupted by a message from the bridge. Two guys in neat tan uniforms, two officers, in other words, say they need to brief the crew about ground rules for the upcoming leave at Bahrain, an oil-rich island just off the coast of Riyadh, Saudi Arabia.

First off there are dress codes: no shorts, no T-shirts on women. These seem sensible for a Muslim country and probably make for better sun protection anyhow. Then comes the news that everybody is to be accompanied by a "buddy" at all times and that seamen under the rank of E-5 (an E-5 would be a slightly senior petty officer) are not allowed to take a taxi unless accompanied by someone ranked E-5 or over. People over E-5 can stay overnight in Bahrain (make reservations at hotels, locate old friends at the Air Force base that is also in Bahrain, whatever) but only if they get their supervisors' permission, and then only "on a case-by-case basis" after the supervisor has reviewed the where, the whom, and the whatever else the supervisor feels he needs to know. For most of the poor enlisteds (generally the younger, non-married guys and girls), the rule is back to the rack by midnight. Falling asleep under a bar stool would seem to be out.

This even bugs some of the older, more settled crew: Narda Looney, an attractive blond petty officer from the ship's Safety Office, who is keeping her long fingernails manicured and her skin unburned to look good for her upcoming engagement to a guy back home, has a few problems with all of this. "I'm, like, almost fifty," she says, "and I need a buddy? I'm an E-four" ("I started late," she adds apologetically), "but I have to have a curfew?"

And if you are a single guy and you haven't touched a woman in a couple of months (except in a purely professional way) and you thought you might check out the "local talent," think again: Advance parties had been ashore to scope out the nightlife and they've put together a list of "off-limits" bars and nightclubs, presumably, sailors told me, those with prostitutes and drug dealers. Worried about how to spend your time on Bahrain if you can't get drunk or get laid? Don't want to blow all your money wandering the souks blowing your pay on gold trinkets?

The briefing officers are ready to address that unspoken concern: "Folks, we have a really exciting list of things to do and see in Bahrain," one of the guys in tan on the closed-circuit TV says heartily. "Maybe this time," he says a bit pleadingly, "you'll want to take advantage of our fantastic package of tours. We've planned a Beach Party Barbecue that's gonna be really fun! We've arranged for sight-seeing by bus!" He rambles on about Jet Skis and hot dogs and Bahrain's historical sites. "I'm thirty years old," mutters an enlisted man near me, "and I can't stay out all night?"

Granted, there are some good reasons for some caution in Bahrain. The island is just a causeway drive away from Dhahran, Saudi Arabia, where nineteen American servicemen were killed when a truck bomb exploded outside the U.S. Air Force's Khobar Towers barracks in 1996. Obviously there are people around who'd like to kill Americans again, and one wouldn't want to give them any excuse. In 1995, two Marines and one sailor stationed on a base in Okinawa, Japan, abducted and raped a twelve-year-old Japanese girl. The Pentagon had to work very hard to placate Japanese government officials who were threatening to order all U.S. military bases out of Japan. Saudi Arabia has not been sending strong signals of solidarity with the United States lately, and another "Okinawa incident" on this shifting and explosive Arab soil would . . . well, it's too frightening to think.

On the other hand, maybe once upon a time the Kingdom of Bahrain was a demure, closeted, otherworldly Muslim port, but now it's full of international bankers and financial sharks of all types, all scrabbling to get their mitts on the emirate's oil money, and the kingdom is voluptuously cooperating. The island has become a fleshpot, a free port, a Hong Kong, a place where American, British, and Australian businessmen and entrepreneurs mingle with white-robed, sunglass-wearing Arabs who roar around in Mercedes, have bodyguards, and keep one ear glued to their cell phones. One soldier described it as "a playground for the sheiks who dart across the causeway in their MBs from Saudi to get snockered and whore around." The nightclubs don't even fill up until about nine or ten—on weeknights!—which would leave enlisted men about one and a half hours to enjoy the nightlife.

Sensing that I was a bit perplexed by the restrictive leave policies, the *Stennis*'s public affairs officers went into high-spin mode, muttering, "Muslim country . . . special situation . . . war zone."

But restrictive leave policies are not particular to the *Stennis*, or to the summer of 1998, or to Bahrain. Every sailor I asked had run into similar policies on other ships and while visiting other ports—even in what one would presume are friendly ports in Puerto Rico and Australia and Canada. As Cmdr. Lesa McComas, in an essay for the *Navy Times*, put it, "The same sailors who are trusted during the day to take apart jet engines, manage million-dollar budgets, sew up lacerations, operate nuclear propulsion plants, and launch cruise missiles are treated like children when they leave ship.

"Whether out of fear of terrorism, crime, or another internationally embarrassing incident—or just because we tend to be the sort of organization that likes to have lots of rules—we seem to be trying to wring the fun and adventure out of the Navy."

Even Times Square, in New York City, has, as *New York Post* reporter Gersh Kuntzman put it, "changed in the post-Tailhook world when the Navy rechristened itself 'The New Navy.'"

"When I first got into the Navy in '83, we'd pull into town, get drunk, raise hell, chase every woman, and see what you could get away with. There were always all-you-can-drink parties for us," one "Old Navy" man told Kuntzman in the summer of 1998. "No one even gets a tattoo anymore."

"They used to fill this place," said the owner of a topless bar quoted in Kuntzman's Times Square story. "But now nothing. I'd love to buy them all a beer. If they come here," the man said wistfully, "the second beer's on me!"

Let's look, for another example, at the plight of a sailor named Jeff Cook, an electronics technician. He had been spending a liberty day in Dubai and was scurrying to get back to his rack on the USS *Kitty Hawk* so as not to break curfew when he bumped into a *Navy Times* reporter doing a story about liberty ports of the Middle East:

"We went ice-skating," Cook reported, with what the reporter said was "mild enthusiasm." "Ice-skating has got to be the last thing I figured I'd be doing in the middle of the desert."

"What Cook really wanted to do, like most men after being cooped up aboard a ship with thousands of other guys, was go out and mingle with some ladyfolk," the *Navy Times* continued. "Without women, many say, it ain't liberty. Cook got a taste of Dubai's nightlife before all the restrictions were levied. As a seaman aboard the *Kitty Hawk*, he was able to do more than even a second class petty officer may do now. In fact, even the chiefs and Marine staff noncommissioned officers who stay out in town can't stay out late. They have to be in their hotel rooms by 1 A.M."

"That's the problem," said Cook. "Dubai is a great liberty port, but we'd never know it because we can't go anywhere." Cook then told the *Navy Times* reporter that he had met "a beautiful Australian woman" at the ice rink who invited him and his friends to come with her to a club. But the witching hour was nigh, so they had to decline this tantalizing invitation. "It's kind of insane," Cook said. "I'm twenty-five years old and I've paid my way through three years of college, but I can't stay out overnight."

The place where the restrictions seem most incongruous is in the Western Pacific: home of ports-of-dreams like Singapore, Guam, and Pusan, South Korea—the place where your dad had his most exuberant fistfights and was entertained by the most enthusiastic and exotic ladies of the night. Now, said Marine reservist Sgt. Matthew Johnson, on leave in Pusan with the USS *Fort Henry*, "the young guys are disappointed. Their dads and uncles were here and they have come in with these impressions, and now it's just totally different."

But once again, there in Pusan, the Navy is right in there attempting "to give sailors an alternative to heading straight for sailor town with its bars and strip joints," as the *Navy Times* put it. Two alternatives offered by the Navy's Department of Morale, Recreation and Welfare for this particular port stop were "a rock-climbing tour that included sights of waterfalls and sheer cliffs, . . . and the Kyung-Ju cultural tour, which takes visitors through an ancient Korean capital city."

For the old guys, rock-climbing just doesn't make it. "We were just a lot wilder," said Chief Damage Controlman David Tallman. "Nowadays everything is a fucking 'incident.' It's just not fun anymore."

Sure, there were a few fights in the old days; sure, some guys came back with gashes in their heads from getting beaned with beer bottles. Sure, some guys even got left behind. In the old days, a *Stennis* crewman told me, they would leave at least one guy behind in every port they visited, usually because the damn fools just fell asleep somewhere. Still, as one senior enlisted man put it in the *Navy Times*, "That is what it was all about. That's what I came in for."

Of course, if the new, more tamed, better-behaved, feminized Navy is going to go after unruly male behavior, it's going to go after hazing and initiation rituals. They are, after all, sometimes violent, frequently childish, often lewd, sometimes downright gross, and seem to serve absolutely no purpose except providing fodder for embarrassing stories in the press and the possibility of those cross-gender misunderstandings that so often turn into lawsuits.

"Back in the olden days," recalled Pilot A, "we did this thing called the Fo'c's'le Follies." (The fo'c's'le, short for "forecastle," is where the ship's pair of mighty anchors live, attached to massive iron chains that are, in turn, attached to giant winches. The space is used for socializing because it is relatively large and—except for the anchors—empty.)

"Each squadron would do a skit," the aviator said. "It was time for us lower-echelon guys—meaning us pilots—to poke fun at the ship if they did something dumb, make fun of the CAG [carrier airgroup commander]—the skipper of the ship, the admiral. It was kind of a free-for-all, a pretty much anything-goes kind of thing. This year the CAG comes out and briefs us about the follies and says, 'I don't want to hear the word *fuck*. I don't want to hear anything that rhymes with the word *fuck*: "duck," "luck." . . . And there will be no personal attacks on anybody.'"

That kind of put the kibosh on the Fo'c's'le Follies.

Crossing the equator makes you a true sailor (or at least more of one than one was before), so an initiation ceremony is in order—and that's where Wog Night and the Shellback Ceremony come in. If you've crossed before, you're called a "Shellback." If it's your first time, you're a "Wog," which, reflecting your pathetic newly hatched status, stands for "Pollywog." As in most initiation ceremonies, the elders get to humiliate, pound on, and generally torture the initiates—and therefore judge whether they are fit to join the world of men.

"We would swat 'em on the butt with fire hoses, put stuff on 'em, put eggs down back of pants," recalled Pilot A fondly. "It was an initiation into a brotherhood that was part of a long tradition."

In the middle of this Fellini-esque bacchanal sat "the Wog Queen," the leader of the revels. The deity on the throne was played by any sailor—there was at least one on every ship—who was willing (or in some cases champing at the bit) to get into a full tiara-wearing, scepter-wielding Glenda-the-Good-Witch-style drag.

Of course, it was dumb. Like much shipboard recreation it was supposed to be one big mindless blowout for guys who, in the case of pilots, routinely risk their lives, or (in the case of nearly everybody else) work in 100-degree heat on flight decks and in engine rooms.

The Navy still allows the Shellback ceremony (well, sort of), as long as it is "supervised" and "monitored" by members of the ship's Safety Department, as long as the guys don't use the shillelaghs—"That was half the fun," said Pilot A. "You could really go around and whack somebody"—as long as the behavior is not "inappropriate," which the brass on a ship named the *Princeton* defined as "behavior that would be acceptable in an open forum attended by family and friends."

Maybe the guys on the *Princeton* just had wilder family and friends. In any case, one night in June 1997 eighteen of the *Princeton*'s sailors got together on their own to hold a Wog Night, slightly in advance of the sanctioned ceremony the next day. One of the Wog victims was a petty officer first class. The Shellbacks tied him down, shaved his chest, and dumped food of some kind on him. Two years back, one of the Shellbacks claimed he had done the exact same thing on another ship without penalty.

But somehow news of the party made it back to the ship's captain, who responded by calling twelve of the revelers to Captain's Mast—an investigative proceeding conducted solely by the captain, who then determines a punishment, sort of like a bench trial. The result of the captain's investigation was that within days, four sailors were flown back to San Diego and processed out of the Navy. One of the booted sailors had recently completed two years of Navy-financed education to prepare for a job—fire controlman—of which there was then a service-wide dearth. Five of the sailors got to stay in but were given reductions in rank and a heavy penalty.

*   *   *

Another feature of the gross, disreputable male is that he fights—sometimes apparently for fun, sometimes to settle scores. In a particularly odd phenomenon, duke-outs have been known to leave men better friends than they were before they pounded on each other. In the olden days, on the all-male ships, fights broke out routinely and they were generally handled the way ships often unofficially handled alcohol: with a "Just don't let me see it" or a "For Christ's sake, take it someplace else."

One young petty officer, found mopping an already-immaculate fo'c's'le floor, said that his last ship, an amphib with an all-male crew, had a different climate. "There were about two thousand of us," he said, seemingly happy for an excuse to stop mopping. "It was an LPD, so they were mostly Marines. If you put that many men together for six months, there's bound to be sparks, and there were fights. They used to break out all over the place, but the attitude was 'You got a problem with me, just take it over there.'"

On the gender-integrated *Stennis*, however, this petty officer's scrapping had gotten him in big trouble—and mopping duty was only part of his penalty. As he tells it, he was only trying to get a guy in his berthing area to get in his rack and sleep off drunkenness acquired on liberty. His shipmate didn't like this suggestion, so he came at him, and our officer had to punch him a couple of times in self-defense.

So, maybe he slanted the story in his favor. He admits he was a little juiced, too, and that that had much to do with why he then bellowed, "You drunken asshole, take this!" while he was doing the pushing.

In any case, the captain called it fighting (not "trying to maintain order in a berthing area"), and in our petty officer's case, punishment included the "loss of a stripe" (from the chevron on his sleeve, a demotion, in other words), a $500 penalty, loss of leave privileges for three months, and twenty hours a week of extra duty (the mopping). On top of all this, he was supposed to report to the Hangar Bay five times in a twenty-four-hour cycle, where he would stand at attention while a ship's military policeman (MP) inspected his uniform for any sort of infraction—a loose thread, unshined shoes, an unaligned name tag. If there was any infraction—and it is hard to avoid with the military's baroque uniform regulations and the fact that you've gotten out of bed at 2 A.M. to be inspected—he would be sent up to Captain's Mast again.

It sounded like he was trapped in one of the circles of hell. "That's a lot for punching a guy once or twice," I said. "I mean, this is a warship!"

"I don't know," he answered, discouragedly. "If the Navy had its way, it would neuter everybody."

The young man's off-the-cuff comment goes to an issue that's deeper than he might have intended at that moment. There is a feeling that manliness, aggressiveness, are somehow disparaged by the "New Navy" and there are worries that a warship manned by men who are more like clerks than Vikings won't perform the same when the chips are down.

As a high-level Army officer who once commanded paratroopers put it, "The kind of guys who love fallin' out of airplanes in the middle of the night also tend to be the guys who like to drink and stuff like that. Trying to build an army from a group of choirboys has to be detrimental to the warrior ethic."

"When you're up there pokin' and strokin', who do you want?" said Navy commander Bill Cullen, the CO [commanding officer] of a Prowler squadron. "The guy who never got a nosebleed?"

The fact is, the kind of guys who are capable and willing (under the right conditions) and even eager (under the right conditions) to pursue and demolish an enemy have some very hot stuff in their veins, and on a long cruise—especially one in a war zone, where one has to stay primed for action, the release that may never come—people build up a lot of steam. In the old days, said F-14 pilot John Gadzinski, who left the service at thirty-three, "we built up a lot of steam and we let off a lot of steam. Now with all the valves blocked off, the only way to let off steam is to walk right out of the Navy."

How Did We Get Here?

"He who is full of courage and sangfroid before an enemy battery
sometimes trembles before a skirt."
—Napoleon Bonaparte

"I need to emphasize a very important message: We get it—and
those that don't get it will be driven from the service."
—Sean O'Keefe, acting secretary of the navy, in a post-Tailhook
press conference, September 1992

So how did we get from the blood, sweat, and tears version of boot
camp, to "Bootcamp Lite," "Camp Jackson," "battle buddies,"
"training time-outs," "confidence course facilitators," and the
"gender-normed" grenade throw, to Army bases that hold special exercise classes for pregnant or postpartum soldiers and allow new mothers
in the ranks to take "bonding breaks"? How did we get to the reserve
camp where the CO has taken to supplying Sno-Kones and balloons for
the kids who've accompanied Mom to field-training exercises?

How did we get to medals-as-party-favors? After the Gulf War, said
one young lieutenant whose job included writing medal citations, "the
Army gave out Bronze Stars to practically everybody who showed
up—practically a 'thank you for coming' thing."

How did we find ourselves with a three-star general (Claudia
Kennedy) who starts speeches by announcing, "This is not your
father's army anymore!" and who recently spent forty minutes explaining to an audience of grizzled NCOs how to hold "sensing sessions" as
part of a new program dubbed COO or "Consideration of Others"?

How did we end up with an Air Force whose latest report on its
weapon inventory read, as a military scholar put it, like it should be

titled "Reach Out and Bomb Somebody," and to just-released POWs who were met on a tarmac by a general who gave each a hug? ("If there was less hugging and more combat readiness, these men probably would not have been captured in the first place," grumbled a retired Special Forces soldier in a letter to the *Army Times*.)

Obviously, much of the transformation from the "Old Military" to the "New" simply parallels a general cultural drift in the United States that brought us, by the century's end, to a government that hovers, wrings its hands, and worries whether everybody's having a good time.

Government nineties-style was obsessed with the self-esteem of its citizens and with avoiding injury—psychic and physical. It tended to express this priority through its biggest institutions. Public school systems, for instance, and workplaces exalted teamwork over competition and safety over risk. A doddering kind of hypochondria filled the land. Since so many new *kinds* of injuries were now validated by the courts and by the culture at large, new classes of victims proliferated, and activities that used to be considered a bit risky (but generally worth it) were treated like virtual minefields of danger. . . . In the midst, for instance, of a supposed epidemic of "acquaintance rape" on college campuses, Antioch College in Ohio instituted its own official student sex code: A person who wanted "to initiate a higher level of sexual intimacy in an interaction . . . must get the verbal consent of the other person(s) involved before moving to that other level. . . . Don't ever make any assumptions about consent." In the late nineties, universities reinstituted loco parentis policies and tried to get rid of fraternities and sororities—while the students marched to save them. At a conference in 1998, school system consultants talked about the need to "resocialize" aggressive elementary-school boys and a curriculum guide by the National Education Association circulated recommending that teachers discourage games of tag and substitute a new game called "Circle of Friends," in which chasing, whopping people on the back, or tagging others "out" was not allowed.

Activities that are not totally "inclusive," that stimulate or encourage competition—thus creating "losers" and winner-elites and losses of self-esteem—were viewed as treacherous. "One of the most overlooked arenas of violence training within schools," said one of the scholars at the conference, "may be the environment that surrounds athletics and sports, beginning with Little League games, where parents and friends sit on the sidelines and encourage aggressive, violent behavior."

Thousands of baby-boom parents must have agreed: Other nineties phenomena included soccer parents who cheered for every play of every kid, schools that eliminated the classification of winner and loser in scholastic contests, and the basketball conference that stopped a tournament to allow an injured player to hobble out to center court and sink an uncontested basket so she could become "the leading scorer in the history of women's basketball" (at the University of Connecticut). Of course, officials let the opposing team have an uncontested basket, too—a feel-good occasion all around.

Naturally, the nineties obsession with "sensitivity" and "inclusiveness" in all things meant that the making of war—which is all about uninclusive stuff like dividing people up as "enemies" or "allies" and hurting other peoples' feelings (and bodies) and winning and losing and blowing up other people's stuff and taking their land and even refusing to give it back!—became even more ambivalent and confused than ever.

For a look at a force riven with ambivalence, agonizing over conflicting directives, let us flash back for a moment to the Middle East, Christmas week, 1998, where the U.S. government was—delicately, tenuously, with much throat-clearing—attempting to wage its first major bombing campaign since Desert Storm.

Once again the bad guy was Saddam Hussein, who had been violating the terms of his 1991 surrender to the allied coalition by continuing to produce weapons of mass destruction (WMD) in basements around Baghdad. For four nights we pounded central Iraq with bombs and cruise missiles. Save for the inconvenient fact that we were dropping five-hundred-pound iron shells filled with gunpowder near groundlings' heads, it must have been one of the most polite bombing campaigns ever: We gave advance notice ("The bombing will commence at . . ."), we bombed (or tried to bomb) only empty government buildings, and so as not to offend local religious sensibilities, we took a night off from bombing in observance of the first night of Ramadan, one of the Muslim world's most sacred religious holidays.

Iraqis observe Ramadan by fasting and remaining celibate during the day but are allowed to resume normal activities after nightfall—so that is when the United States decided it would be most appropriate to bomb. And the right more-in-sorrow-than-in-anger tone had to be maintained. When a young sailor aboard the USS *Enterprise* got a little carried away with the spirit of the thing and scrawled, "Hey, Saddam! Here's a Ramadan present from Chad Rickenberg," on a Navy bomb (he might have been trying to copy the famous WWII photo of a bomb carrying the message "Merry Xmas, Adolf!"), the secretary of defense and his men reacted at once, sending an apology saying they were "distressed to learn of thoughtless graffiti mentioning the holy month of Ramadan written on a piece of ordnance during Operation Desert Fox" and remanded Rickenberg to the captain of his carrier for punishment.

After four nights, Desert Fox was deemed a success . . . and by standards of nineties warfare it was: We didn't have to sacrifice men or planes and the Pentagon did not "lose the public relations battle"— CNN did not roll endless tape of dead Iraqis. (It later turned out that eleven Iraqi civilians had been killed, but in network news terms, the Desert Fox story was "over.") Finally, in the stirring words of Secretary of Defense Cohen, we had managed to "significantly degrade Iraq's capability to produce weapons of mass destruction."

Military tradition dictated a revel for the victorious warriors. Ever dutiful about military tradition and all too aware that U.S. forces stationed in the desert hovered near mass desertion over low pay, accelerated workloads, and the fact that William Jefferson Clinton, who was generally loathed in the military community, continued to be president, the SecDef hooked up with the United Service Organization (USO), which was heading to the Middle East to do its annual Christmas show for troops far from home. Once upon a time the USO came bearing Bob Hope and Playboy Bunnies; for Christmas 1998 the boys and girls got Mary Chapin Carpenter and Carole King. And for only a few minutes at that. Worried that song and dance might be inappropriate during this period of Muslim worship, the American embassy in Saudi Arabia decided the show should cancel and move on. The festivities and the SecDef did move on, but not before Carole King (singing a cappella) on the flight deck of the USS *Enterprise*, found a few moments to lead sailors in a couple of choruses of "You Make Me Feel (Like a Natural Woman)." The SecDef, always on the lookout for the humanizing photo op, got to stir the old stumps a bit with a young sailor. If an Old Salt, a sort of Navy-style Rip Van Winkle, had gone to sleep in

1945 and woken up in 1998 and read the *New York Times*'s photo caption—"Secretary of Defense William Cohen does the 'Locomotion' with Navy Lt."—he might have had a heart attack. Well, the Navy lieutenant was a girl, and, as you could see in the photo, a very pretty one, but the Old Salt probably would have been hard-pressed to decide if that information made the situation better . . . or worse.

War making has never been easy. We are a civilized nation, a nation that has tended to go to war reluctantly and that has often attempted to restore our enemies to full health once we've defeated them. In most of the nineties, we had one of the best-educated and morally aware forces ever. The problem is that war, as George Orwell once put it, is "civilization's reversal."

Civilian values and military exigencies do not coexist easily, and when we sit down to make national security and military policy, we always end up toggling awkwardly in between. The institution of the military occupies an odd place in society's arrangement; it stands next to other major institutions but separate and enclosed: the fortress, the walled, gated monastery on the ridge above the village. Because we recognize that what monks and soldiers are attempting to do (in the one case converse with God, in the other ready themselves to kill or be killed) is unusual, out of the ordinary sphere, both institutions are, to a certain extent, given the freedom to do things their own "odd" way—the Army, for instance, demands that its personnel run around "dressed like trees" (most soldiers' everyday wear is the BDU, or battle dress uniform, which is decorated with splotches of brown, black, and various shades of green to blend into foliage). The services can also manage their people with a separate legal code, one that is much harsher than our regular criminal code. They also get to ignore the Constitution at times. In wartime, for instance, in the interests of national security, the military is allowed to violate the First Amendment by declaring areas and documents off-limits to reporters. As John Luddy, an ex-Marine who now works on Capitol Hill, puts it, "American society tolerates a level of independent behavior that would cripple a military force." "The values necessary to defend the society are often at odds with the values of the society itself," says Army general Walter Kerwin. "To be an effective servant of the people, the Army must concentrate not on the values of our liberal society, but on the hard values of the battlefield."

Still, this is an institution that has a budget of nearly $300 billion, one and a half (give or take a few hundred thousand) million active-duty personnel, and piles and piles of communications equipment, vehicles, and weaponry. It has the raw materials—and some would say the propensity—to become an independent state. You want some civilian oversight of the beast. As President John Adams said to a general of the Continental Army, "We don't choose to trust you generals with too much power for too long a time." The problem is that in divvying up the power both parties must walk a delicate line. Military leaders are, after all, paid to be the war specialists at the table. If we're going to win wars, the services have got to be "given their head" a bit, not micromanaged by people far away from the actual workings of things.

We had less problem maintaining this balance when Congresses and presidents' cabinets included more people with military experience. But this has changed dramatically. In 1971, for instance, 75 percent of the members of Congress had served in the military. In 1998, it was only 34 percent. In 1992, we inaugurated our first president since Franklin Delano Roosevelt who had no military experience, and he tended to appoint people like himself, so that by 1998, as James Webb noted in a speech to the Naval War College in Newport, "for the first time since the formation of DOD by the National Security Act of 1947, when the U.S. became a major power, none of the principals in the national security arena—-the president, the SecDef, the secretary of state, the director of the CIA—have served in the military."

We maintain a military to deliver one specialized, rather unique product. In times of war that product is military victory (usually accomplished by killing people and destroying property, unfortunately); in times of peace, the product is *readiness* to achieve victory. That quality of "readiness" is hard to measure, but the only proper way to do so is to start at ground level with the people who actually have to make it work; in other words, at the "peon" level, with the infantryman and with combat service and support personnel. Then you have to get really concrete about everything that can affect his morale, from boots to bedding to whether he's allowed to get an E-mail account on unit computers and whether he hates his leadership and why. But it is hard to sell a request, for instance, for more money to pay for a vague category called "equipment" (including new boots) when civilian congressmen, and the "experts" who often advise them, have only vague notions of how ground soldiers get from place to place. At a recent conference of military historians and women's rights activists, one panelist, an administrator in the Canadian Army, happened to mention that they were conducting a study about how to construct a better boot for the female soldier. An American history professor sitting beside her looked quite puzzled at this and asked her copanelist why on earth they'd study something like that (until then, discussion had centered on sexual harassment and opening combat units to women). "If your boots don't fit, you can't climb hills," the Canadian officer answered briskly. The professor looked startled, like she'd suddenly been clued in on a very esoteric but crucial secret, and then thanked her copanelist profusely for this revelation.

In the late nineties, veterans of World War II were departing this earthly sphere at the rate of about a thousand a day, taking with them the contribution of "a realism . . . about the use of military force and nature of military institutions," as ex-soldier and military historian Williamson Murray put it. Increasingly there were simply fewer people around with military experience, thus more kids without fathers or grandfathers to tell the war stories and thus more of what columnist and former Marine Phillip Gold called "military illiteracy." Catherine Aspy, a Harvard grad who enlisted in the Army in the midnineties and served for two years in intelligence, says it always seems to her that "civilians expect the military to sort of function like General Electric—it's just there, it just works—and then they are mystified when it doesn't." In the absence of a nice juicy war to sink their teeth into, military pundits spent the nineties dissecting, addressing, Q&Aing, journalizing what was called the "growing gap between civilian and military culture." The gap became such a fashionable topic that by 1999, for instance, the SecDef had taken to traveling around the country, from the Microsoft compound in the Northwest to the Illinois state assembly, to "build more grassroots awareness of what American troops do and the sacrifices they make daily for the nation."

Military illiteracy always seems to be worst among the country's best educated and among baby boomers, who, when forced to think about the armed forces, seem to default to two rather foggy images of just who those people are and just what it is they do. One prevalent image is the Neanderthal. A writer in *The New Yorker* cracked, for instance, that "teachers use the phrase 'military intelligence' as an example of an oxymoron." Baby boomers have watched two wars on television (Vietnam and the Gulf) that tended to make death and destruction look relatively easy. Television is good at showing off, say, a brilliant new plane, but it is bad at capturing the intangible factor of enemy determination, which was a huge factor in Vietnam and a critical factor in our "engagement" in Kosovo. As the *Washington Post* put it in an editorial on Kosovo: "Most Americans are stunned that Yugoslavia is fighting back and won't surrender to NATO's air war. We've become so accustomed to watching televised bomb runs, where munitions hit thimble-sized targets, that it is easy to forget real wars aren't programmed in technical manuals." In spring 1999, R. W. Apple of the *New York Times* pointed out that, in their efforts to stop Slobodan Milosevic, Bill Clinton and Tony Blair, who had "grown up in an age mesmerized by technology," had become overly obsessed with bloodless war and were prosecuting what Apple called "baby-boomer warfare."

In the winter of 1998, with images of Operation Desert Fox and the female bombers who participated filling TV screens, a young, gainfully employed Ph.D. at a cocktail party mused about the prospect of sending coed combat arms units to a place like Iraq. When I opined that male/female physical differences could be a problem in gender-integrated ground combat units, he replied airily, "But does that matter? It's all pushing buttons now anyway." Even the clamor from CNN's pundits about needing ground troops to "solve" the Saddam Hussein problem had failed to override this boomer's *Star Trek* syndrome. Another academic, this one a professor at MIT, wasn't sure how military chain of command worked. He said he was "sick of the military getting us involved in all these things," seeming to forget that in Kosovo the commander in chief ordered the bombing to commence while wary military service chiefs fretted in the background.

Sometimes, however, civilian leaders are reminded of the armed services quite vividly—when they have the social reform itch. As one young soldier put it, "They see us as a million-plus young people trained to follow orders and salute," and their fingers get itchy to experiment with social policy. Sometimes these sweeping experiments at cultural transformation are successful; sometimes they are a disaster.

The integration of blacks—ordered by President Harry Truman in 1948—is one of the glowing successes. After decades of rockiness (there were even riots at sea aboard aircraft carriers), the U.S. military became what is probably the most successfully racially integrated institution in the country, probably the world. It is by now cliché, but a profound lesson nonetheless, that at any basic training camp you'll see black drill sergeants barking at young white men, and that mostly the young white men listen with deep respect—even with the kind of veneration a young man should feel toward an experienced older one.

But civilian leaders and their various enthusiasms can produce bloopers. In the late sixties, for instance, Secretary of Defense Robert McNamara, invigorated by the spirit of President Lyndon Johnson's "War on Poverty," decided he would "salvage lives" of "the subterranean poor" by telling the military ("the largest single educational complex the world has ever possessed") to admit "tens of thousands" of the young men they had traditionally rejected because they scored too low on baseline recruitment office tests. McNamara called the 300,000 men he recruited for this experiment "The New Standard" men; critics called them "McNamara's Moron Corps." Unfortunately the skeptics were right—the Category IVs (as they were called because they were from the lowest, cut off recruit category) didn't adapt to discipline. They got into fights. They deserted. When the Navy, roiled with recruiting problems in the late nineties, began to discuss admitting more CAT IVs (the services then set the maximum at about 4 percent), Maj. Gen. Mark Hamilton, a just-retired Army recruiting chief, said that for the "old-timers [who'd been around for Project 100,000] this would be heresy."

Knowing when to fight or when to accept the sometimes goofy and very often uninformed decrees of Congress (how to compromise) is a tough job. You need wise men with experience on the ground in combat, men who can ask themselves whether Congress's latest bright idea will work on the battlefield or not. In exchange for that wisdom and responsibility, generals and admirals get—in military terms—perks and obeisance fit for a king: devoted aides, ship staterooms with private bathrooms, separate dining rooms, salutes from everyone they outrank, relatively high salaries, and chances to attend glittering cocktail parties with Washington's swells. Certainly seductions are strewn in their paths, but by and large, over time, they've managed to keep their eye on the prize, to represent and explain military values to civilian leaders.

So what was it about the nineties that made military leaders desert their posts and go native—Washington, D.C., bureaucrat-style native, that is? Why did they let civilians, who often have only a very abstract knowledge of what the military actually does, micromanage policy? When civilian leaders decried in a sort of my-goodness-this-should-have-been-done-yesterday tone that it was time for young women and men to share tents, barracks, and the catacomb-like berthing areas of combat ships, why did so many military leaders just swallow hard and follow orders, ignoring their own decades of experience? Why did they give not a peep when civilian leaders railed about the need to dismantle a "diseased" "warrior culture"? Why, as columnist Richard Cohen once put it, did the U.S. military become "one of the most [politically correct] institutions in the country," when the current version of politically correctitude is inherently hostile to the way the military must do its business?

How and Why

For a start, it would have helped the brass's resolve, during the policy fights of the nineties, if the cold war had ended with a bit more of a nice decisive climactic bang . . . something involving guns and tanks maybe, at least a bit louder, with better visuals, something that would have made the victory a bit realer to the man on the street, something that would have highlighted the role of the military in this triumph.

There was no dancing in the streets while "public enemy number one" unraveled, especially not for those in the various cold war industries. One morning in the winter of 1989 I called an arms policy guy I know in D.C. "Hello?" he croaked weakly. "Why are you so sad?" I asked. "Great things are happening! This," I said, reading him a *New York Times* headline, which announced that the Soviet Union was reducing its army by about half, "is a good thing, isn't it?" "For mankind!!" he wailed.

The early years of the nineties sent Pentagon types into a state of dislocation. It would take years for all the tiny, ill-equipped potential enemies of the third world to get up to speed. Searching for a rationale not to reduce military strength, Gen. Colin Powell, then chairman of the Joint Chiefs of Staff, was quoted as saying jokingly, "I'm running out of villains. I'm down to Castro and Kim Il Sung." If you were in the military, or a military contractor, or one of the military's civilian employees, scary words filled the airwaves and the op-ed pages. "We could cut the military budget in half without cutting defense," stormed Jesse Jackson in a speech. "Let's go get the money." A budget director at Price Waterhouse was quoted as saying, "I've been telling my defense clients to expect the worst." Some said we'd all been rendered obsolete by the cruise missile and "smart bombs," that we would never need large standing infantries in "the wars of the future." Some said we could get rid of our "blue sea Navy" (i.e., aircraft carriers and such that don't go close to land). An era of peace seemed to stretch before us— and what does a Department of Defense do if war as we know it is "over"?

The point is, we started that decade with military leaders who were feeling defensive, who were worried about irrelevancy, who felt they had to struggle to justify their very existence—sitting across the metaphorical bargaining table from a Congress that was twitching to carve up the new "peace dividend" and tossing around scary words like *trim*, *slash*, and *shrink*.

The first thing on the congressional agenda at the start of the new decade became the vast project of "downsizing" or "drawing down" the armed forces, which many said had grown too large during the Reagan years.

And throughout the early to midnineties, this was accomplished. Defense spending comprised about half of the federal budget in the sixties; it went to about 25 percent in the eighties, and was 16 percent in 1999. In 1989, we had a force of 2.2 million people on active duty; that was allowed to decline to 1.4 million in 1999, the lowest troop strength number since 1940, the year before Pearl Harbor. Funding for ship and aircraft modernization decreased by 50 percent over the decade. The Navy had 526 ships in 1993 and 333 in 1998. In 1993, the military spent about $125 billion on procurement, but only $44 billion in early 1998. We started the decade with eighteen active divisions and ended it with ten.

But the Pentagon had other problems besides trying to preserve war-fighting ability in an era of budget cutting. While the 1990 Pentagon was busy on one front, in a guerrilla camp, high in the hills (of, say, Westchester, New York, and Ann Arbor, Michigan), another force was marshaling, preparing the battering ram that would finally splinter the fortress gate and make changes in the military's cultural core.

What does one call this other force? Throughout the sixties, seventies, and eighties they were called feminists or the women's movement. The only problem with using that description now is that, as one feminist writer put it recently, "there are no rules" in today's feminism: A sort of Design Your Own Feminism prevails.

Maybe it is more specific to call the group who led the cultural part of the nineties charge at the military the "personal is political" crowd because the goal of groups like the National Organization for Women (NOW) was to draw private life into political discussion, and then into the reach of courts and judges and penalties.

It was inevitable that the personal-is-political crowd would get around to the military. They had spent much of the seventies and eighties focusing on the workplace, the home, and schools, but it had been harder to find a way into that monastery standing outside the gates, the preserve of all that was imperialistic, aggressive, violent, hierarchical, uncompromising, authoritarian.

Sure, in the late seventies and eighties the personal-is-political crowd had paid some attention to the military and achieved some successes. In 1975–76, the all-male service academies, the military's equivalent of the Ivy League—prestigious schools like West Point in upstate New York, the Naval Academy in Annapolis, Maryland, the Air Force Academy in Colorado, where cadets pass a boulder carved with the words *Bring Me Men*—had been told to admit women.

In the mideighties, groups like NOW almost succeeded in adding an Equal Rights Amendment to the Constitution that—depending on judges' interpretations—could have required a female draft. Still, there was plenty to do in the civilian sector; thus, in the seventies and eighties, most feminist/personal-is-political energies were still directed toward "workplace issues," and the fortress stood unbreached.

But at the end of a decade that was largely about the revision of sex roles, it is somehow fitting that they would finally end up at those gates, making their way in, and heading, armed with brickbats, for the symbols and most holy objects at the monastery's core.

Warfare is one of the most central, defining, and primal human conditions and (with small exceptions) the heart of it—direct combat—has been a male-only domain. "Women may be both the cause or pretext of warmaking," notes John Keegan in *The History of Warfare*. ". . . They can be the instigators of violence in an extreme form . . . remarkably hard-hearted mothers of warriors . . . and messianic war leaders."

They have "followed the drum, nursed the wounded, tended the fields, and herded the flocks when the man of the family has followed his leader, have even dug the trenches for men to defend and labored in the workshops to send them their weapons." But, he writes, "women . . . do not fight. They rarely fight among themselves and they never, in any military sense, fight men. If warfare is as old as history and as universal as mankind, we must now enter the supremely important limitation that it is an entirely masculine activity."

And the military made such an exciting end-of-the-century project. In an era devoted to examining, criticizing, and rebuking masculinity, the armed forces were the last preserve where the species ran free. The culture of the military was just so unapologetically male: all that heavy-booted stomping and deep-voiced howling, those cries of "Hoooooooaaaah." Their monosyllabic nouns and verbs—"grunt," "legs"—and rapidly fired acronyms. That habit of running around with protruding objects and stabbing things. And there was the shocking level of lewdness (the way men talk when they are alone, revealed for the intelligentsia in Norman Mailer's blockbuster World War II novel *The Naked and the Dead*). Even the fact that it was then overwhelmingly male (women were 11 percent of the force in 1990) was considered ipso facto proof of sexual discrimination, a clue that one might find a hidden gulag of sexually rebuked, intimidated, harassed women behind the fortress gates.

Of course, heretofore the women's movement hadn't devoted much thought to those women. One of the things that delayed the personal-is-political movement from taking on the military was that it was hard to establish links with female allies within the fortress. Were there allies in there at all, in fact? Reformers discovered that, as one female academic put it on an on-line bulletin board recently, "many military women are as conservative as many military men in sociopolitical beliefs. But does that conservatism mean they can't be or are not feminists?"

(A woman named Pilar Ryan, who apparently walked between both worlds, complained on the same discussion board: "I can understand why people at Penn see me as fairly conservative. What absolutely bewilders me, however, is when a woman will tell me that I am not a feminist because I collude with the patriarchy as a member of the military service.")

There was also a logistical problem. In a country like the United States, we really couldn't demand change in somebody's more subtle behavior until it crossed the line into a legal infraction or made for a civil case that could corral highly visible powerful defendants, whose fate the world would watch. We didn't have a way of going after *culture*—that subtle web of conventions and expectations expressed by what people say in ordinary conversation, and how and where they look at each other, and what they laugh at, and even the way they think. There was no way, in other words, to get at this nebulous web of injustices the reformers called "sexism" because the "injuries" it generated were not recognized in any serious way by criminal or civil law. The psychic injuries incurred in marriages, while dating, or while just flirting were merely seen as the costs of life with other people, especially people of the opposite sex to whom we are particularly vulnerable. As for sexist behavior like, say, the socially incompetent or outright boorish boss who always seems to be wishing your breasts good morning instead of you, there was no way to rap him with the legal code unless he demanded that you put up with such behavior or get demoted, fired, or docked. In the past, a successful sexual harassment case demanded evidence of a quid pro quo. Sexual harassment is covered by civil law and who would want to sue Mr.—let's call him Clooney—anyway? Lawyers wouldn't take the case. Sexual harassment was not a well-publicized charge, judges and juries had not been "educated" as they are today, and there was no money in it. One was only allowed to sue the harasser himself, and you just knew that Mr. Clooney had very, very shallow pockets. The civil sexual harassment suit was not the kind of legal tool with which one could change society as a whole.

By the mideighties, however, a blizzard of legal briefs and books had been making the argument that sexual harassment in the workplace was, in effect, sexual discrimination in the workplace and thus should come under the powerful federal umbrella of the Civil Rights Act of 1964 that forbids discrimination against people on the basis of sex, race, national origin, and religion. Once sexual harassment moved under Title VII (the branch of the act that deals with workplace discrimination), one could sue one's employer, even if he wasn't the harasser himself, and even if he wasn't a "he" but a mega corporation—with very, very deep pockets. Furthermore, though a quid pro quo was still very much a cause of action, the definition of sexual harassment was broadened to include verbal and physical conduct of a sexual nature that creates a "hostile, intimidating, and offensive environment."

The new broadly written and subjectively defined infraction opened up a new frontier for litigation and created a new legal language. A hostile and offensive environment is very difficult to define. Monica blow-job jokes around the watercooler are the stuff of life for some people, a traumatic experience for others. Feminist lawyers argued that we needed "hostile environment" protection because women were sometimes forced to quit a job to get away from a boss who continually made them feel uncomfortable. But what if the boss thinks he is acting normally—by the standards of our overly familiar, crude age—and the employee just happens to be a particularly delicate flower, is the boss a harasser? A vague definition coupled with lawyers smelling money is a dangerous combination. Wherever there is a possibility for confusion (as between men and women most of the time), there is a possibility for injury, and the law gave us a crude template of victim and victimizer, hurtful act and injury, perpetrator and receiver, to fit over the most complex, the most ambivalent, the most highly charged, of our relationships: between men and women, employer and employee, teacher and student.

Thirty years after members of groups like NOW marched in the streets of New York City proclaiming, "The personal is political," the country found itself gathered around TV sets to watch a grim panel of senators interrogating a Supreme Court nominee over a joke he might have made, in a relaxed moment, about a pubic hair and a Coke can. Nobody really knew where "sexual harassment" began and ended and we were still struggling in the early nineties: "Society and the military [are] just beginning to understand that certain behaviors constituted harassment," one congressman explained with great earnestness at the time. But while we tried to figure out what sexual harassment was and what it was not, the new law seemed to take on a life of its own. Our half-finished creation began to toddle around the countryside scooping up victims in its large bumbling hands. Even the president could not escape.

Anyway, in August 1990, if we had been looking at one of those topographical maps of a combat theater, the configuration of the forces would have appeared like this: The embattled Pentagon is now engaged on two fronts—holding the line against the budget cutters while trying to fortify the gates against the culture reformers whose grenades are actually landing inside the compound now and then.

Everyone could have stayed like this for a decade or so, with the Pentagon digging in its heels and conceding a tiny increment here and there, except that a new player, a catalyst, entered the arena:

A solitary plane was seen putt-putting overhead. A lone trooper was disgorged and the tiny figure swayed lazily toward the earth under his big white chute like a wisp of milkweed down. After the figure extricated himself from his crumpled chute and began to slog toward us over the plains, we saw that it was . . . Saddam Hussein—president of Iraq, likely nutcase—come to announce that he had just invaded Kuwait, the portal for the world's oil supply.

The Gulf

Armies don't usually get five and a half months to set up their miniature cities, to spread out on the desert with the tents and the trucks and the boxes of Froot Loops and the computers and the dental supplies and the typewriters and the clerks ready to start typing away on those typewriters and the crates of Chef Boyardee Meals for One, and six-packs of Pepsi, and even rugs sent from home bases in Germany.

The Desert Shield ramp-up—from August 1990, when we began putting troops in tents in Saudi, until January 17, 1991, when the first missile was fired—was agonizingly slow for the families (who waited to hear if one of their own was going to go), for the pundits (who had to keep coming up with things to say), and most particularly for the press corps obligated to "stay with a story" (supposed to be Huge, supposed to be Historic) that was actually, well, somewhat static.

So editors sent reporters out to "find a feature," especially a "human interest" or "reaction" story. Editors are always happiest when the story is time-tested, reader-tested, and publisher-approved—in effect, already vetted, so the first weeks of a New War called for unpacking a popular culture convention called The Tearful Farewell.

Everybody who's looked at Norman Rockwell paintings or watched old war movies knows what The Tearful Farewell looks like. A young man in a crisp new military uniform strides forth, while an assortment of tearful civilians—your basic mom-dad-sweetheart package—stay behind, rooted to the porch. There was a sense of joy in that young man's stride, a sense that he moved in an unfettered way toward action and even adventure.

But in the fall of 1990, when the press corps turned their cameras on the front stoops or the tarmac or the living room, they stumbled upon a genuinely fresh angle: A number of those departing soldiers were women! Often they were the ones tearing up! Sometimes the one left behind wringing hands and looking out the window was the man of the house! And suddenly there were kids . . . tons and tons of kids, toddling into the shot, hanging off the doorjamb with jam-covered fingers, staring at the cameraman with big eyes. Deploying to a foreign land seemed to have become a family affair.

There was a general, domestic-flavored stickiness to the new mobilization. What we were seeing was fifteen years of family- and women-friendly policies initiated after 1973 and the advent of the all-volunteer force. Having to make do with soldiers who choose to join and choose to stay, the forces have had to meet the "competition of the private sector," as a DOD paper put it, by letting them have a normal family life. Having also decided that recruiting goals could not be met without women, many women-friendly policies were instituted, too. The policy of kicking out women who became pregnant or, somehow or other, acquired a dependent child ended in 1975, for instance, along with barring women from schools like West Point and the Naval Academy.

In the mideighties, naval officer Gary Shrout was transferred from his shipboard billet and assigned to join the staff of the admiral who oversaw the Navy's base in Pearl Harbor, Hawaii. When Shrout went to his first staff orientation meeting, the first thing out of the "CO's mouth was 'My first priority is child care.'"

"*My* first reaction," says Shrout, "was 'I've left the Navy!' I looked down at myself and said, 'I'm still wearing the uniform . . . I think.' . . . After the shock wore off, I realized it was the right thing to do. There were many families now. Still, it was such a cultural change from the Navy I'd been in before."

And the family-friendly/women-friendly stuff had an impact. By 1990, 55 percent of the enlisted force was married (in contrast to the mostly bachelor forces of World War II and Vietnam)—75 percent of male officers, 50 percent of female officers. In Vietnam, a serviceman's average age was 19; by the time we got to the Gulf War, it was 26.7. The days of "If the Army wants you to have a wife, it would have issued you one" were over. By 1985, servicemen were married at two times the rate of civilians, in part because you got—and still get—a much better deal if you're married. The most attractive part of that deal is probably the housing allowance, which allows one to live off base or off ship in your own place. For instance, a married E-3 in the Navy (a fairly junior enlisted person) receives a housing allowance of $406 a month in Norfolk, $469 in San Diego, and $850 in Hawaii. Theoretically, a young unmarried enlisted guy or gal could rent an apartment in his or her home port, but young enlisteds are generally not making enough to afford that and tend to be trying to use their free "room and board" aboard their ship as a way to save money for whatever they'll do when they "get out."

And you don't have to be what they call "a traditional family" to get the benefits. In fact, as Linda Bird Francke wrote in her book *Ground Zero*, "the family benefits made the services a particular Mecca for single parents." Indeed, as John Luddy puts it, "it's hard to think of a better place for a single parent." A single mother searching for a safe, friendly, compact community decamps at a military base and finds subsidized day care, health insurance for herself and her dependents, a pension program, a housing allowance, and Family Care Centers to listen to her problems. If she is on, say, a Marine or Army base in the States, she'll probably be living in what appears to be a suburban subdivision—with its own ball fields and playgrounds and supermarket (even McDonald's, Baskin-Robbins, and the like). By December 1990, while we were deploying for the Gulf, there were 55,103 single parents in the 2-million-member armed forces according to the DOD, 17,836 of them women and 37,267 of them men. (You can be classified a "single parent" even if you do not have custody of the child and even if the child lives with someone else.) "In 1989," Francke writes, "there were proportionately twice as many single parents in the Navy as in the civilian population." The services still seem to be a magnet for single parents, most, in terms of ratio, female.

In any case, whether they signed up to serve their country or "for the job security" (as one respondent in a survey on why people "stay Army" put it), now they had to do their duty—in theory, that is.

Well, the editors said, this is not quite the old Tearful Farewell. Still, the gender reversals made for good copy and good television: Here's a gal in camouflage fatigues and a helmet! There's a mom in the cockpit of a plane! Over here's a sailor . . . a girl . . . swabbing the deck, for heaven's sake! The headline writers were in headline-writing heaven. A *New York Post* copy editor once opined that the single best words to put in a headline (alone, but especially together) are *coed* and *inferno*. Thus, "Coed War" was such a wonderful, newspaper-selling way to elicit that tiny tremor of S&M-ish thrill that readers get when women and violence are juxtaposed—all the while appearing appropriately high-minded and properly feminist.

Some rustics (the lower-circulation regional papers among us) saw this as an opportunity for *Private Benjamin*–style humor, but the major papers took the high road by attempting to superimpose a woman over the image of the jaunty young man of World War II.

"With tears and brave smiles," read the lead of an article entitled "Mom Goes to War," "thousands of American mothers are saying good-bye to their families to face the unknown dangers in the Gulf."

The problem with merely superimposing the image of the new female GI over the age-old image of the young male GI was that one simply couldn't silence that interminable yowling when the cameras rolled. In other words, you couldn't get the damn kids out of the picture.

In the mideighties, because of the greater numbers of women and single parents entering the services and because of the more married nature of the services and the increasingly common phenomenon of "dual-service" parents who could be sent overseas at the same time, the services had begun to require that parents of dependent children keep an up-to-date "Family Care Plan" in their personnel file in case their unit deployed. (A Family Care Plan is what it sounds like: an up-to-date, good-faith statement about who will take care of one's kids, just in case of deployment.) One could not deploy, in fact, if one's kids were not squared away. The Gulf War was the first test of the Family Care Plan and it did not pass with flying colors.

Perhaps care plan filers and their COs never expected they would have to use the child care plans. Perhaps they should have been checked and updated more often; perhaps there should have been a greater penalty for filing a plan in bad faith. In many cases during the Gulf War call-up, units got only a few days notice before they were supposed to go overseas, and when the files were exhumed, it turned out that grandmas had died, ex-husbands had remarried and acquired a huge new brood to care for. A Navy study reported that in 1990, a month after the Gulf War call-up had begun, 89 percent of single and dual-military enlisted parents did not have a valid child care plan. Nights before deployment to the Gulf saw many COs and their ostensible troops burning the midnight oil—as parents worked their way through their address books while the CO wondered how many people he'd finally be leaving with.

And so the great kid shuffle of 1990 and 1991 began. Parents turned to friends of friends, sometimes to foster homes. Relatives took care of kids. But that took juggling. Bobby could go to his uncle's, for example, and then have to be flown across the continent to stay with a cousin, because Uncle had been planning a vacation in Florida. Sometimes neighbors pitched in, as with the forty-year-old Bangor, Maine, logger who took on ten children of local single mothers—until a tree fell on his leg and broke it.

Of course, thousands of female soldiers were mounting those transport or commercial planes stoically as soldiers have always done. Reservist and mother Dianna McCoy, for instance, told a reporter, "I'm aware I did not join the Girl Scouts; I joined the Air Force." The nineteen-month-old baby she'd just adopted went off to stay with McCoy's parents while she went overseas with her medical unit. "Of course, never in a million years did I think I'd be called up," McCoy told a reporter. "Now I'm looking forward to it with ambivalence. . . . I'm looking forward to knowing I can make a difference. We're very good at what we do."

Despite plucky women like this, if you watched much TV, it appeared that a great lamentation had spread across the land. Senator John Heinz (R-Pa) wailed in an op-ed about an "emerging symbol of the Gulf War: mothers being torn from their young children," and the possibility of "American children being orphaned by an outmoded Pentagon personnel policy; an Uncle Sam already talking about how to rebuild Iraq, but whose heart turns to stone when confronted with the pain of American kids."

To the but-they-volunteered-for-this argument, Heinz replied, "It is also questionable whether an eighteen-year-old tantalized by offers of tuition money has any inkling of what he or she is giving up in 'volunteering' to leave children yet to be born behind."

A *Newsday* piece began with a grandmother named T. M. Harris "[holding] a framed photograph of her daughter, U.S. Army Reserve Sgt. Sharon Harris and her three children close to her chest. 'War is for people who like it, not for people like her,' Harris said of her daughter who, at 42, was abruptly called to active duty as a medic three weeks ago. . . . 'She called me in the middle of the night, and from that moment on, I haven't stopped trembling,' Harris said. 'She is the sole support of her three little girls and they can't do without her.' "

One Army nurse who was going to Saudi Arabia three months after the birth of her second child wondered to a *Wall Street Journal* reporter "why she and other mothers couldn't serve in hospitals in Europe and bring their children along so 'we wouldn't have to watch our babies grow up on videos.' "

One reason for all this commotion is that in December, as our overseas force was still being installed, the *Washington Post* reported that "one of every four U.S. military men and women in the Middle East now is a member of a National Guard or reserve unit." This, after all, was the new, "leaner" post–cold war force—and it would be wasteful not to use "the weekend warriors." But, Francke points out, "almost forty years had passed since the last major call-up of the reserves for the Korean War. Many modern reservists had been born after the Korean conflict and had not seriously considered that they would be activated."

Also, as Henry Hamilton, a retired member of the Judge Advocate General (JAG) office, notes, "[The commotion] hadn't happened before because we didn't have nursing mothers we were trying to send to war."

Still, it wasn't that hard to find a way to stay behind with your kids. The regulations that govern exemptions from deployment and even discharge from the service are, as Hamilton puts it, "an art not a science." In unofficial, practical terms, the decision to exempt or allow an "out" is made on a pretty local level, like by the captain of one's company, a person you'd see every day, and the wording of the various categories—"for the convenience of government," for "extreme hardship"—are pretty broad. Besides, as Hamilton points out, if someone is complaining about going from the get-go, a CO will generally be "looking for a reason to get this person the hell out of there. A dud will hamper the mission." So many parents sought and got an exemption or even a discharge from the services.

Still, there were no firm criteria for an exemption and since COs were not always so sympathetic to people's desire to stay with their children, other stratagems were employed.

Some filed for conscientious objector status: "My recruiter told me I would never have to go to war, that I would travel and gain skills and an education," said Azania Howze, a thirty-five-year-old single reservist with a twelve-year-old daughter. "I cannot kill another human being. I cannot even facilitate war. It is more caring to fight against war than to make war." Some contacted Congressman Heinz, who wrote in the same op-ed, "Most of the soldier-parents caught in this predicament are not careerists. In fact, most of the people who have contacted my office are just the opposite: They had opted to devote time to their children and were on their way out of the military when they were called up." Some contacted media (like one soldier/mother with a two-year-old daughter who told her story on the *Larry King Live* and got a call from a Saudi Arabian prince who offered to pay for a nanny) and the media was happy to oblige.

With all this drama on the airwaves, by the end of January 1991— with the war just beginning its "shooting" phase—the floors of congressional hearing rooms were filling with senators and representatives pitching bills such as the "Gulf War Orphans Act" to keep parents out of combat zones. Groups like NOW and the National Women's Law Center and the Defense Advisory Committee on Women in the Services (DACOWITS) were watching with dismay. After all, they had won enlarged roles for women with the argument that women did not need and would not ask for special treatment. An ambivalent representative Patricia Schroeder (D-Colo) supported some action to deal with Gulf War "orphans," but warned "we have to be careful that we don't start talking about mommy tracking." The image of soldier-mothers was supposed to accomplish broader social change. As Francke puts it, "Advocates of equal opportunity have long known that interchangeability of father/mother roles is essential to downplay a mother's indispensability to her young children and thereby allow her to pursue a guilt-free life outside the home."

Nevertheless, a lot of women out there—who tended to be in the enlisted ranks—seemed to be making the point that the children were "indispensable" to the mothers as well.

A reservist named Lori Moore had petitioned for a general discharge. "This is all new for America and we're feeling our way blindly through this deployment," Moore told Jane Gross of the *New York Times.* "This whole experience has changed my mind about many things. I hate to say it because it doesn't fit with the whole scheme of the women's movement, but I think we have to reconsider what we're doing. For me, this was a major conflict between two loves. I'm a soldier. I was ready to go. But I produced these kids, and I need to take responsibility for them. . . . There's no question that women can do this. The question is whether we should."

"There are so many feelings; how can I possibly sort them out?" Sgt. Twila Erickson-Schamer told Gross. "I've tried to convince myself that it's going to be OK and displayed that attitude to other people. If I didn't, I'd be in a constant state of emotional breakdown. I'd be crying all the time."

In general, as Gross pointed out, the call-up had become "a dramatic measure of how different this military crisis is from any other in history. . . ." Some parents, she wrote, "never expected the escalating military call-ups or the storm of emotions brought on by first-time motherhood. . . . For many young parents the demands of war are colliding with those of the evolving American family. . . ."

And, besides showing how "family-friendly" we'd become, the Gulf War showed us how we'd shifted from an all-male force to a coed one. The mobilization of about forty thousand women in the Gulf War was "the largest onetime deployment of military women in our nation's history," said Undersecretary of Defense Christopher Jehn. New kinds of jobs that put women closer to the action had opened up, and though women were still barred from "direct combat" (infantry or artillery), the all-important pictures from the Gulf featured women who actually looked like soldiers, helmeted, gun-carrying, as dusty and motor oil speckled as everybody else. Women military police (MPs) were seen directing traffic or shepherding enemy prisoners to holding areas; female pilots were flying supply helicopters and doing repair work on both those planes and other machinery.

If you'd just tuned in to this new television war (with the last television war, Vietnam, as your reference point), it may have looked like the mixed-gender force popped up overnight. Actually, what we saw in the Gulf had been gestating for years.

It's hard to find a place to begin the story of the integration of women. In raw numbers, the number of women connected to the services by nursing has grown steadily since World War I. But in terms of other aspects, there have been four catalytic periods in the history of women in the military: the period after World War II, the period after the Vietnam War, after the Gulf War, and after the annual Tailhook convention of 1991.

World War II

World War II was a heartbreakingly beautiful example of civilian mobilization. The creation of those "citizen soldiers" required the patriotism and contribution of practically every American citizen; over time, of course, that vast mobilization required the conscription of 11 million men. When male bodies began to get scarce, military planners realized that women could fill noncombat positions (clerical positions, intelligence positions, billets as weather forecasters, PT leaders, dental assistants, and more) and thereby "free a man to fight." And so the first of the all-women (i.e., staffed by women and commanded by women), all-volunteer auxiliaries—the WAC (Women's Army Corps)—was born.

The conventional wisdom is that the government took every opportunity to remind WACs (and what the government perceived as an anxious public) that women weren't going to turn into men by putting on a uniform. Much attention has been paid to the training films that reminded the ladies to wear makeup and look feminine, with the implication that being in a separate branch made women feel second class.

But the WAC experience is a nuanced one—and most women emerged feeling exhilarated, not put down. Recruiting posters from World War II suggest that the services offered a dignified, professional, even noble role for women who wanted to join the war effort. Certainly it is a different role from the one dangled in front of men. There are no fatigues or rifles in these posters (as there are today); still, they convey a sense of mission, of importance.

One beautifully painted WAC recruiting poster shows a nightscape: In the background, helmeted men carrying rifles and planes seen in silhouette, as if they are backlit by a bright moon, stream in one direction—presumably toward a battle. In the foreground, as if she has stepped out of this rush of bodies, is a young woman, a very pale-skinned brunette in a WAC uniform. She has stopped and stares apprehensively at the night sky. At the top of the poster it says, "Mine Eyes Have Seen the Glory." Of course, it is a recruiting poster, but unlike posters of today, blaring, "40K for College," this poster actually pitches to one's sense of duty, conscience, and adventure. The poster invites women to share the glory; it says that there are different kinds of glory to be had in a war effort and that the U.S. Army needs and respects the other kinds of service as well.

Certainly some posters stressed the practical. "The Army Has 239 Jobs for Women," reads one caption under a drawing of a trim blond draftswoman drawing on a large wall map. Certainly she is beautiful and feminine-looking, but we're not talking Betty Boop here; she looks with fierce seriousness only at the board—not coyly at the viewer.

All in all, World War II had been a very good model of the way women, indeed whole populations, could aid a war effort, so it is not surprising that in 1948 Congress passed the Women's Armed Services Act (WASA), which authorized permanent status for women in the regular and reserve units of the Army, Navy, Marine Corps, and the brand-new Air Force, which was pulled from the Army's rib cage in 1947.

But WASA gave and WASA took away. In other words, it gave cautiously—as if expressing the queasiness the public tended to feel about women in combat. So, while it authorized a permanent place, it decreed that the number of women in the force could never exceed 2 percent of the number of enlisteds in the "regular" forces. And it included the Combat Exclusion Law, which reassuringly made the boundaries clear: "Women may be assigned to all units except those with a high probability of engaging in ground combat, direct exposure to enemy fire, or direct physical contact with the enemy."

There is a large niche in the contemporary military history community busy unearthing the stories of the handful of women who served on the front lines dressed as men. Academics of this feather gather to compare notes on a Website called Minerva (Minerva was the Roman goddess of war). But curiously, the well-documented role women played, say in World War II, in military intelligence—as spies, for instance—and as nurses is relegated to dusty cabinets, even denigrated. "Except as nurses and whores women have always been excluded from the military," said one German professor in one of Minerva's on-line discussion groups.

Well, it's true both provide comfort, but prostitutes can escape war zones and military nurses are obligated to stay. Throughout all of our military engagements, nurses have been extraordinarily important to our soldiers, but their role is often downplayed. When one talks to them, it is obvious that they radiate a kind of power, that they have been a sort of invisible second leg of the military, the life force balancing the death force, the yin to the killer's yang. "Give us bread and give us roses," as an old labor movement slogan put it. Nurses gave both.

The psychoanalyst Fred Wyatt of the University of Michigan explained that "healing grows along a slender thread of eros." (Actually, he apparently improvised this nugget on the spot when a graduate student came to visit him in a hospital and found him flirting with his nurse.) Soldiers grow rapturous about the experience of, as one Canadian ex-infantry officer put it, "waking up in a hospital bed and seeing a woman's face . . . feeling her touch, her soft fingers."

Vietnam-era nurse Elizabeth Finn worked with both male and female nurses. The men, she says, used humor as the psychic energizer, while the women harnessed (not always consciously) what a psychologist would call the power of transference—wherein the nurse becomes a stand-in for every female who has ever brought comfort and a reason to live, allowing themselves to become, in effect, a sort of impersonal object, "Woman"—a stalk around which the soul, hope, eros, can attach itself and climb. Sometimes they can't cure, and then they provide a good death, which, maybe only karmically, is an essential in a society (and an army unit is a small society) if it is going to be healthy.

Finn worked in a field hospital surrounded by jungle on a base near Long Binh, thirty miles north of Saigon. It was not so much "on the front lines" as surrounded by them, she says, and their base was often a target because ammunition was stored there. When the wounded men were brought into the field hospital, the medics patched them up and threw them back in or, if the injuries were more serious, stabilized them enough to fly to a Stateside hospital. For many weeks the medics had struggled with a young man who'd come in as badly damaged as they'd seen. He was "about twenty," Finn says, "a redhead. He was so badly burned, we had to keep him on a stretcher frame instead of a bed. His kidneys were gone. Parts had been amputated and he had a really bad chest wound." He was conscious most of the time, Finn said, "but he had never talked to us."

Everybody had worked so hard on him to get him in shape to be evacuated to Japan or Hawaii. One day I went back on the intensive care ward; people were standing around looking at him; I knew something was going on, so I went to look, and it was obvious he was dying. I began yelling, "What's the matter! Do something! Get a doctor!" Finally a physician came over and put his hand on my shoulder and he said, "Liz, he's dying. There's nothing you can do."

I was still very upset, so I went over and stood next to him. By now the ward had cleared. I was just standing by the side of his bed looking into his eyes and all of a sudden I had this feeling. "My God," I thought. "What is his mother doing now? What are his sisters doing now? At this exact moment they may be out shopping or working and they don't know what's happening at this moment to their son and brother."

I just kept thinking that he was just a kid. He had never gone anywhere. "He probably isn't even married. He'll never experience being married; he'll never experience children; he'll never see his mother and father again." I thought, "He's never going to see another woman."

I thought, "I guess I have to represent everything to him." I felt that very keenly, that it was good to represent the women in his life—mother, sister, girlfriend. I've always wanted to track down his mother and tell her he wasn't alone when he died. He was surrounded by Americans, he wasn't in the jungle.

Vietnam

The next spike in the gender-integration process occurred after the Vietnam War, but to understand why it occurred, we have to look at the emotional landscape that war left behind. The process of drafting all those American men had been like a battle in itself—a sort of unacknowledged civil war from which we've never really recovered.

There was a brother-against-brother quality in the scene outside draft induction centers: Young men marched determinedly in, sometimes flanked by MPs, while barricades held back crowds of more young men who hooted, pleaded, or lectured at them to turn back.

But, gosh, if you were one of the guys, trying to ignore the chants from the sidelines, you probably wondered if maybe the guys on the civilian side of the barricades were onto something. Call-ups didn't always have to compete with such siren calls from the street.

"Men go to war," an old sea dog I know once said, "because the women are watching," and by the Vietnam draft, women's attention was definitely not on the men lining up to board the transport planes. The antiwar movement was a great moral battle for a lot of people, but it also became the beach, the place where the action was. Humorist P. J. O'Rourke once wrote that one could judge the power of a political movement with a "pretty girl index"—in other words, by comparing the number of pretty girls hanging out at the demonstrations, or collating the flyers in the campaign offices. And "the movement," as it was called, had 'em. And these weren't just any girls. They were purportedly a sort of once-in-a-lifetime anomaly, an improbable new breed who wore miniskirts and went braless, and sometimes even lived in communes and practiced "free love." Who didn't want to hang around for that?

Ever since . . . forever, girls have loved soldiers, but suddenly wearing a military uniform didn't get you laid, it got you scorned. "Girls Say Yes to Boys Who Say No," announced a sort of antirecruiting poster of the time. The counterculture even competed directly with the cosmetic appeal of the military by appropriating the easiest and sexiest parts of militarism. Uniforms could be found at any military surplus store, and it began to be the fashion to wear them—tattered and mismatched, of course. Important-sounding titles and sometimes even guns were available at your local Weatherman chapter. In other words, if you wanted the macho warrior stuff, the streets seemed to offer that, too—and with little chance of getting killed. Anyway, there was just something so embarrassingly grim, so serious, about those lines and lines of soldiers slogging off to war. It seemed infinitely more cool to be a draft "dodger"—even the word implies cunning, lightness, insouciance.

At dinner parties everyone had their amusing draft-resistance stories: so-and-so who had gone to Canada or what's-his-name, the Ph.D. candidate in psychology, who had feigned schizophrenia so convincingly, he fooled the draft board. The proper tone was sounded by a piratical-looking fellow named Country Joe McDonald, who took the stage in the sea of people that was Woodstock to sing:

> Yeah, come on all of you, big strong men,
> Uncle Sam needs your help again.
> He's got himself in a terrible jam
> Way down yonder in Vietnam
> So put down your books and pick up a gun,
> We're gonna have a whole lotta fun.
> And it's one, two, three,
> What are we fighting for?
> Don't ask me, I don't give a damn,
> Next stop is Vietnam.

Operating quietly in the background were people who opposed the war and often made great sacrifices. Sentenced to three years of jail time for urging demonstrators to burn their draft cards, activist David Harris said he could do more "in there" than he could in the streets. Harris was a pacifist, but opponents of the Vietnam War could be found up and down the political spectrum. Senator John Kerry (D-Mass) volunteered to go and "went to it twice—once in the Gulf of Tonkin and once in-country on a gunboat."

On a talk show in spring 1999, explaining why he had once demonstrated against Vietnam but now recommended that ground troops go to Kosovo, he said, "I went because I wanted to win and because I thought, initially, that the values we were being told we were fighting for were, in fact, what they were. I found a war very different from the one that I went to fight. I found a war that was not supported by the country, nor even strategically by the military in the way that we were fighting it. And I found a place that was very different from the one that had been described to me. But I said when I came back that while I opposed the war in Vietnam, I did not oppose the notion that we might not have to fight somewhere in the future."

Senators who have had military experience are increasingly rare. At one time there was a natural back and forth, infiltration, integration, between society's elites and the military's ruling classes. It was natural, for instance, at a summer lawn party in front of the mansions on the bluffs of Newport, Rhode Island, to meet, say, Mr. Vanderbilt's youngest son, who was "just visiting from Annapolis." Debutantes' balls on Park Avenue would be stocked with lovely young West Point cadets for the girls to dance with—and, it was hoped, marry.

But the Vietnam era severed this already-frayed connection between society's elites and the tradition of military service. Harvard lost 691 alumni to World War II. From all the classes between 1962 and 1972, it lost 12 to the Vietnam War.

"The greatest lingering effect of the Vietnam era on our society is that by default it brought about a new notion that military service during time of war is not a prerequisite for moral authority or even respect," James Webb, a decorated Vietnam vet has said. The new student deferments (for students in college or university) seemed, Webb said, "to whisper . . . that some lives are worth more than others. . . ."

The deferments also communicated the government's ambivalence about the Vietnam conflict. The student deferment resonated like a kind of hedging bet—it seemed to say this conflict is worth expending, say, uneducated farmers from the heartland but certainly not our future Ph.D.'s of the Northeast.

In any case, perhaps because of the deep national sense of guilt over this exercise of class privilege, returning soldiers were met with a thundering silence—or sometimes cries of "Baby killer!" One of the generals in Al Santoli's oral history *Leading the Way* describes (briskly and perfunctorily) how he was spat on while walking through the Los Angeles airport on his way home.

In any case, when our engagement receded, the idea of conscription was tainted for the public—again, maybe out of this collective sense of guilt, because we made others go. Conscription was also an easy target, a relatively easy way to explain some of Vietnam's most troubling phenomena—the fraggings, the heroin use, the high number of desertions, the My Lai massacre. Maybe a sort of national rebirth could be achieved with a new era of a force made up of volunteers. Candidate Richard Nixon, then running for president, caught this wave with a promise to end the draft immediately, squaring this position with his conservatism by saying a draft represented intrusive, big government.

After much debate, with everybody on the sidelines worrying how you'd get 'em if you couldn't draft 'em, the all-volunteer force (AVF) was finally instituted in 1973. "Nixon's decision to shift to the AVF in the early 1970s showed the worst possible timing," wrote author Brian Mitchell. "Never was patriotism in shorter supply throughout the fifty states, nor public confidence in the American military at a lower ebb. After an inglorious retreat from Indochina, . . . still shaking the mud off its boots, it was ordered to pretty itself up for a recruiting drive."

Indeed, when the AVF opened up shop—offering new enticements like homier living quarters with actual rooms to sleep in, instead of open-bay barracks—guys did not pound on the doors trying to get in. The high life in the counterculture, the sad standoff that was the prosecution of the war, the taking of huge casualties without victory, the public's contempt for returning soldiers—they all took their toll. Servicewide, only 9.5 percent chose to reenlist; new recruitment dropped as well.

Painfully aware of its less-than-groovy image, the U.S. Army recruiting command pulled itself up by its bootstraps and launched the ringing slogan "We Want to Join You!" Somehow the new slogan just didn't get 'em by the heartstrings. . . .

On the other hand, there were reasons to be very serious about recruiting: The cold war was heating up and nervous military planners wanted a big force. Once again they decided to turn to women. There was queasiness in some camps, but other policy makers argued that women were a higher-quality recruit. Then, as now, women tended to score higher on the academic tests given by recruiting stations; they tend not to get roaring drunk and start fights; they're generally more dutiful. The armed forces "combat service support" sector had been expanding—as bureaucracies are wont to do—and women filled these billets well.

A number of arguments could have been raised: that women, in general, are not as easy to sign up—they show far less "propensity," as the recruiters put it, to join the military—the nation would shake off Vietnam-era demoralization, and that men would be drawn to the services for the age-old reasons they've always been drawn to the services (in fact, only about a decade later, during the Reagan years, with a required end strength of 2.2 million, the services had so many potential recruits, they had to turn them away).

Still, Secretary of Defense Melvin Laird, nervous about the need to assemble a mighty force quickly, directed the services to develop a plan to use more women. According to a House Armed Services report, "The Army, Navy and Air Force were told to plan to double their women's programs by the end of fiscal year 1977. The Marine Corps was directed to plan for a 40 percent increase during the same period. By the end of June 1977, all of the services had exceeded their goals. More than 110,000 women officers and enlisted women were on active duty." One congressman said admiringly that Laird "[brought military leaders] kicking and screaming into the twentieth century" by giving the services two deadlines: ten months to have a female general and flag officers and twenty months to create a viable program for bringing women into Reserve Officer Training Corps (ROTC) programs and the service academies. Laird vowed that if those services didn't make deadline, he'd freeze promotions for all officers waiting to move up to general and flag rank until the "goal" was met.

Other female-friendly policies helped this recruitment effort. While the military was dealing with its personnel problems, groups like NOW and the Women's Rights Project (whose general counsel was Ruth Bader Ginsburg) were knocking down laws that sometimes drove women from the workplace. They had persuaded the Equal Employment Opportunity Commission (EEOC), for example, to issue federal guidelines stating employers must consider pregnancy "a temporary disability" that employers must accommodate, the same way they would accomodate, say, a broken leg. To have special policies for pregnancy would be a form of sex discrimination, since only women can get pregnant. At that time the services discharged pregnant women (unless they wanted to become unpregnant) and were allowed to under the doctrine of "military necessity." In 1972, Ginsburg challenged the "military necessity" exemption, taking on an institution that hadn't had to think much about maternity leave and pregnant sailors with morning sickness.

The plaintiff was a pregnant Air Force nurse who had been offered the option of terminating the pregnancy or accepting involuntary discharge. The Air Force argued that this was justified by its need to "maintain the required pool of men and women ready and available for all military assignments." Ginsburg argued that pregnancy was similar to "other temporary physical conditions" like sports injuries, which the Air Force was tolerating. The Air Force lawyers argued the "compelling government interest" of having fully deployable troops and that the plaintiff had the option of having an abortion if she wanted to stay in the service. Touché, said Ginsburg, and then produced some strong stuff: "If a serviceman and a servicewoman conceive a child, the serviceman is not even disciplined; on the other hand," she argued, "the servicewoman is discharged, regardless of who is responsible for the failure of contraception. If that is not sex discrimination, then nothing is."

Rather than appeal and let these legal issues proceed to the Supreme Court, the Air Force, afraid of letting the Court establish a legal precedent, granted the nurse a waiver from the policy and allowed her to stay on active duty. The services soon found they could live with waivers, and between the years 1972 and 1975, 60 to 86 percent of waivers requested for pregnancy were approved. Soon the Air Force remembered that it didn't want to waiver large numbers of women out. After all, one of the goals of bringing them in in the first place was to meet end-strength requirements, to get the numbers, achieve a force as big as the Joint Chiefs wanted. And it needed those women! Even in an all-volunteer service, as Francke puts it, "women were still leaving . . . at an alarming rate." So, Francke writes, "bowing to military pragmatism . . . DOD ordered the services to rescind their bans on pregnancy effective May 1975."

Leave it to those stubborn "leathernecks" to keep "kicking and screaming" about being "dragged into the twentieth century." In 1970, a female Marine had been discharged for becoming pregnant. Then, when she tried to reenlist several years later, she was turned down, ostensibly because she had a child. The Marines, who are a much smaller, everybody-does-everything force, won the first court go-round by citing unique requirements for "ready and mobile personnel." In 1976, however, a federal circuit court overruled this lower-court decision, arguing that the Marines had failed to show that pregnancy was different from any other temporary disability in its impact on military readiness, even though a pregnant servicewoman usually goes on light duty quite soon after her pregnancy is discovered, is not allowed to deploy aboard a ship, and, because of toxic chemicals and other shipboard dangers, is shipped home if she discovers a pregnancy while under way.

We became the only major force in the world that had to issue maternity uniforms. (At that time, Britain separated a woman at four months. She would need a new uniform, it argued.)

Nevertheless, the size of the female force rose steadily in those years, so that by the time we got to the Gulf War, the percentage of women in the armed forces had inched to 11 percent from 2 percent in 1973. And though women made up only about 6 percent of the force deployed to the war zone, the Gulf War would be remembered as "the largest one-time deployment of military women in our nation's history."

Making this kind of history may have given reporters something to write about, but women's rights activists in Congress and elsewhere were unimpressed. Wearing Kevlar helmets and carrying rifles seemed a mere public relations decoy covering up the fact that women were still denied what Representative Patricia Schroeder called the "real plum jobs"—infantry MOSs, artillery MOSs, and the ability to pilot combat jets.

One place to start a general push for "expanding opportunities" for women was with the 1948 Combat Exclusion Law (CEL), which kept women of the Navy and the Air Force off combat ships and from combat aircraft squadrons. The law was a bit odd politically. The services could not put women in combat with the law on the books, but even if Congress withdrew it, each service still had the right to decide for itself whether it wanted to open combat positions or not. And the Marines and Army were not controlled by the law; they had kept women out of combat MOSs as a matter of policy. So, it was clear that the services liked the status quo. With jurisdiction so muddled, the law was useful as a way to unload this political hot potato on someone else.Congressmen could say that they were inhibited by the law. Anyway, they would reason, the law had been on the books for years because it seemed to reflect the will of the American people, who, polls showed, were "not ready to see women come home in body bags." Meanwhile, the service chiefs could blame Congress for not defeating the law. Secretary of Defense Dick Cheney, for instance, told reporters, "We basically follow whatever direction we're given by Congress in this regard." Said Christopher Jehn, "We are looking to the Congress and to the American people for the answers to these complex questions."

When the troops started trickling back, activists like Patricia Schroeder and Patricia Ireland of NOW were invigorated. The Gulf was generally proclaimed to be "a test of the coed military [which] women had passed with flying colors." Retired general Jeanne Holm, author of several histories of women's role in the military, and a frequent witness in congressional hearings, opined that "the Gulf War had demolished every stereotype. . . . Many old myths that had hindered their progress in the military were demolished." It was time, in other words, "to stop hindering women's progress."

The summer of 1991 found activist organizations packing hearing rooms, buttonholing congressmen in the halls, and appearing as expert witnesses at the innumerable hearings held that summer over the CEL. Representatives Beverly Byron (D-Md) and Pat Schroeder, Senator Edward Kennedy (D-Mass), Senator John McCain (R-Ariz), Senator John Glenn (D-Ohio)—everybody was preparing a bill to kill the law. The CEL only controlled planes and ships, but the general feeling was that if it fell, barriers to ground combat would soon fall as well. The debate, therefore, shifted to the issue of whether the services, as one activist put it, should "provide equal opportunity in combat to both men and women."

A lot of the pro-combat lobbyists' fervor seemed to have come out of a sense that women had basically just "earned it," as one op-ed writer put it. In other words, we'd all just seen them out there in their Kevlar helmets and their Army boots and we'd read about women who'd been "killed in action," "killed on the battlefield" or "in combat"; "proved themselves in battle," and "led units into combat"—a result of newspaper accounts, often by novice war reporters—agog with uniforms and great groaning tracked vehicles—using vague, but terribly evocative, military vocabulary in imprecise ways.

There is no definition of *combat* in the DOD dictionary of military terms. There is one for *direct combat*; a unit assigned to "having as one's primary purpose the goal of engaging the enemy." A person who carries a gun and walks through a Mogadishu street where one hears the sound of guns has walked through a combat zone (though combat zones are usually so large, they can include areas that haven't heard rifle fire in weeks). A person who walks through a Mogadishu street hunting Somali tribesmen is said to be engaged in "direct combat." Women were not assigned to "direct combat" in the Gulf and, if there were any who engaged in it, they have yet to present themselves.

There is also a large difference between being "under fire" and being under "direct fire." "Direct fire," said a fiftyish female Marine sergeant representing her service at a DACOWITS conference, "is when you can see the person who you're shootin' at."

"Thirteen women died in the Gulf deployment," wrote the experienced *Los Angeles Times* reporter John Broder, "five in combat, eight in accidents." Other rhetorical ballast was added: "We must take time to remember the thirteen women who risked their lives for their country despite . . . the discriminatory laws and practices . . . intended to exclude them for combat," wrote Amy Eskind in a *Washington Post* op-ed. She then described how one of the Gulf's female soldiers had been "mortally wounded when she rolled over a land mine as she and six other soldiers took defensive positions during an apparent enemy attack." Recently, a respected military analyst told a national TV audience that "five women died in action" during the Gulf War. Again, lack of specificity and evocative terms combine to paint a picture of stormin', rockin' female Sergeant Fury.

The reality is somewhat less Hemingwayesque. Thirteen women died in the Gulf War theater. One was killed when her supply helicopter was shot down near the Iraqi border. Another helicopter pilot, Maj. Marie Rossi, who had been celebrated for flying fifty miles into Iraq to deliver supplies, was killed when she hit an unlit tower at night—one day after the cease-fire had been declared. Two women were killed in their barracks when it was hit with a Scud missile. The woman Eskind described was riding in a relatively quiet part of the desert in a convoy to pick up some prisoners and bring them back to a central holding area. As they rumbled along, there was a booming sound nearby. One of the medics jumped out of her truck thinking that they were under attack and began to signal to the other vehichles that her truck would need ammunition. Suddenly, her foot touched something explosive—not a mine, the blast was not big enough—and she died from her injuries before she could be brought to a hospital. (It is now believed that she may have stepped on a piece of American ordnace—a bomblet, which is a little glass receptacle of explosive that is released when a missle makes contact.) Another eight were killed in traffic accidents or in other ways unrelated to combat. In fact, more troops, male and female, were killed in traffic accidents in the Gulf War than "in combat."

But why was there this sudden passion for combat anyway—when just fifteen years before many of these same folks had been denouncing war? Actually the passion was about *the right to be in combat*. Call it the "equal rights in the workplace" rationale. "Barriers based on sex are coming down in every part of our society," declaimed Senator Kennedy, as he introduced a bill to rescind the CEL, and "women should be allowed to play a full role in our national defense free of any arbitrary and discriminatory restraints."

Oddly enough, in the lobbying for equal opportunities for women, one rarely heard anything about what effect any of this would have on readiness.

"Certainly women should be able to go into battle if they want to," stormed Sally Quinn of the *Washington Post*. In *Tailspin*, a book about female aviators, Jean Zimmerman looked at the Navy and saw "the hopeful beginnings of a gender-neutral workplace." A few sentences later, she complained that "the cockpit of a military warplane, along with combatant ships and submarines [are] the only workplace in America that [are] still legally off-limits to women."

And if the military was indeed just another workplace, then there was a steel ceiling in some career paths as far as women were concerned. Female officers who have wanted to move up to flag rank—general or admiral—have complained that one can only move into the upper echelons if one has had combat experience. As Amy Eskind put it, "The Gulf demonstrated that combat exclusion policies do not keep women from dying in war, they just keep them from advancing to the highest ranks in the military."

But all this clamor for the right to kill and die had a bloodless, legalistic quality. The women lobbyists never showed any particular visceral love for combat—"the stern joy which warriors feel in foemen worthy of their steel," as Sir Walter Scott once put it. Their lobbying was not to be mistaken for any sort of enthusiasm for fighting. In fact, many pro-combat-for-women proponents said quite openly that the point was to make the world a more peaceful place.

Betty Friedan made the point in her book *The Second Stage* and in an essay written in 1975 after a visit to the newly integrated West Point.

> I leave West Point, as the first female cadets are about to graduate, feeling safer somehow because these powerful nuclear weapons that can destroy the world and the new human strategies therefore needed to defend this nation will hence forward be in the hands of women and men who are, with agony, breaking

through to a new strength, strong enough to be sensitive and tender to the evolving needs and values of human life—if only the last gasps of threatened machismo do not stop this evolution.

The view persists, as one can see in this 1998 Website posting from military historian Erin Solarno, an ardent supporter of opening combat jobs to women:

> I think we would profoundly change the military virtues I love so much. I think it is harder to kill when you might give birth. I think it is harder to send people to their deaths when you are capable of feeling a young human grow under your heart for nine months, and then bring it into the world through great labor, and raise it until it is grown—and still, it will always be yours. I do not think women have to give birth, or even be physically capable of giving birth, to have a much different attitude towards life and death than men have.

Another meaning of combat exclusion for the proponents was and still is far more subtle but far more charged—not just about changing world events but about changing social structure. As NOW president Pat Ireland put it in a press conference during the Gulf War, "Exclusion promotes the view that women are weak, inferior, and need to be protected." "Combat exclusions contribute to a powerful symbolic message about the appropriate roles of men and women," wrote Madeline Morris, a law professor at Duke University, who later became a consultant to the secretary of the army.

> [Exclusions] . . . retain as exclusively male many of the most stereotypically masculine roles. [It is important to change] military culture from a masculinist vision of unalloyed aggressivity to an ungendered vision. . . . The perpetuation of the exclusion in its present form limits potential effects on the gender and sexual norms of military culture that might be gained from a more thoroughgoing integration of women . . . and limits the cultural change likely to result from the presence of women in the forces. . . . We might expect that a truly thoroughgoing integration of women throughout the services would do much to undermine

group norms featuring a constellation of attitudes including hypermasculinity.

As lawyer Anita Blair, chairman of the Congressional Commission on Military Training and Gender-Related Issues in 1994, put it: "As a result of my work on the commission, I became convinced that the objective for many who advocate a greater female influence in the armed services is not so much to conquer the military as conquer manhood: They aim to make the most quintessentially masculine of our institutions more feminine."

There was, I suspect, a glamour issue: What it came down to was that men have been allowed, at certain times in history, and only after paying a huge price, to bask in the special glory and adoration that comes to soldiers returning from or marching off to war.

The "equality for glory" argument often expressed itself with what I thought was an odd focus on death and a certain misunderstanding of what it is we feel grateful to the departing soldiers for. Certainly part of that flush of feeling comes from thinking about bravery—"This person is going to risk his life for me!"— but a very big portion of that rush comes from our enthusiasm over what a soldier *does*, not what is done to him. He—and I don't know if women will ever feel this way about other women—is going to *smash* that guy so he can't harm me or my family. But throughout the CEL debate, the female cravings for battle have always seemed peculiarly masochistic (as opposed to the more sadistic pleasure men seem to derive from the image of the warrior). There were too many entreaties that women "be allowed to die for their country." "Women have achieved full citizenship except in one area: their right to put their lives on the line in combat," stormed Judith Youngman, an instructor at the Coast Guard academy, during a 1998 conference. A reporter for the *Atlanta Journal-Constitution* quoted Representative Beverly Byron and Representative Pat Schroeder as saying that women proved their right to fly combat aircraft by serving, dying, and being captured in the Gulf War. A female official of the Carter administration had once opined that "women have a right to die for their country." Jean Zimmerman wrote that "[combat exclusion] was as if one of the most mystical potions of all—the blood of the martyred warrior—had been reserved by males for their exclusive use. Women did not have the right to die fighting for their country."

But after all, the willingness to face danger or sacrifice one's life is only half the equation. As Gen. George S. Patton, Jr., once put it, "No bastard ever won a war by dying for his country. He won it by making the other poor dumb bastard die for his country."

What one wants for one's tax dollar—for soldiers are really federal employees paid out of the public till—is that rare creature who can go into harm's way, be able to stay there for as long as it takes to close with the enemy (often a long time), and then neutralize that enemy—by capture or killing or whatever it takes. A number of qualities are called for, many of them trained—not just the willingness to face danger. Actually, a soldier too willing to die is dangerous.

But by late summer 1991, it became clear that Congress had painted itself into a bit of a corner by suggesting that the Combat Exclusion Law existed mainly to protect women. Number one, paternalism was totally out of fashion in the early nineties, and number two, the supposed worst fear of the American public had happened—women did come home in body bags, and there was nary a peep.

And despite the idea that women POWs would be tortured horribly and used as a way to incite or demoralize male prisoners, the Gulf's two female POWs came back relatively unscathed. Melissa Rathburn-Nealy, driver of a supply truck, was captured along with a male soldier when they strayed off course on a delivery run and got lost in the desert. It seems the Muslim captors actually enjoyed having a Western woman around to gape at. When she was released, she called her parents to tell them that she was OK, that her guards had been "beautiful people," who had told her she was as "beautiful as Brooke Shields and as strong as Sylvester Stallone."

Maj. Rhonda Cornum, a flight surgeon, was taken prisoner when a medevac helicopter she was riding in to fetch a pilot who'd been shot down in Iraqi territory was itself shot down. She did not fare as well. Later she admitted to congressional investigators that several Iraqi guards had taken advantage of her two broken arms and the ropes tying her and had fondled her breasts and penetrated her "digitally." However horrible this must have been, in harsh unsentimental military terms, as Cornum put it, it was not really a big deal. The bottom line was that the horror scenario—of women tortured to gain concessions from men—had not occurred. And the American public remained silent over the body bags.

Certainly it is especially tragic when a blooming young woman is cut down at the beginning of her life. However, these were probably not the images of death and torture service chiefs and congressmen had been alluding to when they talked about delicate American sensibilities. It's more likely these veterans had remembered the gruesome treatment of male POWs or the defilement of male corpses they'd seen in Korea or Vietnam. It's more likely they'd visualized front-page photographs of, say, a female corpse rotting in the sun, with a bayonet stuck through her neck.

Still, the pro-women-in-combat forces were psyched. Schroeder and other activists all over the nation argued that if the Combat Exclusion Law was in place to protect women from danger, it was now obvious that they were already in danger, so why not just go all the way and ditch the law? "The Persian Gulf War," said Shroeder, "helped collapse the whole chivalrous notion that women could be kept out of danger in a war. We saw that the theater of operations had no strict combat zone, that Scud missiles were not gender-specific—they could hit both sexes and unfortunately did." Said one pilot, "Women serving in combat is a moot issue. We were there."

"In the eyes of Congress and the nation, Desert Storm did more than vanquish the Iraqi Army," opined NBC producer Naomi Spinrad. "It wiped out cultural taboos that American women should not be wounded, captured, or killed facing an enemy." (The women-are-capable-of-dying-too argument, again.)

Of course, there were other issues to consider before deciding to put women on front lines as combatants (like whether as a whole they would make adequate support for the soldiers they flanked, whether they could march with an eighty-pound pack and an eight-pound rifle and still have the energy to hit the ground and begin shooting), but these questions traversed very dangerous territory indeed. The arguments that remained unsaid involved the real career-killing assertion that perhaps, just maybe, men simply make better soldiers than women and that the hassle of combing the ranks for that one woman who could perform to "male" standards would cost more in time and money than the services had to expend.

Ever since the implementation of the AVF, the Pentagon has anticipated that the day might come when it would be ordered to open infantry and artillery, and it has been quietly commissioning tests of women's ability to do things like take a two-mile hike loaded up with a sixty-pound rucksack, a rifle, and supplies of bullets.

From 1977 to 1982, the Army tried training platoons of men and women together and putting them through what was then standard infantry training. The results were not encouraging, but a number of top-echelon reporters (who found themselves examining the issue of gender-integrated boot camp when it returned in the nineties) have never been able to locate the records of this experiment. Even Army brass couldn't find records. Gen. William Hartzog, then head of U.S. Army Training and Doctrine Command, was reduced to testifying: "We had one experiment that occurred between 1977 and 1982, for which there is not a lot of data remaining. It was given up in 1982. The best I can determine from historical reading from some very terse reports was the perception that the men's performance in that gender-integrated training at the time slipped to accommodate the women involved in the training."

In general, there was an entire alternative and not-so-positive way of reading the Gulf War data: News outlets like the Associated Press ran wonderful lead paragraphs about "women pilots streaking over the desert as part of an invasion," but when it turned out that one tenth of the female crew of the repair ship *Acadia* had left midcruise because they'd become pregnant, the *New York Times* relegated the news to a back page of the A section and a two-inch column of terse wire copy.

There were other kinds of worrisome stats. The conflict between mothering and soldiering had postwar ramifications as well as prewar. As Linda Bird Francke reports in her book: "While fathers evidently felt little conflict between war and children and actually resigned in lower numbers at the end of 1991 than they had the previous year, 982 American mothers would resign by the end of 1991, an increase of 22 percent over 1990."

Nevertheless a certain momentum had been set in motion. If you were a congressman running for reelection, worried about your "gender gap" stats, trying to redeem yourself for some past wrongdoing, the women-in-combat issue seemed to be a relatively cheap church to pray in. You could do your tithing without worrying that the effects would come back to haunt you. The Gulf War was so easy! Peace was upon us. Nobody really believed we'd have to use our troops again. In the summer of 1991, anybody who was *anybody* was on this CEL thing—Democrat or Republican. As Melissa Healy of the *Los Angeles Times* put it, once again invoking the "death right" concept: "Emboldened by public acceptance of the death and imprisonment of female soldiers during the Persian Gulf War, Congress is getting set to eliminate the last statutory barriers to allowing women to serve in combat."

Since it was beginning to look as if President George Bush was going to sign one of these CEL-killing bills, Congress turned to the next hurdle: the service chiefs who would have to be persuaded to change their exclusionary policies. The summer of 1991 was full of House and Senate Armed Services Committee hearings designed to persuade the "dinosaurs" to change their ways. A *New York Times* headline read, "The Services Have a Few Things to Learn About Women" and was illustrated with a photo of four chagrined service chiefs sitting in a row at a hearing-room table. If the service chiefs dragged their feet, at least the congressmen would look as if they were concerned. But nervously and with some backing and filling, Army and Marine chiefs refused to agree that putting women in ground infantry would be a good thing. Luckily, they could put off definitive statements for a year. President Bush had put together a commission to study the issue of women in combat, and the commission's recommendations weren't expected for another year.

What the service chiefs didn't know was that in about three months something would happen that would make reasonable discussion impossible. A convention held over that coming Labor Day weekend would be used to sweep away post-Gulf exuberance, replace the picture of the triumphant pilot with the image of the brute, and in general kick out the tiny foothold the brass had just gained by winning the Gulf War.

Tailhook 1991

"After Tailhook everything was about gender."
—George Delgado, U.S. General Accounting Office, National Security and International Affairs Division, Spring 1997

There's a reason newspeople dial up Charles Moskos when they are searching for a native guide to lead them through the dark continent that is the U.S. military. Sure, Moskos, often called "the country's preeminent military sociologist," publishes more than anybody else (at least in venues people actually read), churns out reams of those always-handy statistics, and can always rattle off the authoritative sound bite. But what people really like is that, in the middle of one of the most divisive, passionate, and politically "sensitive" issues of this decade, Moskos can be counted on to float serenely down the center, a voice of calm, balance, and moderation. When a just-inaugurated President Clinton stumbled into a minefield by declaring that the military should officially accept gays in the ranks (in many units, they had been unofficially accepted for years), it was the mild-mannered, moderate prof, "Charlie" to his friends, who was summoned from Northwestern University to help the president draft a gays-in-the-military policy (it became known as "Don't Ask, Don't Tell") that would make the services slightly less crazy than the one the commander in chief was proposing.

When this professor, who writes in the journals of military sociology with an academic's reserve, says, "The Tailhook convention of '91 was the worst event for the Navy since Pearl Harbor," you have to know this was big.

Everyone agrees that Tailhook (it's called simply "Tailhook" even though there have been some thirty other Tailhook conventions) changed everything. In the months after that Labor Day weekend conference, "one could hear the sound of a culture cracking," former representative Patricia Shroeder told writer Peter Boyer. Boyer has called the scandal the beginning of "the Post-Tailhook epoch . . . a period of perpetual penance." A pilot talks matter-of-factly about the "Post-Tailhook Armed Forces." Even a sober bureaucrat from the General Accounting Office (GAO) uses the term *Tailhook* as a signifier like B.C. or A.D. "So what's the big deal about Tailhook?" I ask him after he's started yet another sentence "After Tailhook . . ."

"Well, you know," he said with a shrug, "after Tailhook everything was about gender."

If Tailhook was a milestone in the "gentling" of the military and a marker in the seismic shift in the way it approached gender issues, it is also something of a milestone in the history of distorted news coverage. This was the era of Anita Hill versus Clarence Thomas, the cry "You just don't get it!" rang in the air, and the "gender gap" was supposed to be a crucial element in winning elections. Women had become the third rail and, terrified of being seen as "blaming the victim," reporters suspended their normal skepticism and abandoned the practice of checking both sides except in the most perfunctory way.

The Tailhook story has been so distorted that it seems to have become a kind of Rorschach inkblot for people's feelings about the sexual politics issues of the nineties. In fact, Tailhook-the-Media-Creation (it was subsequently turned into an "NBC Movie of the Week" and other entertainments) never seems to have been *about* what actually happened. This was mythmaking filled with iconic figures: the brutal warrior and the raped female. And was it just coincidence that this image of the brutal, destroying, imperialistic military was regenerated just months after America was supposed to have exorcised its "Vietnam syndrome" and rediscovered a kind of simple WWII-era affection for its armed forces?

Most civilians (including many of the congressmen with the power to mete out blame) seem to have come to believe that Tailhook was some kind of cataclysmic breakdown in the social fabric—the weekend two thousand naval officers went berserk and assaulted . . . well, in press accounts over two years the number jumped from five women to twenty-six to about sixty to at least a hundred, so the average civilian probably visualizes something on the scale of the rape of Nanking.

Who could blame them when editorials titled "Stone Age Warriors" roared about female guests "forced to drink from a simulated rhinoceros penis and run a gauntlet of drunken gropers" (*New York Times*)?

Or when the *Chicago Tribune* fulminated that "[f]liers engaged in a disgustingly libidinous bacchanal in the hallways and hospitality suites of a Las Vegas hotel, sexually harassing or assaulting at least two dozen women, including more than a few officers"?

Or when Peter Jennings announced on his evening news program that he intended to put "a human face on the worst case of sexual harassment in the Navy's history," a scandal that had featured "the so-called Gauntlet . . . set up in one of the hotel's corridors for the specific purpose of targeting and sexually molesting women"? "Navy women have not come forward because they are afraid for their careers," he intoned. "The Navy knew that this sort of sexual abuse was a ritual at this annual convention . . ." but had sinisterly "covered it up."

Or when Representative Patty Murray (D-Wash) thundered to fellow HASC members that "the Tailhook matter is a sordid, sleazy stain on the U.S. Navy . . . a scene of drunkenness, debauchery, vulgarity, and violence"?

The reality is, as Tailhook '91 attendee and F-18 pilot Vic Weber puts it, "the Tailhook convention had been raucous and rowdy for years. . . . The senior leadership could have put a stop to some of the more 'offensive' behaviors such as leg shaving and hiring exotic dancers anytime." In other words, everybody knew that Tailhook was Tailhook. All that had changed was the lens we used to look with.

A number of facts got lost in the reporting: The events were not organized or paid for by the Navy but by a private organization, the Tailhook Association (the name refers to a slender metal bar on the rear of an aircraft that hooks a restraining wire on a carrier deck), whose convention planning committee included female Navy officers. There were three incidents of "sexual assault" that a reasonable person might consider "criminal," not "dozens and dozens," as the *New York Times* once reported. Last but not least: Hundreds of women guests and a sprinkling of female officers held up their end quite respectably in the "drunkenness, debauchery, and vulgarity" department.

When investigators from DOD's Department of the Inspector General (the IG) finished crisscrossing the country interviewing every female they could find who'd attended the convention, they published a report listing each person they defined as a victim and the way in which he or she had been abused. Their final victim tally came to one hundred, including seven men and a number of women who had demanded that the IG publish a disclaimer in their case study making clear that they had not wanted to be counted among the victims of Tailhook. We actually can't know how many of the women counted as victims were actually included against their will, because some of the women's disclaimers were not published for one reason or another.

An additional "reluctant" victim (her case was listed in the tally without the disclaimer even though she told people close to her she didn't want to be listed) was the late Lt. Kara Hultgreen, a Navy pilot, who attended Tailhook '91 along with most of her squadron of A-6 pilots.

Hultgreen was twenty-six that summer, a gorgeous Amazon, well-liked, who was sometimes affectionately called "The Incredible Hulk" because she was nearly six feet tall and had a statuesque but muscled build. Like everybody else, she attended the conference in civvies, in this case dangly earrings, red lipstick, a cleavage-enhancing black lace camisole that was mostly covered by a black blazer, a black miniskirt, and four-inch pumps that showed off her long, shapely legs. When she strode into the party and joined a knot of male aviators talking on the floor, the general reaction from the sidelines was "Wow! Who's that beautiful woman?" then—this being Vegas—"Is she a hooker?"

"She's a hooker," one of the men from Hultgreen's squadron shot back (meaning that she hooked restraining cables), "but not the kind you think. That's an A-6 pilot." Some were so drunk, they'd long since lost the ability to understand such distinctions: One desperately drunk man (he committed suicide after the Tailhook investigations) looked at Hultgreen and must have seen only "Woman"—maybe more precisely "Babe." Since he was then so drunk he was literally slithering around on the floor, he slithered over and shot a hand up her skirt.

In the months afterward, practically any woman who had been at Tailhook was much in demand for TV or print debriefs, and at one point Hultgreen found herself with Fred Francis, a TV reporter and commentator.

"Were you assaulted?" Francis asked.

"No," said Hultgreen. "What happened to Paula [Coughlin—the original Tailhook scandal complainant] was criminal, malicious misconduct. What happened to me was irritating, and easily handled, and then blown out of proportion. The vast majority of my peers never have and never will require sexual harassment training. They were taught by their parents to treat people with dignity, good manners, and respect."

But, Francis probed, "a guy actually grabbed you?"

"One person who had a lot to drink thought he was being clever, witty, and charming. I made it clear that his advances were unwelcome. I told him, 'I'm an officer and an aviator; touch me again and I'll kill ya.' When he came back, he had obviously only heard the 'touch me again' part and interpreted that as an invitation. So I decked him. He crawled away, and we all commented that he was an idiot."

"And none of the men around you jumped to your defense?" pressed Francis, who seemed determined to go back to the studio with tape of tears and wobbling chins.

"It wasn't necessary. I took care of it myself. I didn't need any help," Hultgreen said coolly. "Had someone been trying to maliciously and violently overpower me, there is no doubt in my mind that everyone would have rushed to my aid. I didn't need it."

Aviators' real home is in the air; they touch down occasionally as part of a ship's air wing or to spend some time at their home base, and, like all military personnel, they are always being shuffled around. It can be argued, and Tom Wolfe does, that, as keepers of "the right stuff," the bond between aviators is particularly strong. So, every year since 1956, when the Tailhook Association was founded, a bunch of Navy and Marine fliers headed for the same spot for a weekend; the forum was the annual Tailhook Conferences and Symposiums.

"It was a great place to go and see people you hadn't seen in years," says a female jet pilot. "Your old buddy that you lost track of in flight school: You hear he's in such and such a squadron; you'd go find Admin [the hospitality suite his squadron has rented] and ask about him and eventually you'll find him. It was like a big reunion." (Like most young aviators, she doesn't go to Tailhook conventions anymore.)

In 1963 the association moved the annual conventions to Las Vegas, a good central location for personnel at the Navy and Marine bases that dot the West Coast from San Diego to Whidbey Island in Washington State.

It was not all partying by any means. Conference days were full of lectures and panel discussions on aviation issues of the day. Nights featured formal dinners, sometimes award dinners, followed by informal socializing. The most senior military leaders often attended "on orders" precisely because hanging out and floating around the place was a good way to bump elbows with the men, get a feel for rank-and-file morale. Often they took the podium at question-and-answer sessions. The young officers who attended these Q&A's tended to be more direct when they were off duty and wearing civvies (which erase rank and service affiliation) and on neutral territory—that is, not their ship or their base. Often contractors (or wanna-be contractors) from companies such as Northrup Grumman, Raytheon, and Bell Labs took over a huge exhibition hall. They set up booths with blinking neon, product demos, free trinkets, and video loops pitching new jet engines, and the place began to resemble a military-tinged Disneyland or a high-tech carnival midway. With all these festivities, it was possible to just spend the day being sociable with old friends and high muck-amucks and then scurry off to bed, which is exactly what some high-ranking officers and married people attending with spouses did.

Nevertheless, people like that were in the minority. Over the years, as the association's enrollment grew, so had attendance at the annual conference. Given that the attendees were aviators—typically very cocky, fiercely energetic men in their twenties and thirties (with a sprinkling of aggressive, tough young women)—the reputation of the convention as "a rip-roaring, raging, drunken bachelor party" traveled around the country via word of mouth. Legend even had it that Secretary of the Navy John Lehman once lay down on the floor in a hospitality suite with a twenty-dollar bill in his teeth so a stripper could pluck it from his teeth with her vagina.

Like the Navy itself, the attendees respected tradition and protocol . . . well, their own sort of protocol: It was traditional that each squadron rented its own hospitality suite and did things their way and there was usually fierce competition over who could be the most outrageous, the most memorable, the one the aviation community would talk about for years to come. Out on the open "public" floor, tradition operated as well. There had been some guy who dressed up as "The Barber of Seville" and opened a little stand on the main floor offering "free leg shaves" for women walking by. He always attracted a long line because he did a slow, sensuous, maniacally thorough job using techniques he'd purportedly learned on liberty in Asia. Watching a woman getting her legs shaved rather fetishistically by a young man was mildly titillating for spectators, but it could become racier when the occasional prostitute or really frisky average-gal hiked up her skirt and demanded a "bikini shave."

Another tradition was the rhinoceros dummy supplied by the Marine Corps Tactical Reconnaissance Squadron 3 out of El Toro, California, who used it to decorate their hospitality suite. The gimmick was that the rhino in the "Rhino Room" (as the suite was called) was fitted with a dildo hanging where his penis would be. When a new woman entered the suite, people would bay at her to "pleasure the rhino" or "beat the line" (deep-throat the rhino past lines set by previous contestants). If the suite bartender deemed the performance good enough, he would pull a lever releasing "Rhino Spunk"—a white frothy mixture of Kahlúa and cream. Some women needed no encouragement to "pleasure the rhino," others were urged on by the crowd and pressed forward.

Then, of course, there was the infamous "gauntlet," a central feature of the Tailhook investigations that would come later. Here men would line the sides of a hotel corridor just off the central pool patio, grab passing women, and try to pass them down a line of touching, exploring hands—a sort of X-rated car wash maneuver.

This was no party for shrinking violets. One Navy base's newspaper a year before caught the flavor in their report on that year's Tailhook.

"The good news," announced the *Flying K* newspaper, "is that all the Redhawks [a squadron based there] returned home relatively unharmed and none were convicted of any crimes, felonies, that is."

The *Flying K* described the "interesting lectures and demonstrations" and the nights "characterized by celebration, joviality, and debauchery." After listing the total amount of booze consumed in the Redhawks' suite (40 kegs of beer, 450 gallons of margaritas containing 315 liters of tequila—15 cases of liquor in that room alone), they inventoried the objects thrown out of the suite's window: "everything but the squadron commander," as reporter Gregory Vistica put it in his book *Fall from Glory: The Men Who Sank the U.S. Navy.*

"The couch failed its initial spin evaluation and suffered complete strike damage," the *K* reported; in fact, "the garbage cans proved, to the dismay of the 'engineers,' to be more aerodynamic than the couch."

Furniture destruction was such a feature of Tailhook conferences that the Hilton had taken to asking for five-figure damage deposits. Sometimes the Hilton got to keep some of that deposit—as at one Tailhook convention when a line of men and women formed a "pressed ham" (a row of naked butts pressed against one of the floor-to-ceiling windows) until a picture window broke and sent shards of glass falling on heads on the pool patio below.

Ever since those dashing men of the Royal Air Force waved jauntily from World War II newsreels, aviators have been objects of romantic fantasy. And the late eighties/early nineties only made them more so. In 1986, Jerry Bruckheimer, who said at the time that jet pilots are "the rock and roll stars of the sky," unleashed his elite-pilots-in-training-at-Miramar-Air-Base movie *Top Gun. An Officer and a Gentleman*, which took place at a training school for Navy officers, was about local factory girls who saw the snappy white-jacketed guys as their tickets out of the boonies. Then there was "The Gulf War," a four-month CNN special also starring American pilots.

The women required for all this mayhem were not hard to find. Officials seem to have been unable to estimate how many women—military or otherwise—attended. Observers have tended to guess about two hundred women total. (It was sometimes hard to know who was civilian and who was military because most everyone was in civilian clothes.)

Investigators' records show the women came from all over. For some, whom Zimmerman calls "the jet-jock groupies," the convention "was a sort of annual pilgrimage." Some were tourists—visiting Vegas with girlfriends in groups of two or three. Some were female officers from the aviation community who came on official business or, like the men, just to hang out and catch up with old friends. Many were "pros": "the huge corps of Vegas working girls who descended upon the convention like modern-day camp followers," as Zimmerman puts it. Some were locals, waitresses and students, who may have read about the convention from flyers sown around town like the one that read: "Join the Intruders for an evening of imbibing, chicanery and debauchery. Las Vegas Hilton, Suite 307 . . . We stay up Longer . . . and deliver Bigger Loads."

According to Zimmerman in *Tailspin*, a book that celebrates female aviators of the nineties, "The carrier pilots who attended the convention expected, if they saw a woman at Tailhook, that she either wanted to get laid by an aviator or . . . was a prostitute or dancer. And in 90 percent of cases that was true."

This particular convention may have been fueled with an unusually potent mix of euphoria and anxiety. The general feeling was that we—the nation and the military—had finally gotten over Vietnam. A kind of we're-OK-after-all, we-can-win-goddam-it! spirit had been restored. Pumped by the fast, surgical victory, the conference's organizing committee proclaimed that Tailhook '91 would be "The Mother of All Hooks" (a reference to Saddam Hussein's prediction of "the mother of all battles").

The troops that were still straggling back in early September came back to congratulation and euphoria but also to the grim news of budget-cutting and "drawdown." No one knew who would survive. The venerable F-14 community had been told to expect a 14 percent personnel cut. Upgrades on that plane were canceled, which meant that the program would eventually dwindle and die, effectively meaning that aviators in F-14 squadrons (and the ones preparing to go into those squadrons) would have to find a new career. (In a downsizing, in the tight world of naval aviation, there would be no spots flying a different kind of plane when there were plenty of others who had experience flying that plane.) Of course, with Big Daddy Congress in a more parsimonious mood, competition among the siblings grew fiercer, especially for naval aviation and the Air Force, who, it could be argued (though not too loudly!), have overlapping abilities and missions.

Reporter Greg Vistica makes the controversial case that naval aviators returned angry, feeling that the Air Force got most of the sortie action while Navy aviators sat by impotently, kept at arm's length from the action by their unwieldy supercarriers. In fact, the Gulf War only added to a quiet ongoing debate about whether we actually needed a big fleet of awesome "blue sea" vessels at all. None of these third-world strongmen seemed to operate out of battleships.

Maybe the most unsettling thing of all for the aviator community was that outside the fortress gates shouts were getting louder and closer. Practically every day a news story appeared about the clamor in Congress over whether to put women in combat jets and on combat ships. At one point a group of uniformed Navy officers had marched through the halls of Congress, going from office to office to lecture legislators about rescinding the Combat Exclusion Law. (Why they were allowed to breach regulations and lobby in uniform is a question for another day.) And just that morning, on the first day of the 1991 Tailhook symposium, a Q&A session that touched on the subject turned, as a female pilot put it, into something like the "Jerry Springer Show." "There was a lot of heat and discontent in the room and a lot of the male JOs [junior officers] were expressing their opinions pretty vividly and the female JOs were yelling back."

Other factors are the aviators' personality and their pressure-cooker lives. "There's only one guy flying the plane and that's the aviator," explains John Gadzinski. "Even if an admiral comes flying with you, he has to sit in the backseat and you're in charge. If he wants to do something, he has to ask you. So the aviator has the experience of saying, 'Fuck you! You want me to fly the plane or not?' Meanwhile, the average nonflier is down there sitting around worrying if the name tag on his uniform is on straight."

But to live at this pinnacle, to win the privilege of flying the government's multimillion-dollar flying machines, one agrees to work under constant scrutiny, to have one's work evaluated by Olympic skier standards, and to subject oneself to a fate determined by inches and seconds. Every landing, even if it is just to keep up the chops, is filmed and graded by fellow officers who stand at the stern of the boat. Then the grade is posted in the squadron's ready room for all to see. Moving at Mach 2, where a second of inattention could mean death, calls for hyperawareness. A little thing like hooking the last of the flight deck's four restraining cables or a habit of "boltering" (deciding to abort a landing and circle around so you can try again) could end your days with the squadron. Everyone wants your job and there is always the hot breath of younger aviators in the pipeline who can claim faster reflexes, better eyesight, and a cardiovascular system that just might hold up better under lung-crushing G forces. The gist is, as Chuck Yeager used to say, "flying and hell-raising—one fuels the other."

The truth of the Tailhook '91 imbroglio is in the details, and the most meticulously reported account of the convention and subsequent investigations is in the book titled *The Mother of All Hooks* by a Newport News, Virginia–area reporter named William McMichael. To convey a sense of the convention on those nights in 1991, McMichael used the eyes of an aviator/everyman named Lt. Gregory Geiss.

If Marine Squadron 3 always brought their rhino, Geiss was developing what he thought was a witty signature Tailhook MO for the Labor Day weekend conference. He came to the Vegas Hilton with a palm-sized card listing "The Ten Steps of Drunkenness" from number one "[I'm] witty and charming" to number ten "I'm invisible. She won't notice if I reach up and grab her tits." The joke was to get a woman to read the card and just as she's getting to number ten . . . Gotcha! Since Geiss repeated the gag with any woman who struck his fancy as he ambled through the halls, you could say that the Geiss experience is actually a trove of survey data (using the respected "random selection" method) on female participants' responses to sexual harassment.

After getting a bit of a buzz going, Geiss begins his rounds. Two Live Crew's dance hit "Me So Horny" is blasting from speakers in the packed open space next to the pool patio. The leg-shaving booth is doing a lot of business. Guys are "zapping"—which means slapping a sticker with a squadron logo on a passing female body part—and ball-walking (pulling your genitalia through your fly and then walking around like *everything's completely normal!*), and doing "the butt rodeo," wherein you bite into a girl's unsuspecting backside and try to hang on as long as you can while she swats at your head or tries to shake you loose.

Geiss tries the card gag first on a waitress. "She giggles and dashes off, minutes later she returns," McMichael writes. "Geiss tries a tweak this time; she exits and comes back again. Geiss, who wasn't attracted to her, moves on to a suite where he meets a female Navy lieutenant, married but at the conference without her husband. He grabs her breasts; she responds by grabbing his testicles, both dissolving in laughter, a scene that they would repeat during the course of the conference."

Not every woman thought the card was funny, but many of them were veteran Tailhook attendees or military officers like Kara Hultgreen who "took care of the situation" and strolled on. One woman standing near a group of Navy friends tells her friends what Geiss has just done and the men chase Geiss away with a chorus of "Hey, man, that's really not cool." Other women respond by socking Geiss in the gut, squeezing him back—in the genitals; a few pull out tasers (a kind of stun gun) and threaten to zap him.

At one point in his increasingly Hieronymus Boschian travels, Everyman Geiss shambled over to the infamous "gauntlet." Before he could get much of a look, however, a woman "jumped into him, wrapping her arms and legs around him, and knocked him down. They landed on the carpet, with the woman on top. 'Hello,' she said and Geiss returned the greeting as the fliers nearby roared with laughter; they chatted and both went on their way." Even the "gauntlet" had a lot of eager takers. "Some younger women passed through repeatedly. One group of four college-age women worked and giggled their way through the thicket of men, one woman pushing the next along." "Indeed," reported Greg Vistica, the reporter who broke the Tailhook story and prodded the Navy to take action, "for every one woman who resisted, there were many more who couldn't wait to walk down the Gauntlet and be manhandled."

National media without exception (as far as I can see) cast women as big-eyed, sexless Paulines (as in "The Perils of . . .") who venture into, say, the rhino suite just looking for a nice cold Coca-Cola after the scorching Vegas sun. What was almost completely omitted from news accounts (as if editors and producers were so puritanical, they couldn't countenance the idea of switched-on female sexuality) was the almost equal amount of female cutting-up in the corridors and ballrooms.

Take the practice of "package checks"—for obvious reasons a largely female Tailhook tradition. You'd spy an attractive unit—across a crowded room, as it were—weave your way over, take an appraising handful, and bawl, "Package check!" It cracked 'em up every time.

"Some women chose to stroll topless through the crowd," wrote Greg Vistica. On different occasions, he claimed, female naval officers had bartended topless. Like all male/female interaction with a sexual component, even the gauntlet experience varied with who was on it, what a woman's expectations were (i.e., whether she entered it by choice), her mood, time of the night, and who was doing the groping. At one point the whole thing was suspended when a woman who had just gone down the line yelled, "I've lost my pager," and everybody (gropers and gropees) fell out to search for the device.

At around 11:30 on the second night of the conference, a twenty-nine-year-old naval officer named Paula Coughlin came out of the elevators onto the third floor, the party floor, and began to walk down the infamous gauntlet corridor. Coughlin was a former helicopter pilot who'd landed a job as an assistant to an admiral stationed near D.C. She had been in the service a long time (in fact, she complained that she was having trouble "breaking in" her new boss). As an admiral's aide, she was very much in the loop; she had attended Tailhook many times before, knew the raunchy ways of the aviation community, and was no shrinking violet herself. One reporter who has spoken with her many times said that "she talked like a longshoreman."

Searching for a friend, she began to walk toward the dim corridor. She didn't recognize any of the men, but one must have recognized her because he began to yell, "Admiral's aide!" Earlier in the evening, the guys hanging around would have taken this as a good reason to "wave off"—aviator jargon for aborting a carrier landing. Maybe there was resentment at the fact that women now occupied coveted positions like "admiral's aide," maybe they disliked her hard, sinewy body and her spiky hairstyle because, in a world of encroaching women, that represented more evidence of women trying to be men. In any case, Coughlin's unexpected trip down the "gauntlet" seems to have taken on a harder, more sadistic edge.

As Coughlin walked by one man, she felt him grab her by the hips from behind. Coughlin, who is five feet four, was pushed and lifted down the line that had suddenly formed. She screamed, "What the fuck are you doing?" She was able to wrench around and look the first grabber full in the face, then she screamed the question again when the next man clutched her. There was more rough fondling and grabbing by several more men. Through much of this she kicked and bit—a hand and then a forearm—until, she said, she drew blood. Even with (or maybe because of) this obvious resistance she felt another hand thrust itself up her skirt and attempt to pull her underpants off. Finally, she was able to wrench herself free. Dazedly she walked away and found a male friend. After she had calmed a bit, they went back to the hall to search for the perpetrators. Not finding them, she sat for a while trying to recover from her shock and rage and then went to bed.

The other case of criminal-level mishandling involved a seventeen-year-old girl, a civilian who had found her way to the party and gotten so drunk, she could hardly stand. She was nearly unconscious when someone scooped her up and started a hand-over-hand stadium surfing maneuver over the heads of the densely packed crowd. Suddenly people who were then supporting the girl spotted a security officer. A general panic ensued. Whoever was then supporting the girl attempted to lower and/or dropped her in his haste to split. Hours later, hotel security guards found her unconscious (from alcohol, it was later determined) lying on the floor near where the mosh pit of the night before had occurred, naked from the waist down. In the morning the girl reported the incident to the Las Vegas police.

The next morning Lieutenant Coughlin rejoined her boss, Rear Adm. Jack Snyder, and here the story turns into *Rashomon*. As an illustration of how elusive a commodity the truth can be, there are at least five books that cover this sequence in detail (it turned out to be crucial), each one slightly different. McMichael's account says that Coughlin sat down to breakfast with Snyder (aides and their bosses are supposed to be inseparable) and at some point announced, "I was almost gang-banged last night by a bunch of fucking F-18 pilots. But we will talk about that later," and that Snyder umm-hmmm-ed but seemed preoccupied with other things.

One account says that Snyder claimed he never heard Coughlin's comment; another says that Snyder has said he heard the account but didn't think much about it because "Paula always talked that way." Months later, when the story had grown "legs," Paula Coughlin announced to a national TV audience that her boss had told her, "That's what you get for hanging around with guys like that."

All in all, the consensus is that Snyder didn't seem to realize at the time that Coughlin was really serious. Still, a few weeks later, after the story came back to him via the office grapevine, he immediately called Coughlin to his office, listened to her account in detail, took copious notes, and drafted a letter that he hand-delivered to his boss, Vice Adm. Richard Dunleavy, the highest-ranking aviator in the Navy.

Apparently, as so often happens in bureaucracies, the letter sat on a desk for several weeks. So Coughlin drafted her own letter and sent it to Dunleavy, as well. Coughlin's letter then made its way to Jerry Johnson, then vice chief of naval operations. Johnson seems to have jumped as if he'd been goosed. The Clarence Thomas hearings were then under way and it was not the time to appear insufficiently concerned about sexual misconduct charges.

Vice Admiral Johnson immediately convened a branch of the Navy called the Naval Investigative Service (NIS) and ordered them to fan out across the country to find the men who had assaulted Coughlin and/or the four other female complainants, and/or evidence of any other criminal-level assault. An oversight panel made up of senior NIS and DOD personnel was also appointed.

So far things were neatly contained within the Navy chain of command, which is the way the services like to do things. That ended when the Tailhook Association's president sent his customary postconference debrief memo to the fleet. It read, in part:

> Without a doubt this was the biggest and most successful Tailhook we have ever had. . . . Our very senior leadership . . . were thoroughly impressed and immensely enjoyed their time at Tailhook. . . . [Nevertheless] I have had five separate reports of young ladies, several of whom had nothing to do with Tailhook, who were verbally abused, had drinks thrown on them, were physically abused, and were sexually molested. Most distressing was the fact an underage young lady was severely intoxicated and had her clothing removed by members of the Gauntlet. . . . Tailhook cannot and will not condone the blatant and total disregard of individual rights and public/private property! I as your president will do damage control work at regaining our rapport with the

Las Vegas Hilton and attempt to lock-in Tailhook '92. We in Naval Aviation and the Tailhook Association are bigger than this.

The memo was leaked to Greg Vistica of the *San Diego Union*, a key newspaper in the West Coast naval community. Warned by Vistica that the story was going to run, Johnson hastily added a woman to the oversight panel. Barbara Spyridion Pope, then assistant secretary of the navy for manpower and reserve affairs, who was quoted in an interview a year later as saying, in reference to boot camp training, "We are in the process of weeding out the white male as a norm. We're about changing the culture."

So far the nation was distracted from this racy story by the Thomas hearings. But legislators west of the Mississippi noticed the story, particularly Senator John McCain, who was running for reelection against an opponent who attempted to discredit him by telling constituents that back in his Navy aviator days, McCain had attended a Tailhook conference or two!! McCain joined the chorus of denunciations of the Navy and even took the floor to call for a full congressional investigation. (Later he would use a campaign endorsement from Paula Coughlin in promotional material—even though Coughlin had violated Navy regulations to endorse a candidate.)

Meanwhile, the NIS was not what you could call fired up for a countrywide search of the ranks. The operation was still smarting over the highly publicized *Iowa* debacle in which they had identified a "perp," effectively let him be pilloried in print, and then had to retract the charge when they couldn't find enough evidence to support it.*

---

*On April 19, 1989, crewmen on the USS *Iowa* were loading propellant into one of the guns in the battleship's number-two turret, in preparation for firing one of what Vistica calls its "Volkswagen-sized shells." Instead of a successful firing, there was a cataclysmic explosion that destroyed the turret and immediately killed forty-seven sailors. At first, investigators searched for a physical cause, but were stymied. When they learned that one of the men in the gun crew who had been killed had left a life insurance policy giving $101,000 to another member of the gun crew—one who had survived—they began to develop psychological theories of sabotage or suicide. The theory was that Clayton Hartwig, the deceased, and the survivor Kendall Truitt had had some kind of attraction and/or love affair that had gone bad. The NIS scoured Hartwig's home and found somewhat innocuous material that they used to profile Hartwig as someone with the know-how to sabotage and the temperament to engineer a revenge killing—a "dangerous loner" who had a fascination with bombs and sabotage. Truitt found himself attempting to correct assumptions about his sexual orientation to the press, to friends, and to family. Finally, without enough substantial evidence to prove one of the theories, and under a barrage of accusations of "rushing to judgment," "defaming a dead man," and so on, the NIS withdrew its theory.

Understandably they felt queasy about rushes to judgment pushed by public opinion, a hysterical press, and grandstanding legislators. There was also the practical problem of getting evidence to make solid court cases out of a milieu in which nearly everybody involved had been howling drunk, where the crowds had been huge, the lights dim, and where there had been lots of jostling and manhandling naturally (and surreptitiously) as people attempted to squeeze through the melee. To make matters worse, all kinds of characters had slunk in and thus were untraceable via Navy records. In fact, the man who had dallied around Kara Hultgreen's backside turned out to be a member of the Australian military. As Rear Adm. Mac Williams, the newly appointed chief of investigations for the NIS, put it, they "didn't have a fart's chance in a cyclone."

Another problem was that Coughlin (she had not let the press print her name but was working furiously behind the scenes) couldn't offer much in the way of descriptions. After months of poring over photographs of servicemen, she had pulled only one picture of a guy who she said might be "the large, light-skinned black or Hispanic" who'd grabbed her from behind and effectively initiated the mean trip through the gauntlet. When the investigators found the man matching the picture, he turned out to be a Marine named Gregory Bonam. Indeed, he had been at Tailhook, but the NIS investigators were dismayed to find that he was widely considered to be sober and church-going, that he was the son of a Tuskegee Airman (the black aviators corps), and that he had cancer. The consensus around the NIS was something like "Well, that's just great; we've got one suspect and he just happens to be black." Already the *Navy Times* letter pages were beginning to fill with letters accusing the Navy of antiblack bias.

The pressure for scalps was becoming quite intense. The dogged reporter Greg Vistica was beginning to write stories with heads like "Navy Brass Accused of Ignoring Molestation Reports." Barbara Pope, the only woman on the NIS investigation oversight panel, was beginning to mutter about "old-boy networks, foot-dragging, and clubbiness." A scalp was needed and quick, so Coughlin's boss, Rear Adm. Jack Snyder, a former fighter pilot who'd been honored as "best pilot" and best squadron CO, was relieved of his command "for failing to take timely action to investigate Tailhook sexual-abuse complaints."

But Pope was still gnashing her teeth. She wasn't terribly interested in all this diddling around with the junior officers who primarily did the carousing, she wanted the big boys, leadership, and told Williams to bring in the squadron skippers and higher. If they didn't seem cooperative, she suggested to Williams that he relieve them of their duties by using a good all-purpose charge like "lack of confidence." But Williams was still wary of moving too fast; the veteran lawyer thought a judge in a court-martial hearing could call this "exerting undue command influence." Never mind the moral arguments, practically speaking, "undue command influence" could get a case thrown out of court.

One of the things frustrating Pope was that there seemed to be a fleetwide rebellion under way; aviators were closing ranks, resurrecting the code that dictates that you don't rat on your wingman (you'll be flying with him someday). Many aviators were using "evasion" skills they learned in a standard military course called SERE—Survival, Evasion, Resistance and Escape—where fliers learn to cope if taken as prisoners of war. Some were merely clamping their lips and citing the Fifth Amendment right not to incriminate themselves. Even this caused arguments back at the ranch.

When Williams told Pope that the guys had a point, Pope argued that "there's a major difference between [invoking the Fifth Amendment] and lying to investigators." Even Adm. Frank B. Kelso, Jr., the chief of naval operations, second in command to the secretary of the navy, was mad:

"Mac," he asked, "is it true these people have a right to remain silent?"

"Yes," Williams said, "it's their constitutional right. As a lawyer I'm not bothered by that."

"Well, I am," Kelso fumed.

It was like the "New Navy" was duking it out with the "Old" as Williams and Pope raged at each other in meeting rooms and sometimes even in Pentagon halls. The arguments always tended to get into the larger background issues:

"What you don't understand, Barbara," Williams said, "is that men in the Navy don't want women in the Navy."

"Mac, you don't get it," she replied. "Yes, some men don't want women in the Navy. . . . Things were easier when women weren't there. But if men can't accept women and integrate women into the military, then they shouldn't be here."

At one screaming match in one of those endless Pentagon halls,

Williams insisted to Pope: "You can't understand. Men's hormones are different, and as a female, you can't understand. Men look at women as sex objects."

"Sure, men and women are attracted to each other," Pope exclaimed, "but you learn to control those desires and feelings."

Finally, after a cost of $1 million and as many man-hours, the NIS issued a voluminous bound interim report. The three suspects they had been able to find so far had, as McMichael put it, "a resoundingly low sound to it." To come up with the number sixty-five, they began counting anyone they interviewed as suspect.

This piddling result did nothing to assuage the fever for perpetrators; calls of "Cover up" and "They just don't get it" rang out.

Obviously bigger guns were needed. Enter Derek Vander Schaaf, head of the Inspector General's office at DOD. Vander Schaaf blasted the NIS for failure to broaden the investigation to include "cultural problems" and went to work vowing to investigate those as well.

By then it was the summer of 1992 and Tailhook the news story got the personal focus it had been lacking in the form of Paula Coughlin, who decided to come out of the shadows. In press coup terms, her public debut was spectacular. On June 24, she appeared on the front page of the *Washington Post*; that night she began a three-part series about Tailhook on ABC's *Nightly News* with Peter Jennings. Jennings listened in his fatherly way as Coughlin wept and told her story.

Among the national audience was President Bush. He called Coughlin the next day to invite her to the White House and was photographed consoling her—and, some reporters say, crying himself. The next day, Secretary of the Navy H. Lawrence Garrett III was told to pack his bags because he had visited the Rhino Room and had not exerted influence to stop the events under way. (Garrett admitted he had visited the suite but insisted it was early in the evening and that all he had seen was some guys standing around drinking cocktails.) Bush issued a short statement, just a few paragraphs, omitting the usual thank-yous for years of distinguished service. In other words, in the subtle world of military protocol, the career naval officer had been disgraced in front of the nation.

Without a SecNav, Bush began a search for a replacement and in the interim appointed J. Daniel Howard as acting secretary. Howard, a civilian who had spent most of his career in public relations, wasted no time in leaving his mark. A couple of days after taking charge he called three hundred flag and general officers to an auditorium for what he called a "Come to Jesus" meeting, then he delivered a jarring speech:

> I think it is important to underline that what happened at Tailhook was not just a problem with the integration of men and women in our ranks . . . it was just as much a problem with the toleration of Stone Age attitudes about warriors returning from the sea. . . . [We need] to dismantle a decaying culture. . . . Anyone still wasting time disparaging women, fighting their integration, or subjecting them to sexual harassment is a dragging anchor for the entire Navy and Marine Corps. Anyone who still believes the image of a drunken, skirt-chasing warrior back from the sea is about half a century out-of-date. If that's you, we don't need you, because we've got places we need to go, and not much time to get there.

The new marching orders were clear. The thought sequence driving the new orders went approximately like this: Don't allow anything resembling sexual harassment in your ranks and make sure the women in your unit don't have anything to get mad about. Navy culture (like the rest of U.S. culture) is shot through with sexual harassment. Sexual harassment is encouraged by the macho culture of the military and adding women and making them more "visible" would dilute that culture and ensure that women could serve in safety. Many seemed to believe the eradication of sexual harassment in all its varied forms was worth whatever it took, even if innocents were scooped up in the pursuit. Mused *Time* magazine's Margaret Carlson: "For the moment, perhaps the only way women can make their point is to take a few admirals down with the ship."

The problem was, again, that nobody knew what this heinous, career-ending offense actually looked like. And official definitions such as this one—"Sexual harassment is identified commonly through many behaviors ranging from 'dating behaviors' and improprieties common in interpersonal relationships, i.e., jokes, gestures, unwanted pressures for attention, to other acts that are criminal in nature"—did not help clarification much.

Ten days after civilian Sean O'Keefe, the new SecNav, who would serve until Bush left office, took over, he called a press conference and announced that he was going to pull the expected promotions of two popular admirals because one had allowed his staff to send out a newsletter that contained a mild joke comparing women and beer, and the other had been in office when a female Naval Academy cadet was chained to a toilet—ostensibly as part of one of the hazing games that are common among trainees. On September 24, O'Keefe told the press: "I need to emphasize a very important message: We get it." Then he announced a cavalcade of new measures designed to "enhance professional opportunities for women" in the Navy and the Marine Corps and to "deal with the culture, environment, and attitudes that contribute to sexual harassment and gender bias." By December, he declared, the Navy would have a hot line to provide "advice and counseling . . . to any member who might be involved in an incident of sexual harassment regarding her rights and responsibilities and options to resolve the situation."

He promised to "review the sale of sexually explicit publications in Navy exchanges"; "to assess whether cutbacks in the Navy and Marine Corps will disproportionately affect women's careers and develop a plan to ensure that they are not so affected"; to develop recruiting strategies "to attract women into nontraditional careers" in the Navy; and to " review policies affecting pregnancies and single-parent families and modify them if need be."

Firings now appeared in the press almost every day. In a remarkable burst of self-destructiveness—or defiance—a group of fliers at the Miramar Naval Base held their annual rave-up called the "Tomcat Follies"—named for the F-14 Tomcat fighter. This time, however, the men added an obscene jingle to the general silliness telling Pat Schroeder she was invited to perform a particular sex act—on them. Though the skippers of the two squadrons were out of the country when this occurred, they were relieved of command. Schroeder told the press: "I think [brass] now realize that culturally they have a terrific problem. They have a group of people who don't believe that things have to change."

Everyone started getting with the "cultural change" program and there was an I'm-thankful-to-Big-Brother-for-punishing-my-counter-revolutionary-behavior tone to the new declarations offered up by officers at the most vulnerable (i.e., visible) rank levels. By July 3, 1992, as President William J. Clinton was preparing to take office, Adm. Frank

Kelso, his appointee for chief of naval operations, told a HASC panel that "until Tailhook, we dealt too often with sexual harassment at the local level, one case at a time, rather than understanding it as a cultural issue." Regional commanders were beginning to see the light as well. On July 10, Gen. Henry H. Shelton (now chairman of the Joint Chiefs of Staff), then commander of the 82nd Airborne Division based in Fort Bragg, North Carolina, told his staff: "Recent military and civilian scandals have shown us that sexual harassment is more prevalent than previously thought. I expect all commanders to become personally involved in monitoring their units' awareness of the prevention of sexual harassment."

HASC held a hearing and one panelist echoed what seemed to be a common concern: "If we only constrain or control behavior, inherent tension is built into the force, which may weaken it. Successfully changing attitudes leads to self-motivated soldiers who are more cohesive, leading to a more effective organization."

In the summer of 1992, HASC promised to do its own report focusing on "cultural beliefs, attitudes, and perceptions about women . . . which are [at the root of sexual harassment]." "Unless we can change stereotypical *thinking*" [emphasis added], one representative said, "sexual harassment training will likely prove ineffective." Once again the chiefs were presented with the equation: Get rid of sexual harassment. Sexual harassment is a result of men thinking that women are unequal, thus worthy of "abuse." If you let women do everything men do, men will respect women enough to stop "sexually harassing" them.

Throughout all this bustle at the Pentagon and in the hearing rooms of Congress, the DOD IG investigators were literally crisscrossing the world to "interview" aviators who attended Tailhook '91. It was a period that Navy aviators everywhere describe as "Stalinesque." Even Representative Randy "Duke" Cunningham (R-Calif) complained in a HASC hearing that he had had "a dozen calls this week from military wives saying that a DOD IG showed up on their front doorstep and used abusive—I use their comment—Gestapo tactics."

F-18 pilot Vic Weber never even hung out on the Hilton's pool patio or in the Admins where all the incidents had happened. He'd come to Tailhook to have a party with a few close friends in a suite many floors above. His troubles started, however, because the party's organizers had hired an exotic dancer and later in the evening, according to the testimony of someone who had been there, the dancer had performed oral sex on one of the men. Given its new broad "cultural" mandate, the IG wanted to talk to people who'd attended *this* party as well.

These guys came out to the ship with an agenda. They didn't appear to care what they found, [just] anything with which they could hang someone and answer the call for blood. Anyway, I gave them a factual account of my time at the convention. Some months later, they came out to my squadron in Jacksonville, Florida, to interview our Tailhook attendees again. They gave us a transcript and summary of the previous interview. Mine was riddled with mistakes of wording and outright alterations of what I said. In several cases in my squadron, the [interview] summary was heinously inaccurate. Anyway, about halfway through this interview these guys had sufficiently angered me enough to the point where I asked them about the gross inaccuracies in my ROI. I said, "You guys are either completely incompetent, or something sinister is going on with these ROIs. What's going on here?"

Well, that didn't make them happy. The bad cop guy (standard good cop/bad cop technique) starts yelling at me saying that I was a liar and they were going to bring me to Norfolk and prove I was a liar. I said, "Well, I guess I'll see you in Norfolk." In the end, I realized that these were just guys under pressure from everyone to get results that would satisfy the blood lust over Tailhook. In some cases, they would take a guy's foggy recollection of how an event occurred, and contrast it with another guy's recollection. They would then pick the guy they thought was lying. In my case, a guy in my squadron had said something that was 180 out from what I had said. They brought me to Norfolk and grilled me about the entire Tailhook weekend, trying to drum up inconsistencies, which, of course, there were—all minor—like little half-hour time recollections found in interviews that took place months, and in the end, years, apart. Finally they had me where they wanted me—caught in a [n inconsistency]. The guy in my squadron who said something different from me had been given full immunity, so they reasoned that I had to be lying. At one point in the interview, my lawyer comes outside and says to me that I was nailed because my squadron mate had said something different than me. (My young Navy lawyer was in way over his head.) They bring me back in making a big deal about how they are giving me a chance to come clean. Bear in mind that this was just a little fact, not some huge thing that would matter either way in the outcome. The IG just saw it as a way to break me down. I wasn't going to break because I hadn't lied. They spent so many dollars on me alone in airline tickets and time just because they assumed I had lied.

Another pilot who attended the exotic-dancer party was Cmdr. Robert Stumpf, the commander of the Blue Angels demonstration team—that squadron of crack pilots who fly in astonishing formations at air shows around the country. He'd been trained at Miramar's elite Top Gun school and earned a Distinguished Flying Cross, the Navy's third-highest decoration for valor, for sorties in the Gulf War. It looked for a while as if he had come through "Witchhook," as aviators called it, unscathed. The Navy had approved his promotion to captain. The Senate's Armed Services Committee (SASC) gave it a thumbs-up and the promotion was confirmed by the full Senate. Then SASC began receiving anonymous phone calls insisting that the committee "take another look" at Stumpf's record.

This "new look" at Stumpf's record took a year. SASC would not tell Stumpf's lawyer what the allegation had been or what methods and sources they were using in their investigation. Stumpf was never allowed to appear before the committee to offer rebuttal—verbal or written—to the mysterious misdeed. Finally, SASC voted to turn down the promotion, and a seemingly cowed Navy brass retracted their earlier go-ahead as well. By way of explanation, a SASC spokeswoman told the press that "we looked at the broad scope of his record, and his activities at Tailhook were such that we didn't feel his promotion was warranted." Many military stars pleaded for the promotion, citing Stumpf's contributions to his service, but SASC stood firm. Denied a promotion in the "up or out" armed forces, his career effectively over, the star pilot and war hero left the service at the age of forty-four.

By now the IG was claiming they had evidence of eighty assaults. In fact, they had so many files on suspects that the lawyers who had to review them were getting overwhelmed. One problem was that there was confusion over the question of what constituted a crime. Two of the female lawyers, Capt. Bonnie Potter and Capt. Carolyn Deal, were in favor of hammering commanders who had allowed strippers in their Tailhook '91 hospitality suites and anyone who had touched the strippers.

According to McMichael, the male lawyers "argued that you can't prosecute people for exercising their constitutional rights." And even if you went back to the Navy's internal officer's code, which prohibits behavior not befitting a gentleman, the question was "how to punish officers for behavior that had been institutionally condoned—if only tacitly—for as long as anyone could remember." After all, they argued, commanders of various West Coast naval air stations were still allowing strippers to entertain at officers' clubs on a weekly basis. Could you really say the officers were guilty of sexual abuse? After all, said one, "being touched kind of goes along with the job if you're a stripper."

One of these lawyers, a Lt. Cmdr. Henry Sonday, found himself increasingly disturbed by the IG's tactics. One of his files pertained to a guy named Janssen who was charged with streaking the pool patio around midnight. Janssen was a little fish, but with some pressuring, he might deliver "goods" on bigger fish. The IG had promised him immunity from prosecution if he could produce damaging material on more senior men at the party. Janssen's lawyer, a Navy attorney named Pat Padgett, had been assured by a DOD IG agent that they would grant Janssen "transactional immunity," wherein a witness trades testimony for immunity from prosecution in the matters he testifies about *and* new allegations that may surface in the future. Janssen offered what he could recollect and found himself being prosecuted anyway. Why? Turns out, the DOD IG didn't even have authority to offer transactional immunity. What they'd *meant*, they explained, was "testimonial immunity"; the witness was immune in matters in his own testimony but still legally vulnerable if material was supplied by someone else! Darn those slippery legal terms! Other lawyers were amazed at the flimsiness of many of the cases the IG had collected and worried that their efforts were being wasted, since it looked like many of the cases couldn't stand up in a trial. Nevertheless, as McMichael puts it, "they plowed forward. 'If nothing else,' [one of the lawyers] was heard to say, 'the defendant's attorney feels it will serve as a form of punishment and the publicity will ruin their careers.'"

In late April 1993, Vander Schaaf's IG was finally ready to reveal to the world what *actually happened* at Tailhook.

A day or two before the report was slated to come out, Admiral Kelso called a press conference to tell a crowded Pentagon pressroom: "We cannot undo the past, but we sure can influence the future. . . . Tailhook brought to light the fact that we had an institutional problem in how we treated women. In that regard it was a watershed event that has brought about institutional change."

When the report was finally handed out, the reporters in the briefing room weren't paying much attention to a desperate official. They were busy nudging each other over the grainy photos and admiring the foldout artist's renderings of the party produced in full-color at a cost of $10,000. Even the lowliest stroke book would have disdained most of these grainy snaps, but they were a lot racier than the usual Pentagon pie graph: There was one of a guy wearing a huge rhino horn on his head, another of a fellow setting his alcohol-saturated breath on fire with a Bic lighter, another of a nude woman, surrounded by male onlookers, standing astride a man who is lying facedown on a carpet; she looks like she is about to do one of those shiatsu spine walks.

The report's opening paragraphs declared that "misconduct at the 1991 Tailhook Symposium was more widespread than previously reported by the Navy. . . . Eighty-three women and seven men were assaulted during three days of drunken parties in Las Vegas."

The introduction was followed by sections entitled "Butt Biting" ("For the most part, male officers at the Tailhook convention bit the buttocks of female officers and civilians. However, at least three instances of civilian females biting males on the buttocks were reported") and "Chicken Fighting" ("Dozens of witnesses stated they observed 'chicken fights' in the Hilton Hotel pool. These chicken fights involved women sitting on the shoulders of male aviators in the swimming pool and attempting to remove the bathing suit tops of other women").

Newspapers rushed to press with page-one stories, while the all-comedy cable network Comedy Central staged nightly readings from the voluminous document.

No names were mentioned, but finally there was some detail about the alleged victims. Victim Number 43, for instance, was a nineteen-year-old student who resided in Las Vegas. According to the report:

> She and her friends arrived on the third floor of the Hilton Hotel at approximately 9:30 P.M. and exited the passenger elevators. As they walked down the hallway to the administrative suite . . . she found she had to push her way through the crowd that lined both sides of the hallway. She was pinched on her buttocks while she walked through the hallway. She could not identify anyone who was in the hallway at that time.

There were even seven men, such as Victim Number 84, a twenty-nine-year-old Marine captain, who testified that "two women pulled his shorts down to his knees."

Victim Number 35 was a twenty-six-year-old Navy lieutenant. The report states that "while walking through the hallway, he was pinched on the buttocks by an unknown woman. A short time later he was grabbed in the crotch by a different woman. He retaliated by pinching the woman on the buttocks."

And there was Victim Number 14. When she attended Tailhook '91, she was new to the Navy and beginning pilot training. Now in her early thirties and still an active-duty naval officer, she told me her version of events:

> What I saw looked like a big fraternity party—a lot of guys and girls guzzling drinks. It appeared to me that anybody with common sense could find the places they wanted to be depending on what they were looking for. . . . It was so crowded that you would have to be able to see through people to see into anybody else's admin, to see the stuff going on.

When she went back to Lemoore, her base, just before Halloween, the investigation was then under way:

> I'd already heard from the guys how the interviews were going. They seemed like very hostile exchanges, antagonistic interviews, yet when I went in and sat down, I had a female interviewer. Her

whole approach was "Oh, you poor thing, it must have been so terrible for you," and I thought right away, "This is completely different than what I've heard the guys say about their interviews." It seemed they thought I was gonna spill my guts about some terrible thing that happened and it was pretty obvious that they were digging . . . looking to create something, to twist my words. They'd ask questions like "Were you sexually harassed?" and I said, "No," and they said, "Well, the operations officer at your squadron reported that he was walking down the hallway with you and somebody grabbed your buttocks!" I said, "Yeah, well, somebody did and I turned around and said, 'You get a free bowl of soup with that shirt,' and kept walking." He was really drunk and it was no big deal, but my operations officer felt he was afraid to not say that that happened; he's worried about his career. . . . He thought, "If [she] comes in here and says this happened and I didn't already report it, I'm going to be sunk, so I'm gonna tell him it happened before she can." I told them "he was probably concerned about his career based on how your interviews have been conducted." I told her "I don't consider myself to have been sexually harassed. I consider myself to have handled the situation and moved on," and she said something like "Well, nonetheless it was [sexual harassment]." The other thing that annoyed me was that they acted like there was more that I wasn't telling them, like I was withholding information.

I was like "God, I'm just starting my career off and I'm already, seemingly, in a world of shit!" . . . I didn't know the [buttock-grabbing] guy; I told them I didn't think I could pick him out of a lineup. . . . So that was the incident that made me Victim Number 14 in their little book. Then the phone calls started. After that interview I went off to flight school, and I got a call: They were setting up this thing to fly all the women from Tailhook to D.C. for this debrief. . . . I said, "I don't care what you guys thought you found, I think you're making a lot of stuff up and I'd like the number to the Fraud, Waste and Abuse hot line because I think they need to be notified you're intending to spend government funds to fly a bunch of prostitutes to D.C." But I was worried that if I didn't go that that would negatively affect me. I believe they ended up not doing it. I was in the middle of flight training when they called me to another city for a sit-down with the IG. They asked all the same questions as before. They told me they thought maybe my butt pincher was also one of the goose guys of the gauntlet, so they wanted me to come up with more information on him. They asked, "What color was his hair?" By that time, I was deliberately being a smart-ass. I wasn't gonna tell 'em; I didn't care. . . . I even said, "You guys got the good guy/bad guy routine down to a science here." . . . It was such a crock of shit. They asked me if I was part of the gauntlet. I told them that I had seen a female gauntlet. (The first night I was there, there were women that were lined up, wives who had come with their husbands, friends of the guys.) They didn't want to hear about that. They never said anything about it. It was definitely a witch-hunt. . . . They considered anything fair game. I didn't even know if the guy who pinched me was an officer; he could have just been some business dude who was up there soaking up the scene, but that didn't matter to them.

I started to get annual phone calls, first from the assistant for naval personnel [*sic*], a female, asking, "Are you being treated okay in your squadron? Any fallout, any backlash?" and I said, "You're a captain in the Navy?! What a waste of your time! I absolutely can't believe we're doing this."

Apparently the report—or the thought of the press coverage that would result from the report—shook military leadership. Just five days after it was published, on April 28, 1993, Clinton's new SecDef, former Wisconsin congressman Les Aspin, issued a historic order. "The services shall permit women to compete for assignments in aircraft, the memo said, "including aircraft engaged in combat missions." The Navy would also "develop a legislative proposal . . . to repeal the existing Combat Exclusion Law and permit the assignment of women to ships that are engaged in combat missions."

We will probably never know the full financial costs of the Tailhook investigations, but the morale costs and loss of talent have been astronomic. A 1999 damage inventory taken by the *Navy Times* counted "14 adimrals and almost 300 naval aviators" whose careers had been tainted or ended, and "thousands more" who were affected when "officer promotion board results were screened, and officers had to sign papers stating whether they or anyone under their command attended Tailhook '91 and thus should receive "special evaluation." An "event that should have taken at the most a week," wrote James Webb, had become a permanent state of being and had acquired a "casualty list which read like a Who's Who of Naval Aviation."

Many, like Bob Stumpf, were the Navy's best and brightest. In the Navy tradition of "the captain goes down with his ship," many men who had only tenuous connections to the party were penalized severely. For example, Rear Adm. Riley Mixson, chief of the Navy's Air Warfare Division, was a decorated veteran of two wars, had spent many years at sea, and is profiled in Al Santoli's oral history about Vietnam veterans who went on to assume command in Desert Storm, men who, Santoli says, effectively "rebuilt the U.S. military" after the demoralization that filled the ranks in the post-Vietnam years. Mixson was listed on the planning commission of Tailhook '91—in name only. During the planning phase, he was in the Red Sea commanding three battle groups in the Gulf War. He did stop in at Tailhook '91, very briefly, but was horrified by what he saw. He left and immediately fired off a report to his superiors telling them that the conventions had to change. Irregardless, Secretary of the Navy Dalton gave Mixson a letter of censure for his role in the planning (however tiny). The letter was enough to kill Mixson's chance for a third star and the opportunity to become commander of the Navy air forces in the Pacific Fleet. Shortly afterward, he retired.

For cases like these, where a CO was very far away and hadn't even been told what some of those in his command were up to (on their own time, I have to add), the charge of "failure to exert command influence" was often deployed. Sonday, the lawyer who had worried about bad legal process, was given the hook, as was Mac Williams, who had led the first investigation, the one that failed to produce enough scalps.

Webb warned that the investigations "would reverberate for years," and reverberate they have. In 1995, the DOD implemented a new promotion procedure that, according to Adm. Kenneth Haynes (Ret.), "transformed the promotion process, removing naval service criteria and substituting criteria in the new scale of sensitivity to women." The new DOD ruling allowed "alleged adverse information" or "unsubstantiated allegations to be added to files." The new revised promotion instructions (DODI 1320.4) read: "Normally the [DOD] does not report alleged adverse information or other unsubstantiated allegations to the Senate. However, in extraordinary cases, *such as where the allegations received significant media attention* [author's italics] or when [SASC] brings allegations to the attention of the [DOD], the secretaries of the military departments shall include a discussion of the unsubstantiated allegations in the nomination package."

Elaine Donnelly, who was one of the only people with access to media who noticed this subtle change, pointed out that this simple line of text in a fairly esoteric DOD procedural instruction created and normalized a "death by media" weapon. Now anybody with an ax to grind could simply call a reporter, tell a harrowing story (it is only an "allegation," of course), and then sit back and wait for the "discussion in the Senate over the candidate's fitness. Fearing feminist retribution, some may fail to protect the rights of their own subordinates who have been accused of wrongful discrimination." The effect in the ranks was that women in the services (whether they liked or wanted or approved of this status or not—and there are many who think this favoritism was odious) became virtual "untouchables" in regard to performance reviews and disciplinary violations of the "he said/she said" type.

Though the congressional review system continues to this day, by about 1996 the Navy had effectively dry-cleaned its leadership, flushing out the old, installing the new. "Quite simply, the essence of that warrior culture has been severely diluted this decade," Bob Stumpf wrote in 1998. "Politically inspired social edicts enforced since Tailhook '91 have rendered a ready room atmosphere so different now that it is nearly unrecognizable."

People who remained could see that the new leaders were a new breed, more careerist, less focused on military values.

What had been demolished during the Tailhook "witchhunt" or "purges" was the long-standing belief that "loyalty up" would be met with "loyalty down"—a most important ingredient of successful combat, since men cannot follow a leader into danger unless they trust that he has their welfare, as well as the mission, in mind.

Says John Gadzinski:

Before this Tailhook thing came over, [Navy aviation] was like a real brotherhood, but then anybody who tried to stand up for what they believed was right was fired, retired, forced out of the military, humiliated. It was like when Stalin shot all of his officers. All these [new leaders] care about is how they look; everything has to look like a Hallmark TV special. The new operating principle is politically driven and politically correct as opposed to letting operational reasons drive the agenda. They start treating people in this whole different way that has nothing to do with the military. It didn't used to be like that; all you're trying to do is to keep from getting in trouble [with the people who drive policy]. There comes a point when anyone with a conscience has got to get up and say this isn't right . . . but they've fired all those people.

In 1993, Paula Coughlin announced her intention to resign her commission because, as she stated in a letter obtained by NBC News, "covert attacks on me . . . have stripped me of my ability to serve." She retired in the Virginia area and eventually won $5.2 million and $400,000 in suits against, respectively, Hilton Hotels and the Tailhook Association. By 1998, the Navy—and a year later the Air Force—began to experience what the *Navy Times* described as an exodus from the services. Schools for flight instructors are called "American Airlines U" because after receiving their million-dollar training, pilots depart quickly for jobs with commercial airlines. "Why Won't They Stay!" "The Navy's Worst Pilot Retention Rate in at Least a Decade," and "Navy Pilot Resignations Are Up 30 Percent This Year," howled the *Navy Times* headlines.

In the spring of 1998 I was sitting at a luncheon table at an annual meeting of the Defense Advisory Committee on Women in the Services, a group of civilian women who are appointed and funded by the DOD for three-year terms to monitor the treatment of female personnel, to be, as one proudly put it, "the eyes and ears of the SecDef" in the field and in the fleet on matters pertaining to military women.

The theme for that conference was "Diversity is our strength" and banners with this slogan were everywhere. Appropriately enough, the luncheon started with "a diversity prayer," then a procession of speakers declaring things like "In today's Army people issues are important" and "We must keep the pressure on to train and sensitize each other to value differences. We must allow ourselves to be challenged mentally and physically."

I was sitting next to an Army officer of around forty. His face was an interesting blend of Asian and Hispanic; his body was lean and muscular; he wore wire-rimmed spectacles and had a shiny shaved head. Like most of the sprinkling of men in the audience at DACOWITS functions, he did not look happy. Then again, he didn't look unhappy either. He didn't say much and maintained a neutral, sort of disengaged expression on his face. Unfortunately, or so it seemed, he turned out to be a public relations officer for West Point. PAOs are the most dutiful dispensers of the party line, and I gloomily prepared myself for an hour of exchanges in the "Yes, comrade, the grain harvest is indeed the best it has ever been—another tribute to Big Brother's wisdom" vein. Happily it turned out that he joined the Army to drive tanks, was never happier than when he was driving tanks, and was only just assigned to public affairs, probably because that is where the Army seems to send its best and brightest these days. (Apparently, this is where the real battle is.) Best of all, like most, he was a secret heretic.

I asked him why it is that someone with a natural affinity for driving tanks should be transferred. There are many reasons, he said, but he thinks one is that the brass now believe field leadership, combat leadership, is not an inherent talent, that it can be taught to virtually any soldier. That lead to the subject of "natural warriors" and whether such a thing exists.

The question isn't particularly important anymore, he said: "Soldiers who are natural warriors don't get promoted because they also tend to be outspoken and say insensitive things." And then he told me the story of one of his favorite combat leaders in the Gulf who had suffered this very fate.

"It often strikes me as ironic," he mused, "that these days people like Patton and Schwarzkopf would never have made it past basic training. . . ."

FIVE

"Sex and Lies and Aircraft Carriers and Bosnia and . . ."

"All the media normally says is 'Of course, men and women in the services never do anything so unprofessional as even think about sex, except for a few patriarchal males and fighter pilots and drill sergeants and some Marines, all of whom will shortly be discharged from the new PC military.'"
—Karen Dahlby, age thirty-one, former lieutenant, Air Force

"This isn't Olympic diving. We don't get extra credit for an added degree of difficulty."
—Lt. Col. Stephen Smith, to the Presidential Commission on the Assignment of Women to the Armed Services, circa 1993

The sun has nearly slid into the sea on the western horizon as the floating city chugs along through the warm Gulf waters. Shadows grow longer on the flight deck and the catwalks and now there is the occasional cool breeze as a reminder that nights in desert regions can be as cold as the days are hot. It is twilight, *le heur bleu*, as the French say. Just like most everybody else on the planet, the young crew of the *Stennis* feel that little twinge of melancholy, a little twist in the gut, at the blue hour. Soon it will be time for "darkened ship"— when lights are turned off or dimmed to a sickly ochre or bloodred— and the little city will seem to close in on itself entirely.

Most everybody feels the melancholy, the loneliness, the someone's-walking-on-my-grave shiver, around this time. It's the reason Australians have "sundowners" and Americans have "Happy Hour"—to generate light and body heat and keep the chill at bay.

And, in fact, around about seven o'clock there is a kind of Happy

Hour vibe down here in the Hangar Bay, that great steel Carlsbad Cavern of space where about half the ship's fleet of planes are parked for the night for maintenance. This is enlisted country—the kids are in charge! Commissioned officers come here some during the day, but they have little reason to stay because the supervisors on this deck are young petty officers. Anyway, there aren't too many dour-looking guys with shoulder boards walking around, and so, despite the video cameras mounted on the walls ostensibly to deter equipment sabotage (and sexual misconduct, the kids say), and the security officers who occasionally sweep through looking for "people in the nooks and crannies," as one of the ship's legal officers put it, there is some life and sense of freedom.

There's always something going *on* in the Hangar Bay. Any time of day or night—or so it seems—agile young mechanics can be found at work, twining themselves around helicopter rotors or sitting cowboy-style astride the fuselage of F-18 jets. Often someone will unroll a big mat and hold kickboxing classes or tournaments or an aerobics class— all dutifully gender-integrated. For many, however, this is "The Lido" (a term coined by bemused junior officers on a different gender-integrated ship)—the place where the thousands of junior enlisteds can cruise and mingle.

Once you've met somebody, there are plenty of places to go to get to know them better. In fact, as one serpentines through the vast steel forest of parked machinery (as long as two football fields) stooping to avoid decapitation by a jet wing, taking a detour to avoid the massive E-2C Hawkeye (a sort of mini AWAC), one keeps coming upon shy courting scenes, like something out of Gainsborough, a man and a maid, except here they sit in the shade of a fuselage and not a spreading tree.

Just off the Hangar Bay at the very bow of this deck is a dim space the enlisted kids call "the smoking sponson." It's a really popular place to congregate because it's one of the few where you're allowed to smoke, and also because there is no bulkhead at the area's bow-most end—nothing except a loose, billowy, tacked-up cargo net between you and the feel of real sea air and the sight of the prow cutting through the inky waters.

Outside the sponson all one can see are the bobbing orange tips of cigarettes and silhouettes of the socializers. Inside it feels very much like your average sports bar on "Ladies Night": By the light of one naked, low-watt bulb, one can pick out clusters of anxious males, laughing a little too loudly while surreptitiously tracking the movements of the one or two female seamen who have wandered in and bestowed themselves on a few lucky men. (The man-to-woman ratio on the *Stennis* is great for the women; hard on the men, seamen say.)

"Association," says twenty-six-year-old Debra Maxey, the ship's librarian, delicately, "is highly discouraged. They're not *saying* you can't do it, but basically you can't. More often than not someone is taken off the ship for being in a couple.

"During the day [the smoking sponson] is just a place to get away from work, but at night they can get away with talking to the person who . . ." Here modesty seems to snarl the pretty midwestern girl's ordinarily elegant sentence structure. "Well, the person who, if they were caught together too much other places, people would start to wonder.

"You have to remember," she says gravely, "that a majority of the ship are men, so a new female is 'fresh meat' . . . so to speak. That's the main thing about females and males on the ship; they are lonely—all of 'em are. It's a very lonely type of job; you're very far from home and it's like being on an island with very little choice of who you're with.

"But that's why they hang around the Hangar Bay. Period. I knew a girl who came the same time I did. She would go, put full makeup on, do up her hair, and then put on her jogging clothes to go exercise in the Hangar Bay, and after running she would walk around. That's how she met most of her boyfriends."

The late nineties—about eight years into America's experiment with the world's biggest, most-deployed coed force—have produced one solid finding. Here it is: To everybody who asked, "So, are they having sex?" after I'd been out "in the field," I can now report that, yes, as a general rule, it is safe to assume, and the data and survey instruments definitely indicate, that men and women and girls and boys (and combinations thereof) in gender-integrated units have plenty of sex.

This may not seem like earthshaking news to the troglodytes who believed, as one soldier put it, that the military's gender-integration plans hadn't factored in enough "healthy respect for the sheer cussedness of the human animal," but it could be a bit of a revelation if you've spent the last ten years listening to the Pentagon or mainstream media.

Throughout the Gulf War ramp-up, when there hadn't been much to write about, a few of the more uncouth regional newspapers snickered about the possibility that GI Jane and GI Joe might find themselves on night guard duty under that big ole desert moon, but the upscale urban broadsheets—like the *New York Times*, which did a boys-and-girls-in-the-Gulf feature with the subhead "No Time for Fraternizing"—reproved us roundly.

"Despite what might have been expected under the circumstances, the returning troops spoke of following the rules when it came to members of the opposite sex," proclaimed the *Times*. "On the working level 'it didn't matter if you were a female or a male, living there was hard. You just made the best of it, the best you could,'" said Specialist Manuela Caballero. Lisa Foster, twenty-three, another very junior enlisted, told the reporter, "Sex was not supposed to happen. 'No fraternizing,' they told us. You knew you couldn't have anything like a relationship, you know, a real close relationship, so you got to be good friends in other ways."

Actually, time is what some support units had plenty of. There was no television, no alcohol, you were warned not to go more than a few yards away from your base, and the food was boring, so, as Sgt. Mary Rader told President George Bush's Commission on the Assignment of Women in the Armed Services in 1991, troops deployed in Saudi found other ways to occupy themselves:

> Our company [a supply unit] only has 69 people and it was very heavy in our E-4s and below. It didn't just stop there. We had a captain and an E-4 having an affair, and he went to a sexual harassment board for it. I had a female officer who had an affair with an E-5 male that she worked with. . . . We had one female in particular that we could not keep out of one of the male bunks. She was caught sleeping in the male tent more than once. We had females and males that would go to guard duty together and be caught necking, and they're supposed to be out there protecting us.

Lt. Kyle Smith's clerical unit, also stationed in the desert, but way to "the rear with the gear," had time on their hands as well. In his very funny unpublished memoir "If I Die While Sipping Tea," Smith describes days spent picking sand from orifices and clothing, considering which direction to position his standard-issue aluminum cot (to catch the breeze should one miraculously happen by), and endlessly searching for a slightly less disgusting toilet and slightly more palatable food. What he craved was something that wasn't freeze-dried, embalmed with preservatives for the year 2012, and cosseted as if it were nuclear waste in industrial-strength plastic—something, in other words, that was not an MRE (a Meal Ready to Eat, otherwise known at the time as Meals Rejected by Ethiopia). Smith's version of a big night in the Gulf was the time he gorged himself on Kellogg's Cocoa Puffs and Froot Loops after discovering the cache in a supply truck.

A Yale grad who had sold his soul to the ROTC in exchange for college tuition, Smith could usually be found curled up in his tent with books about military history like the biography of Winston Churchill. (Smith especially thrilled to Churchill's line "War, which used to be cruel and magnificent, has now become cruel and squalid. In fact it has been completely spoilt.") Smith's troops, on the other hand, had more social pursuits. Twenty-five of his women soldiers—6.4 percent of his little combat support unit—were shipped home midtour because they had become pregnant.

"When people are overseas, they play," says an Army officer who spent more than a year commanding a mixed-gender support unit in Honduras, matter-of-factly. It is, in fact, quite a military tradition, and one would think, with the military habit of cataloguing, recording, debriefing, and postmorteming, this little statement would be recorded in some DOD tome under the heading "Lessons Learned." (The term *Lessons Learned* gained currency after the Vietnam War as a sort of abbreviation for salvaging something from a bad situation.)

"In '84 I became a battalion commander of a support battalion in Honduras which was about twenty to thirty percent female," says this officer, who now works close to the top in the Pentagon. "One day, my boss, a colonel, came to me and said, 'People are screwing like minks!'

"My boss was never real clear about his policy, because he couldn't be clear about what he wanted," he recalls. So believing that "if you set up a rule you can't enforce, then all the other rules come tumbling down and you lose discipline across the board," he told his troops:

" 'OK, this is the policy: There is no policy. I don't care who screws who, but the rule is, you show up for work at 6 A.M. You do PT. You stay out of trouble. You don't drink too much.'

"[For work performance] there was this one standard," he says. "There would be no consideration given for anything. There were no breaks given to anyone. I guess I was cold and heartless and everyone knew it, because I didn't care if someone dropped dead in the road—I would just get someone else. The result was [sex] became a nonissue. There were no gender issues in my command unit in my fourteen months overseas."

Many of the officer's people, men and women alike, remember the deployment as Bali Hai, a little interlude of Jungle Paradise. He still meets people who tell him how great it was and ask him if there's a way to get assigned there again. One ingredient in the happiness and smooth functioning was clearly his strong command and clear rules, but he also says he thinks the Shangri-la-like state had a lot to do with the fact that everybody was, as they say, gettin' some. Thus "the men weren't competing over women, so there weren't those kinds of disruptions." Most of his female soldiers were overt or all-but-admitted lesbians, happy to find so many of their own, perfectly happy to keep company with each other. As for the men, "there were always Honduran women which the Army soldiers could have whenever they wanted."

This officer was among the many I met who seemed to prove that you can't generalize about "the military's" attitude toward gays. Of course, there are some four-star homophobes in the services, but it is a huge institution filled with all kinds of people and all kinds of feelings about serving with homosexuals. Male homosexuality gets particularly harsh treatment sometimes, in part, because men in combat zones must be able to develop deep, loving, protective feelings for each other and they are better able to achieve this if they know a clear line is enforced, if they know that their mates will not step over that line, and that an arm around a shoulder is not the beginning of a come-on. Often enough, though, the practice of expelling homosexuals has more to do with the danger and inappropriateness of sexual love as opposed to platonic love in general, not something about homosexuality in particular. What needs to stay "in the closet" in war zones is sexuality, period. Generally, what soldiers most respect is the ability to do your job and being a cooperative member of the group. It is—or was—a society all about conformity. So generally what would get anybody in trouble, gay or straight, was flaunting one's sexuality, coming on to fellow soldiers—dressing or acting in a sexually provocative way—and so disrupting "good order and discipline."

In 1988, shortly before he resigned as secretary of the navy, James Webb saw the "overseas syndrome" in action as well: "During a staff meeting with Secretary of Defense Frank Carlucci, I reported that I had been informed that 51 percent of the single enlisted Air Force females and 48 percent of the single enlisted Navy females stationed in Iceland were pregnant," Webb wrote.

Carlucci, who had announced in the first weeks of his tenure that he wished to remove the Reagan administration's policy of restricting women from combat, was unconcerned. "What else is there to do on Iceland?" he replied, drawing titillated chuckles from several sycophantic male military officers at the table. Needless to say, there was no follow-up on this or any other systemic failure, and the uninformed military was given the word through the grapevine that passes from Pentagon aide to general's aide and on down the line, that no matter what written policies might have existed, the leadership was not concerned about sexual fraternization.

As for the nineties deployments: A July 1996 article in *Stars and Stripes* reported that in Bosnia, from December 20, 1995, when the deployment began, until July 1996, one woman had to be evacuated for pregnancy approximately every three days. "It's no different from appendicitis," snapped a civilian public relations spokeswoman when I asked if Operation Joint Endeavor command considered this a problem. Anyway, she sniffed, the pregnancies may have occurred on leave with husband or boyfriend. But not necessarily all . . .

"It's going on all over the place," acknowledged Capt. Chris Scholl to *Stars and Stripes*. "They've locked us down, so what else is there to do?"

But where, in that bleak, damp landscape, could one go? After all, as a spokesman at Tuzla Air Base put it, "the Army does not prohibit heterosexual relations among consenting single soldiers [unless they are supervisor/subordinate in the same chain of command], but it does not provide facilities for sexual relations."

No problem. "Where there's a will there's a way," Scholl explained. Trysting spots, he said, tended to be the backs of Humvees parked on a deserted airstrip, tents, latrines, even underground bunkers—if you could hack having icy water dripping on your head. (According to women-in-the-army policy officer Lt. Col. Robert Carrington, by 1999 things had simmered down. Perhaps the familiarity of coed tent living was breeding, if not contempt, then sexual disinterest.)

In "olden days," before leaving the harbor, the Navy treated its sailors to their now infamous anti–venereal disease films. "We called them the Mickey Mouse movies," says one Old Salt. " 'We're going to watch Mickey Mouse movies!' we'd tell people. We thought it was funny the way they combined cartoon characters with the grossest details of venereal pathology." (This Old Salt got medical training when he left the service.)

"There was one called something like *But She Seemed Like Such a Nice Girl!*" he recalls. It featured a sailor who comes back from shore leave with a suspicious discharge, he doesn't tell anybody, is then too ill to help when there is a fire aboard ship, and thus ends up bobbing around in a lifeboat saying something to the effect of "If only I had used protection!" At one point the film cut from "this handsome actor to a stark depiction (they must have used a photo from a medical text-book) of his genitalia, which appeared to be rotting and falling away in shreds . . . the most frightening damn thing I ever saw."

The "New Navy" may have put a dent in syphilis problems by banning visits to foreign cathouses, but now it battles unplanned pregnancy—which is not terribly surprising given that most of its female population are nineteen to twenty-four years old and in their most nubile and fertile years, and that they ship out with males of the same age, preoccupied with the biological imperative to fertilize everything in sight. Navy officials maintain that the rate of pregnancy among their active-duty female population at any given time is about 10 percent, a rate that is almost identical to the civilian population, they point out. It's still a very controversial number. Many ship's captains claim higher numbers, and while news articles will mention the number of women flown off a ship while it is under way, they hardly ever report the number of women who do not deploy with the ship because they discover they are pregnant a short time before. Narda Looney of the *Stennis* told me that the number of women originally assembled for the *Stennis* for the tour she was now on seemed much larger than the number of women who eventually left with the ship. She suspected that there had been quite a few pregnancies.

Since Navy surveys show that 61 percent of onboard pregnancies are "unplanned" (usually because a contraceptive wasn't used, not because it failed), contraceptives are always available and videos with such titles as *Give Yourself a Chance* urge their use. Aside from personal testimonials from young male and female sailors about how difficult life had become with an unplanned baby, the film counsels women that it's perfectly acceptable to refuse sexual advances and reminds men of the various ways their behavior can be construed as sexual harassment. "Pregnancy and parenthood are compatible with your Navy or Marine Corps career, but only when you're ready to make the personal choices and sacrifices necessary to raise a child," says a soothing voice-over. "The fleet isn't a nine-to-five, commute-to-work-every-day kind of job. It's a military force. And all Marines and sailors must be ready to deploy with their unit anywhere at any time. Your unit works as a team, with each member as a vital part. If you can't deploy, everybody is let down."

Meanwhile, sex was and continues to be fairly "Rampant in the Navy," as a *Navy Times* article headline put it. "On the coed ships there is more fraternization than you can ever imagine," said a female officer. "Everyone has a few drinks, everyone gets a little horny, and then a young female [here the officer is apparently talking about shore leave] wakes up in the hotel room with all the male seamen of the damn deck department. . . . If you locked a civilian office building down for six months, the same thing would happen—humans are humans."

It was this legacy—including much-publicized Navy "Love Boats" like the *Acadia* and *Yellowstone*, on which 31 percent of the female crew became pregnant—that helped shape the highly restrictive shore leave policies in effect today. Ship commanders seem to act as if they're sitting on a keg of dynamite, as if any movement outside a proscribed range will detonate it. The idea was if you don't let guys go to whorehouses, they won't come back boasting and talking dirty and generally, as the sexual harassment regs put it, "creating a hostile and offensive environment" around the girls. Also, if you offer your crew plenty of wholesome entertainments (tours, barbecues, Jet Ski parties), the kids won't get drunk on shore leave and forget that "a sailor is just a sailor." Ironically, some of the policies intended to desexualize and professionalize sometimes have the opposite effect. Ordered not to go to houses of ill repute or to the divier bars while on liberty, a group of male and female sailors from the aircraft carrier USS *Abraham Lincoln* simply made their own party. In the fall of 1998 they holed up in a Hong Kong hotel room and precipitated what the Navy called "a group sexual incident," an off-duty party that degenerated into "multiple sex acts" that was discovered when one of the female sailors went to the *Lincoln*'s security office and reported that she had been sexually assaulted. (After an investigation by the Naval Criminal Investigative Service, three women and seven men were discharged from the service, while another man faced a court-martial for sexual assault.)

In the fall of 1994 the USS *Eisenhower*, the first of a new class of bigger, faster, nuclear-powered aircraft carriers, pulled away from its Norfolk dock for its inaugural cruise. You'd think the press pack would assemble every time one of these steel behemoths actually proves it can float, but this departure was especially mediagenic. Finally (after a lengthy period of "reconfiguration," adding bathrooms, creating new sleeping areas and such, at a cost of more than a million dollars) here was the debut of the post–Combat Exclusion Law Navy, the Navy that could now assign women to combat ships (like carriers) and the combat jets they carry.

Four hundred women were on the *Ike*, about 10 percent of the crew. Actually, mixed-sex crews should not have been such an earthshaking event. Women have served on medical ships since the early twentieth century and on "tenders" (repair ships) since 1978, but this was a *carrier*, the stuff of newsreels and Tom Clancy novels, so the press stampede was enormous. "Not a day went by without another reporter coming aboard," says John Gadzinski, who had been assigned temporary duty as a PAO for this tour. Once again, as in the Gulf, the "Coed Cruise" was billed as a test of the coed military and the beginning of a glorious new era. In a predeparture article *Time* magazine quoted a male aviator who predicted that the ship would reverse some of the opposition to women in combat. Still, he says, "the good-old-boy network will continue, except you won't see it. It will be like the Klan in the Deep South."

When the six-month deployment was over, *Time* glowingly post-mortemed this "Historic Experiment":

Before the ship had even begun sea trials last summer, the Navy's macho diehards spread warnings that women, ordered on board by Congress, wouldn't perform as well as men aboard the nuclear-powered carrier. . . . Mixing the sexes in cramped quarters for so long, some critics argued, would turn the *Ike* into a Love Boat. . . . In fact, the naysayers will be sorely disappointed, as *Time* discovered during an exclusive visit to the ship last month. While the integration of the sexes in such close quarters created some delicate dilemmas and awkward moments, the *Eisenhower*'s mission was a resounding success. . . .

But Gadzinski, then thirty-three, who had also worked as an LSO (landing signals officer, someone who grades each jet pilot's landing) on the flight deck, found the experience so depressing, such a sign of the direction of "the New Navy," that he left the service a year later—taking his costly fighter pilot skills with him. The commercial airlines were only too happy to add yet another overqualified jet jock to their growing collection of ex-Navy aviators.

"We called it the 'Emperor's New Clothes' cruise," Gadzinski rages. "Everything was set up for the basis of appearances—particularly anything to do with the fact that we had just gone coed.

"There were some great women," he says, but too often women were simply used as photo props, as when inexperienced female seamen recruits from administration departments like data processing were leapfrogged to the control tower and the flight deck to make a pretty picture for the VIPs on their walk-throughs.

"It was going to be a successful cruise; it was going to be a showcase cruise; it was going to be a great success; and that After-Action Report was written before we even pulled out of port."

In the evenings, Gadzinski and his fellow officers (guys in their mid-twenties to midthirties, usually married with kids) used to stand on the observation balconies a level above the floor of the Hangar Bay to gawk at the young enlisteds milling on "The Lido." Since the enlisteds' mess had much the same vibe, they called that "the Food Court." When the boys and girls of the *Ike* finally paired off, they had to be fairly inventive (an enlisted sailor, sleeping like a sardine in the catacombs of the ship, couldn't exactly invite a girl back to his "rack"), but finding really cool, illicit locations for sex seemed to be part of the game. After one tired of pedestrian trysting spots like the ship's laundry, barbershop, photography lab, and chapel, you could achieve a real coup by sneaking up to the top of the ship and doing it in the captain's gig—the captain's private transport craft berthed on the top deck. "When people heard about a couple who'd gotten up there," Gadzinski says, "the general attitude was 'Way to go!'"

One day some of the ship's public affairs officers were called in to deal with a pregnancy, a shipboard problem that seemed more unusual then than it does now:

"We had a young girl, a seaman recruit who worked in the control tower, who turned up pregnant and decided to have an abortion," Gadzinski recalls. As the ship was about to cross into unfriendly waters near the Mideast and Bosnia, arranging for the procedure was complicated, and they had to wait until they were passing through the Strait of Gibraltar to minimize the distance a helicopter would have to fly to carry her to shore and back to the ship.

In the spirit of "pregnancy is no different than appendicitis," Navy PAOs like to stress that ship staffs have to fly people off for broken legs or appendicitis as well, but Gadzinski hated the whole thing and not just because the timing was bad. When he was able to articulate his disquiet, he turned to another officer and said, "This is a boat where our job is to put bombs on target, missiles on target, and make sure that things get done. How can you reconcile this with the object of this nuclear-powered warship?" The other officer, who had the air, Gadzinski says, of a "political officer in the Soviet Union," just looked him "straight in the face" and said, "The world is changing and this is going to have to be an accepted part of our life and there's nothing we can do about it."

But maybe leadership should just loosen up about this sex-in-the-ranks thing. Maybe the penalties and the breaking up of couples and security patrols are all signs that, as the women-in-combat proponents keep saying, military leadership "fears change" and are grabbing any excuse to keep women out of the military simply because, down deep, not for any practical reason, *they just don't want women in the military*. Maybe the sexually satisfied armed services will be happier; maybe they'll whistle while they work, be less cranky about long deployments in remote outposts, be less volatile, better suited to high-tech work in the supposedly imminent world of the "warrior-technician." In an effort to stem the "exodus out of the services" and to compete with the civilian world, which has, in theory, been pulling people away, all the services have been paying serious attention to this nebulous thing called "Quality of Life."

In the nineties we saw the Army go from combat boots to Nikes, from open-bay barracks to dorms—at one point there was even a proposal to give officer candidates private rooms while in officer training school. (This was shot down quickly, but it's a sign of the desperation level that somebody even thought to propose it.) The Army is so anxious to make new recruits happier that boot camps now offer "sensing sessions" in which they can complain about the food, their sleeping accommodations, or the conduct of a drill sergeant. The Navy has put masseuses, gyms, psychiatrists, E-mail (the little change that made the most difference), video movies, cappuccino, and soft-yogurt machines aboard ships. Maybe sex-with-service, sex as close as the next barracks, would have no more effect than the unlimited frozen yogurt available in the officers' wardroom—just another quality-of-life improvement.

Actually, it doesn't matter whether we think a sex-condoning army would work or not. The big practical problem is that military leaders who can't decide what they think about sex in the service are thoroughly committed to two conflicting plans, and thus constantly toggle back and forth betwixt them, which means that people in the ranks are now hit with so many regulations about so much minutiae, many of them inherently conflicting, that they lose their respect for orders overall.

Imperative Number One mandates expanding gender integration until the force looks "more like America." This sounds just great to the folks in Washington, a matter of moving chess figures, or toy soldiers, around the board, but for the midlevel commanders actually responsible for delivering the results, things are quite a bit more difficult. For example, since we've already opened the "easy" MOSs in combat support, the new mandates may mean opening jobs that are considered really tricky to integrate—like putting women in submarines (a prospect that makes the most grizzled Old Salt reel) or into the MOSs that are not classified as "combat," in that their primary mission is not to engage the enemy with deadly force but that in practice often put the soldier in close combat. These MOSs, the remaining symbols of "gender inequity" or "institutionalizing female inferiority" or what-have-you—supposedly glamorous, inarguably status-conferring—are thus the object of constant lobbying and scrutiny.

For two half days and two full days and nights the DACOWITS meets to banquet, toast, cocktail, and "formulate new requests for information [RFI]," "build matrix[es] for [future DACOWITS] issues," draft RFIs, and "generate policy recommendations for the sec-retary of defense."

It discusses issues such as "gender discriminatory language in per-formance evaluations for servicewomen," ways to identify "indicators of optimal utilization of women in the services," and how to phrase its recommendation that the secretary of defense "require the services to develop and agree on a set of core questions that establish a standard-ized assessment to study sexual harassment and ethnic issues."

In addition to the biannual conferences held in cushy hotels in mili-tary cities such as Tampa, San Diego, and Austin, the committee is required to take an annual trip to visit women of the U.S. military "in the field" in an attempt to hear and "address their concerns." These fact-finding tours—that can take them to all points around the globe—produce reports and sheaves of recommendations. Over the years, since its founding in 1951, the committee has lobbied to raise weight limits for women, designed better fitting uniforms, improved the maternity uniform, rescinded the Combat Exclusion Law, and put air-conditioning in barracks.

After one such fact-finding tour—that had included stops at Ameri-can bases in Aviano and Naples, Italy—it returned and held a briefing session with military officials to announce that Italian men, civilians working on the bases, were pinching American servicewomen! Worse, after chatting with base commanders, it had been "very dismayed to find" that commanders "had heard about the situation," but had done nothing. Is it possible, it asked the gathered officials, that the Status of Forces agreement between the United States and Italy (that prohibits the prosecution of Italian civilians by the U.S. military) was keeping American commanders from taking action?

Approximately 90 percent of all military MOSs are now open to women because of the efforts of groups like the DACOWITS, but the committee continues to chip away at the edifice of the (still) male-dominated military. This step-by-step effort has worked for the services: each MOS that is opened becomes like a precedent-setting court case. In other words, each newly opened MOS sets up the question: If this MOS, which is so very similar to that MOS in this and that respect, is open, why shouldn't the other be open? In many cases, not wanting to oppose the DACOWITS too stridently—wanting to avoid a battle that the press would probably spin as entrenched men versus nobly struggling women—the services have capitulated. And so the chipping continues. But as the DACOWITS gets closer to the core of the military machine—ground combat troops (its raison d'être)—the opening process gets harder. The Army, for one, has begun to plant its heels. For the last two and a half years (as of this writing), DACOWITS has been focused on opening all jobs aboard submarines, on Multiple Launch Rocket System (MLRS) crews, and Special Operations Force (SOF) pilot spots—"the Cadillacs of equipment that the guys want to keep themselves," as one member of the DACOWITS class of '99 put it.

Members of the DACOWITS are only allowed to serve for three years, so institutional memory becomes a problem; there are always "newbies" around who haven't got their bearings yet. Every DACOWITS conference is assigned flanks of military representatives, "mil reps," from each service to handle DACOWITS questions and to explain their services' policies. DACOWITS is reputed to be quite powerful, to have the ear of the SecDef, so briefing sessions with the "mil reps" has come to resemble a dog and pony show, with each service spending much of its time attempting to prove that it is the most woman-friendly—the least deserving of the DACOWITS ire. "Hello! I'm here from the Air Force," says a tall blond officer, starting his presentation. "The service, I'd like to remind you, in which one hundred percent of MOSs are open to women." DACOWITS tending is not a popular assignment among military officers and NCOs. Often one hears them complain about having to "reinvent the wheel every year."

Submarines, obviously a closed system, turn up on the agenda every few years. In 1999, for example, the DACOWITS sent a request for information to the SecDef, stating that the possibility of putting women on submarines seemed not to have been studied. Actually, the Navy has been "studying" gender integrating subs for quite some time. In 1993, with the perennial clamor to integrate subs in its ears, DOD got a bunch of engineers and sociologists and what-have-you together to look at the various "issues" involved when you put a group of young men and women in a stuffy tin box two thousand or so leagues under the sea for six months at a time. Engineer David Stanford, the study leader, recalls that on the issue of of infrastructure alone, his commission concluded "to accommodate women on current operational attack-class submarines and comply with the existing Navy privacy guidelines, you'd actually have to lengthen the sub"—build an extension—at a projected cost of "hundreds of millions of dollars." "It's like the inside of a clock," says Stanford, "there is simply no extra space . . . anywhere!"

In the summer of 1999, maybe because of DACOWITS's lobbying, the issue of women on subs resurfaced. Secretary of the Navy Richard Danzig met with officers of the "silent service" and told them it was time to "embrace that kind of change."

"I would call attention to your demographics," he said. "It worries me. The most Narcissus-like thing about creating something in your own image . . . is the continuous existence of this segment of the Navy as a white-male preserve . . . when the world is changing in fundamental ways. . . . I am not animated by some feeling of affirmative action or political correctness," he said, but he warned that "Congress and political power are changing. More and more we see the role of women increasing in that regard. As that is the case, if the submarine force remains a white-male bastion, it will wind up getting less and less support when it requires resources. . . ."

He used the word *woman* only once in the speech and when a reporter asked him whether he was "saying that he would support women being introduced on submarines," the SecNav answered, "I think the answer is we need to figure it out."

Several weeks later a group of women midshipmen (Navy ROTC cadets) spent several days on a sub as a training exercise, with more such exercises planned.

Another perennial DACOWITS project are SOF helicopter pilot spots. And every year, the Department of the Army sends its version of a Trojan horse, Lt. Col. Robert Carrington, forty-two, a West Point grad and former infantry commander. A short man with thinning blond hair and the face of a twenty-two-year-old in a Norman Rockwell illustration, he speaks low and evenly, blushes frequently, and then unleashes a mind as quick as a Tomahawk cruise missile—one more example of the way the services have been deploying their best and brightest to public affairs. (Public affairs, in fact, is the only department whose budget actually went up during the drawdown of the eighties.) Twice a year, at DACOWITS conferences, Colonel Carrington is charged with gently telling the group (still about 90 percent female) some variation of "No, ma'am, the Army has not changed its position. SOF pilots collocate with combat units and units that collocate with combat units are still closed to women because combat units are ones whose primary mission is to engage the enemy—something women are currently not allowed to do." When there is the inevitable torrent of protest, he dutifully (Carrington says he has made the same presentation for several years running) cues up the overhead projector, then gets ready for the parsing, the sifting, the Talmudic discussions of what constitutes "collocation," what constitutes "collocation" "direct," and so forth.

In one of these sessions, he finds himself forced to diagram the components of an army on the ground: "Light infantry walks, jumps out of planes, or is foot mobile," he explains. "While heavy infantry, those are your tracked vehicles, tanks, and Bradleys. People are assigned to specific jobs among these components."

A DACOWITSer has been listening intently and jotting on her pad. "But," she probes, "the placement of those different components and their collocation with each other could get kind of mixed up in a battle, couldn't it?" "It usually does, ma'am," says Carrington wearily. "It can all fall apart, this plan of battle." "Thank you," says the DACOWITSer, with an air of "there will be no more questions, Judge."

"I guess what I'm struggling with," volunteers an earnest thirtyish professor of communications theory, "is once the risk rule goes away, this notion of primary versus secondary mission, I understand what you're driving at. It's a categorization, it's a definitional issue, and what

I'm missing is the defense of primary versus secondary mission given what sounds to us like similarity in job descriptions in some instances. What they're doing, where they're doing it, isn't any longer the trigger; it's the relationship to the job of the people they're doing it for.

"Primary mission," she adds, looking soulfully at Carrington, "is a trigger that appears to be a definitional one and I understand that is something DOD had imposed on you."

On another day, the DACOWITS are parsing DOD's rationale for keeping MLRS crew billets closed to women:

"For one thing, they are on the front lines," Carrington explains, "which means that the MLRS crew is in a very close collocation with units whose primary purpose is to engage the enemy in direct combat."

A fiftyish female DACOWITSer, who had been listening with narrowed eyes, sees her opening and pounces.

"Then why are the Patriots [missile systems] open!?"

"Their targets are very high in the air, ma'am," says Carrington weakly. "Also, they operate from the rear." She looks blank at that, so Carrington takes a deep breath and begins, "In a combat zone, you see, we have an area called the front . . ."

Spokesmen like Carrington sigh over the difficulty of getting civilians to understand the difference between piloting in a Special Forces unit and, say, flying supplies to a base camp. Sometimes it's easy to see how civilians just don't seem to get these things.

This, after all, is the institution that created the term *collateral damage* (to avoid the messy subject of dead civilians) and the term *POV* ("personally owned vehicle," instead of car) and the term *internally displaced persons* for Kosovars fleeing Serbians. Sometimes the new phrase comes out of the military's need for absolute precision—after all, one wants to distinguish between "internally displaced persons," who are still in their homeland, and "refugees," who have been forced to leave. On the other hand, at least in the gender-integration debate, the techno-speak has a way of distancing us from the intangible, ground-level, qualitative elements—which is exactly where the problems occur.

Every year, for instance, in its attempt to "respond" to the ladies of DACOWITS, the Army breaks out the old "SOF Rotary Wing Mission Profile" overhead transparency. It states that SOF pilots may be assigned to "missions which would collocate with ground combat units" (and women are still barred from direct combat) in "staging areas, forward aircraft refueling points, hide sites, enemy airfields, and advanced operational bases." Flying into a "forward aircraft refueling point" sounds like your basic milk run. So what's the problem? In other words, once again, proponents of unlimited, immediate gender integration are kept, and keep themselves, in a sort of parallel universe, a sort of one-dimensional, freeze-dried, diorama Army where you don't hear bullets flying by, and your rucksack straps aren't cutting grooves in your shoulders, and your feet aren't practically drowning in sweat in your leather lace-up boots.

For a more concrete, simple-English description of a few days-in-the-life of several SOF pilots, maybe Army reps at DACOWITS conferences should read aloud from the book *Black Hawk Down*, a journalist's second-by-second account of what happened when several helicopters full of Rangers, Delta Force guys, and other immensely qualified, no-kidding warriors crash-landed in a narrow, dirt street in downtown Mogadishu swarming with mobs of vigilantes armed with automatic weapons and copter-killing, shoulder-carried rocket-propelled grenades (RPGs). Most of us are at least familiar with the story of Black Hawk pilot Michael Durant, who was dragged from the rubble of his crashed bird, nearly beaten to death by a mob, then rescued by Somali officials who threw him into a holding cell, where he lay on a dirt floor for twenty-four hours with a fractured back and a broken thighbone that poked out of a deep gash in his leg. Obviously the man was strong as a bull or he would never have survived.

Whether or not there are women that could qualify for this job (and I suspect there are a few of the weight-lifting, triathlon-running female pilots who could), the brass must expect many sparks if they attempt to gender-integrate these small, elite, tightly bonded all-male units. The social dynamic problems just start with the fact that the helo pilot, because he's the guy with his hands on the controls, is charged with getting the fighters to leave the relatively safe confines of the agile bird and fast-rope into chaos below . . . and do it fast, so the pilot can get out of there with the copter intact. The pilot thus becomes the de facto leader of the group, and he gets the men to do their jobs by projecting supreme confidence in the mission, supreme confidence in his own flying abilities, and by pumping up a sufficient level of let's-grind-their-pathetic-asses-into-the-sand macho—in short, by being (at that time and in that place) the most shit-kicking crazy motherfucker alive, the guy you would rather commit hara-kiri for than disappoint.

Still, the brass are attempting to move toward an ideal of seamless, well-bonded mixed-gender units while they simultaneously pledge allegiance to a second principle: that intimate relationships destroy unit cohesion, readiness—you name it. As Dennis J. Reimer, former army chief of staff, put it, "We are committed . . . to providing an atmosphere that is free of sexual harassment and free of the conditions that spawn sexual misconduct." Recently retired NavSec John Dalton has said that one of his primary goals was to have "the Navy Department . . . lead society as a model for gender relations."

Retired Army major Lillian Pfluke (a member of West Point's first gender-integrated class) expanded on this theme on the influential Washington, D.C.–based radio show hosted by Diane Rehm. Broadcast in 1997 when the nation was still digesting "Aberdeen," the conversation started with the cases of alleged rape at the Maryland Army base and moved with disconcerting swiftness to the subject of consensual sex rather too seamlessly, as if they are one and the same. "All of these things," said Major Pfluke, who seemed to include rape in the "things," "even the lewd glances, even the unwanted remarks and the love letters, are threats to unit cohesion, and threats to unit cohesion are threats to military readiness, so we have to root out every last bit of this stuff and really drive it home that none of this stuff is welcome. If we're going to have a strong and ready army, then we have to have well-bonded units, and that sex stuff has no place in those kinds of units."

Obeying these dual commandments leaves the services walking a very narrow strip of ground with mines on either side. You have to have some sympathy for midlevel leadership's quandary. Many of them aren't true believers like their Pentagon cohorts, they're just guys trying to carry out the mission du jour: They know they must encourage cohesion in their mixed-gender units (as an essential part of unit survival, and because this is the way armies are simply supposed to look), while avoiding the wrong kind of cohesion—the kind that would be a distraction, the kind that would stimulate jealousies, lovers' spats, and babies.

All of this means that nearly ten years into its vision of a "gender-neutral," "gender-blind" force, the U.S. military is more preoccupied with sex than ever, racing around like a frazzled camp counselor. The nitty-gritty details that generally don't figure into Mount Olympus's sweeping vision—like how to keep people in their bunks after hours—have ended up generating a cascade of new policy, much of it all *about* "gender." From coming up with a more figure-concealing work uniform to propagating the "three-second rule" (in which recruits were told that looking at the opposite sex for longer than three seconds could constitute sexual harassment), the upshot is that the regulation of sex and deciding how to cope with its various aftermaths have become a major military occupation.

All of this is complicated further by the fact that officers and NCOs are never supposed to talk about the root cause of all this policy formation. To say, for instance, that way too many of your "females" are dropping out of basic training because of leg injuries could be a career-ender—you've helped further a "negative stereotype." And maybe they're only underachieving because of sexist attitudes in your command; maybe you are allowing a demeaning climate to exist—and suddenly things aren't looking so good for your promotion prospects. The services operate on two tracks simultaneously, all the time insisting it's one track.

"It's one of the great paradoxes," says former JAG lawyer Henry Hamilton. "On the one hand, we're going to throw them together saying they're all the same, and then there are a million little exceptions and rules to keep [women] apart and treat them special."

Trying to walk this delicate line—trying to fulfill competing directives—or "endeavoring to protect our women soldiers [from sexual harassment] while they learn to protect our country," as NBC News put it without a trace of irony, means that COs learn to practice a kind of doublethink, or that they begin to take all regulations less seriously, which may have been a factor in the Aberdeen Proving Grounds mess, in which advanced individual training instructors were convicted of rape for fraternizing with trainees.

It's especially demoralizing when a CO is just trying to follow orders but gets whomped because the orders cancel each other out in some way. After Hamilton left the Army, he represented an officer who fell victim to "the great paradox from an equal opportunity perspective of giving women equal opportunity and having to protect them." (Any CO who has, say, a rape or an abduction on his watch is going to get in trouble.)

Hamilton's officer-client had been commanding a unit in Bosnia. Many of his troops were in a new MOS category called Civil Affairs, which looks a bit like the old Peace Corps ("We are facilitators," a civil affairs officer, Col. Michael Hess, told the *Los Angeles Times* while on patrol in Bosnia). The soldier walks around nearby towns, gets to know people, has a bit of a chat. (Obviously, it's easier to conduct one's peacekeeping duties when local people are with you.) Earlier, a Civil Affairs female alleged that she had been abducted and raped by two Czech soldiers she had met. She was sent back to the States; the Czechs resolutely claimed that the whole thing had been consensual, and the American command decided it had "no jurisdiction" to prosecute the Czechs. The only thing to come out of the imbroglio was a new U.S. Army policy for the Bosnian theater informally called "the two-female rule," which dictated that women could not leave base without a companion.

The trouble for Hamilton's client started when one of his female soldiers believed she should be able to command a "cell"—a small unit of Civil Affairs people. It would be good for her career, she said. The problem was that Hamilton's client commanded "an odd number of females." He couldn't just yank Female X, say, out of her job and put her with Female Y so Female Y could have an escort in her new job. People were spread around the neighboring countryside and, of course, they were working where their particular skills were needed. Unable to find a second female "battle buddy," he couldn't give her the job. Believing she had been blocked on her climb up the career ladder, the woman filed a sex discrimination suit against her CO. "He really got nailed," Hamilton says. "It took me about two years and thousands of dollars on his part to get him off."

The zone of safety for the CO is made all the narrower by the sexual harassment definition the Army has adopted. Here, from the *Congressional Record*, is a senior Army officer's recitation of that policy, his own comments, and formal policy:

It is important to note that sexual harassment is identified commonly through many behaviors—ranging from "dating behaviors" and improprieties common in interpersonal relationships, i.e., jokes, gestures, unwanted pressures for attention, to other acts that are criminal in nature. The Department of Defense and the Army agree that sexual harassment centers on the linkage between gender-based behaviors and attitudes which contribute to the coercion of the victim, or at a minimum, a reduction of the individual's or the group's standing within the organization. . . . Army Regulation 600-20 defines sexual harassment as "a . . . form of sex discrimination that involves unwelcomed sexual advances, requests for sexual favors, and other verbal or physical conduct of a sexual nature, when: . . . such conduct interferes with an individual's performance or creates an intimidating, hostile, or offensive environment."

Basically it's the same one used in the civilian workplace, but the military milieu is not the civilian workplace. For a start, civilians are not "owned by their jobs," as former Air Force lieutenant Karen Dahlby puts it; civilian employees can get away from the people they work with at the end of the day. And one half of their lives is entirely private—not open to their bosses' scrutiny. In the intimate, physical world of the deployed military there are just so many more chances for a stare, a joke, an "inappropriate touch," or a "condescending remark." And, of course, the definition is vague enough to encompass all kinds of love and lust stuff, like a relationship gone bad. Where is the line, for instance, between the behavior of a jilted lover—pleading for another chance, hanging around just to catch a glimpse of the beloved—and "stalking"? We are still, in other words, dealing with a vague charge in which perception is all—as Debra Maxey found out when the ship's chaplain, her boss, became convinced she was flirting with every man who visited her library desk to check out a book. She says she is just a friendly person and, after all, she "had to talk to them to check a book out." He told her to stop flirting. She wasn't sure what she was supposed to stop. The chaplain decided she was "disobeying orders," a very serious charge, and she was sent to the ship's captain for an Article 15 hearing—in which the ship's skipper plays both judge and jury. The captain decided she was innocent of any wrongdoing, but she was concerned that the Article 15 paperwork stayed in her file, where it might have caused promotion problems if she had stayed in the Navy.

In fact, this is one reason why mixed-crew ships are so often seen as hotbeds of "sexual harassment"—not because the ships or bases are full of marauding predatory men but because, under current definitions, the man/woman thing can morph into sexual harassment charges at the drop of a hat. Describing a case he'd been called in to adjudicate, then vice admiral Skip Bowman inadvertently provided a brilliant example of how the old man/woman dance looks after one has applied a template made up of today's regulations:

"What started off as benign fraternization turned quickly into harassment," he told a reporter. "In both cases, the senior felt he was getting signals of receptiveness, but the junior felt she was being over-run, enveloped by this thing, and quickly wanted out. She couldn't get out of the arrangement, because she had already sent these signals of acceptance. Now the man was taking advantage of those signals. It went quickly from mutually accepted inappropriate behavior to unwanted advances or behavior."

Says one surface-warfare officer: It is "nontraditional missions such as the sheer monotony of managing gender integration . . . and making sure that your personnel do not engage in sexual misconduct" that turn life into "sheer drudgery." Still, he can take some comfort in the fact that his counterpart in the civilian workplace is bearing a similar burden.

On the other hand, the military, for all kinds of reasons, takes a special hit on the sexual harassment issue, and the cost in morale is much more drastic here. The press has long had a keen interest in linking the aggression of the military to aggression against women. During the Aberdeen mess, the Army was portrayed, as journalist Hannah Rosin put it, as "a rotten old boys' network, . . . hiding a cauldron of hostility and even violence toward women . . . under a carapace of order and discipline. . . ." In other words, the Okay Oatmeal Corporation doesn't have to labor to put out oatmeal under constant accusations that the stuff is carcinogenic, but military personnel of the nineties have to listen to accusations that the very qualities that allow them to do their job—aggressiveness, mental toughness (often manifesting itself as "a lack of sensitivity")—are in themselves corrupted, toxic.

In 1998, for example, *Time* magazine ran an excerpt from the book *Ground Zero: The Gender Wars of the Military*, one thesis of which was that the military has a "goal of disparaging . . . the female sex" manifested, for example, in the way it has allowed "sexually demeaning language [to] continue to pervade the services," thereby "bonding men in platoons, squadrons, companies—whole divisions and fleets of men." (Thereby excluding women, the author seems to imply.) Author Linda Bird Francke quotes Gloria Johnson, a Navy airman at school in Orlando, Florida, as saying, "We find ourselves cursing and swearing every two seconds"—as if the language is used deliberately as a ploy to drive women out and a woman can only survive if she "degrades" herself by mimicking this behavior. The "cultural forces . . . at work within the military . . . dictate the harassment of women," Francke writes, and they are so ubiquitous that even the "age-old hierarchy of military rank . . . continues to provide a vehicle for the sexual pressuring of junior women."

So how do the Francke-esque images get into the public mind? Well, partly through the press, which seems to love the almost S&M-ish juxtaposition of brutal uniformed men and victimized women.

But actually, one of the main promulgators are the military brass themselves, who try to show that they are diligently trying to cleanse their diseased culture by ordering study after study, attempting to gauge the incidence of sexual harassment in the ranks. Year after year, since the mideighties, they have hired the people who most distrust military culture and who find sexual harassment around every corner; they publish studies portraying military life as a veritable hell on earth for women in the services; the press runs headlines full of brutal men and victimized women—further evidence "that the military has a long way to go as far as women are concerned"—as one senator put it. On the other hand, if one reads past the executive summaries of these studies to the part about methodology, one has to ask what exactly is being surveyed here? The existence of mutual, consensual sexual interest or the frequency of incidents of bona fide sexual harassment?—which, as I understand it, must be so pervasive, so persistent, so offensive, and so obviously unwelcome that it eventually degrades a person's job performance. Between the lines the researchers seem to be reporting incidents of flirtation and sexual interest; unwilling to acknowledge female consensuality, they call that abuse, harassment, even rape.

In the scandal people now call "Aberdeen," female consensuality was the ghost in the machine. One simply ignored the concept. In November 1996, the Army got its version of Tailhook at the Aberdeen Proving Grounds in Maryland, a base where weapons are tested and where post–boot camp recruits bound for weapons-related MOSs go to learn their trade. (The phase in which a recent recruit learns his specialty is called advanced individual training or AIT.) Officials at Aberdeen called a news conference to announce that female AIT trainees had accused two drill sergeants and one captain of sexual malfeasance, including rape. Both drill sergeants were black, had fine military records, and were married with children. The drill sergeant who had attracted the most accusations was thirty-one-year-old S.Sgt. Delmar G. Simpson. He was accused of raping three of his female AIT trainees (all of them more than once), of sodomizing (which can mean fellatio) two other women, and sexually assaulting three more.

The country seemed to be riveted by the image of drill sergeants actually *raping* women in their command and the press frenzy was enormous. Sensing a full-fledged scandal in the making, the Army moved quickly to demonstrate its openness; whatever you do, one could almost hear the brass saying, we are not going to be accused of "cover-up" like the Navy. The Army set up a toll-free hot line so soldiers could report incidents of sexual abuse by training-base staff without giving their names. The hot line, noted the *Washington Post*, seemed "to have touched a nerve"; allegations started to come in from other Army bases such as Fort Leonard Wood, which also has a large female population.

In almost two months, the hot line had taken 6,600 calls. The majority were obvious hoaxes or petty, but 950 seemed credible enough to merit real investigation. The amount of personnel and resources assigned to the scandal was becoming enormous. For each credible-sounding report, an investigator from the Army's Criminal Investigative Division had to travel all over the country to the alleged victim to investigate futher. The CID was also charged with interviewing every woman who'd trained at Aberdeen since January 1995. CID investigators were working eighteen-hour days, seven days a week; thirty investigators alone were at work at Aberdeen. By December, the investigators suspected that fifty-one women had been assaulted, while twenty-five drill instructors were under scrutiny.

Finally, in spring 1997, Simpson went to trial facing nineteen counts of rape and thirty-five other offenses. As one young female Aberdeen trainee after another took the stand, two things became clear. First, the base had been out of control for a long time. One of the trainees who charged Simpson with rape, for example, said the whole thing came up because she had questioned one of Simpson's orders and he began "picking on her." She said she went to his office to "tell him off," but when she got there, he pushed her farther into his office and had sex with her. Other witnesses described Army transport buses littered with used condoms and liquor bottles, drill sergeants kept lists of trainees they called "locked in tight" and passed the lists around, consensual relationships were common, and female trainees (who usually admired their hunky-looking, slightly older drill sergeants) often schemed to sleep with trainers, as trainee Ruth Brown put it, "because they think it's going to get them somewhere."

Second, the actual "rapes" were extraordinarily ambiguous—as "murky as human motivations," noted the *Washington Post*. One twenty-one-year-old ex-trainee, who alleged that Simpson had raped her five times in one month, also told the courtroom that on one occasion, after this relationship had been established, Simpson came to her barracks after lights-out and, in front of her wide-awake roommate, asked her to meet him in his office. She got there first so she sat on a cot to wait.

"You knew these were essentially dates to have sex?" asked one of Simpson's defense attorneys. "Yes," she said. Even though he never used force, she said she responded because she "felt like his pet, his dog" and that she would "just take it . . . because [she] knew it wouldn't be long." Another woman testified that she reported to Simpson's office knowing that he intended to have sex with her and took a shower while she waited for him to arrive. She did it, she said, because Simpson had told her that she "owed him" because he vouched for her when she was facing discharge for a disciplinary infraction.

In other words, the Aberdeen testimony revealed that the Army had adopted a definition of rape that was quite different from the one in the civilian world. In the civilian world, rape is forced sex. The concept of force has been expanded to include "threat of force" ("comply or I'll blow your head off"), on the sensible theory that one shouldn't be penalized by the law for choosing to save one's life even if it means surviving a rape. But none of the alleged rape survivors testified to physical force (and there was no physical evidence to suggest force); occasionally they reported a belligerent and authoritative or bullying tone, but nothing that would have met the test of "a threat of deadly force."

What we were seeing here was what JAG Hamilton called the Army's "emerging doctrine" of "constructive force"—in which the power differential between trainee and trainer is assumed to be a kind of preexisting force, a permanent, inescapable implied force.

"Consensual sex between a trainee and an instructor does not exist," as one official put it. In a case without physical evidence—based purely on "he said/she said" testimony, "constructive force" was the cornerstone of the Simpson prosecution. The relationship between a drill sergeant and a trainee "creates a unique situation of dominance and control," explained one of the trial judges. "They are commanded to follow a drill sergeant's orders." "Nonsense," railed Frank Spinner, one of Simpson's defense team. It is "paternalism to [assume] that women are unable to distinguish between an order to run up a hill and an order to lie on a bed."

It was strange to hear such rationales coming from a southern military court. It was more like an idea that one heard in law school halls in the Northeast. In fact, constructive-force theory was much like something one had been hearing from a feminist lawyer named Catherine MacKinnon, who wondered in print "whether consent is a meaningful concept." As long as men held the power in a relationship—and MacKinnon assumed that they always did—pure consent, consent that was free of any iotas of coercion, was not possible.

Isn't it strange, asked journalist Hannah Rosin in a *New Republic* article, that "[t]he most tradition-minded, socially conservative, and overwhelmingly male institution in America has . . . embraced a theory of sexual intercourse that belongs not only to feminism, but to feminism's more radical wing. On the central question of the trials—whether or not the sex was consensual—the United States Army has proved itself less a disciple of Rambo than of Andrea Dworkin and Susan Brownmiller."

Months into the CID's search of the country, months after the country had grown familiar with the photos of black drill sergeants looking shamed and young white female recruits in tears, the Baltimore chapter of the NAACP called a news conference to introduce five recruits who had testified against Simpson and other Aberdeen drill sergeants. The five young women, some of them crying, said that they had been bullied into making statements, that in some cases the CID told them they had committed fraternization (a consensual relationship with someone of a different rank), but the CID was willing to overlook it if they told it what they knew about on-base rapes. One of the group, Pvt. Brandi Krewson, told reporters that she had "agreed to tell them what they wanted to hear in order for them to leave me alone." Another trainee told reporters that her relationship was consensual, but that "they pushed me and pushed me to say [she had been] raped. But I would not do it. It was not the truth."

Two years after the first accusations against him, Simpson was found guilty of eighteen counts of rape, his rank was stripped to private, he lost any pension benefits he had accrued as a staff sergeant, and he was sentenced to twenty-five years in jail.

As at Tailhook, the focus turned to culture. Trying to demonstrate that they were not the Navy—that is, not covering anything up—Army Secretary Togo West did what secretaries do when trying to show they're on the ball: He established a commission ("over 40 military and civilian personnel") and told it to go forth and "[assess] the human relations environment in which our soldiers live and work, measured in terms of the dignity and respect we extend to one another as an army."

Eight months later the panel (which had been advised by academics like Professor Madeline Morris, who, a few years before, had recommended that the military cast off its "masculinist identity" in favor of an "ungendered vision"), came back with a report stating that "47% of the female troops polled reported they had been sexually harassed" and "the human relations environment is not conducive to engendering dignity and respect among us [because] passive leadership has allowed sexual harassment to persist."

As in Tailhook days, news stories full of sinister language followed. Under the headline "Army Finds Wide Abuse of Women," the *Washington Post* reported that "endemic sexual harassment . . . is undermining the integration of women in the largest branch of the armed forces." Once again, as with Tailhook, Congress, the holder of the purse strings, made menacing noises. Senator Olympia J. Snowe (R-Maine), for one, called the report "a scathing indictment of the climate and leadership" of the Army. Once again there were charges that an incorrigible, irredeemable military culture had attempted a cover-up. Two commission consultants—the aforementioned Morris and another academic, Dr. Leora Rosen—charged that the commission had been "planning to conceal important facts from the public" by not including questions Rosen had designed that asked soldiers if they viewed X-rated movies, went to strip clubs, or made dirty jokes. The point, Rosen said, was to follow up on an interesting correlation she had observed between these habits and high levels of sexual harassment on bases.

But how *did* the panel come up with their numbers? The researchers gauged experience through questionnaires distributed to soldiers in classrooms or by mail. Most questionnaires asked if a fellow soldier or supervisor had "treated you differently because of your sex (e.g., mistreated or ignored you)," "made sexist remarks," "stared, leered, or ogled you in a way that made you uncomfortable," "touched you in a way that made you feel uncomfortable (e.g., laid a hand on your bare arm, put an arm around your shoulders)," and counted the responder as a sexual harassment victim if any of those boxes were checked. The panel also convened focus groups, but they seem to have used the comments to support their analysis. The "hard" data, in other words, still came from the surveys.

Another panel survey merely asked troops, "Have you been sexually harassed?" but noted, many pages later, "[w]hen asked to provide examples of sexual harassment, male trainees' answers covered a wide range of behaviors from 'simply talking to women' to committing rape."

"I don't think it can be explained," a male trainee said. "It depends on the individual." Female soldiers also seemed to be confused over definitions:

Most [female] trainees are able to generalize parts of the Army's definition of sexual harassment without truly understanding that inappropriate behaviors may lead to and include sexual harassment. . . . These trainees view such acts as consensual behavior or flirting. In trainee focus groups, most trainees indicated that sexual jokes, sexual comments, and touching are common and are often not viewed as offensive by either the perpetrator or the recipient. There are, however, some trainees who do not like or condone such actions or language.

Did anyone ever imagine that the services would spend so much time prodding and poking and policing their coed ranks? At least in their statements for public consumption, service chief after congressman after four-star general say things like Senator John McCain, who admitted that he thought "this was much harder than we expected."

One of the reasons we now find them so surprised, according to Lt. Cmdr. Patrick Vincent, writing in the Naval Institute magazine *Proceedings*, is their "surrealistic refusal to acknowledge" and "pathologically uniform, puritanical denial of human sexuality among military leaders." Vincent, now in the Navy Reserves after nine years on active duty, described a congressional hearing held in the late nineties to "discuss" the eternally probed subject of gender-integrated boot camp, where any mention of the climate produced when "sexually active high-school-age youths displaced from home for the first time [are] isolated in close quarters together . . ." seemed "to be beneath consideration, an affront to the notion of boot camp enlistees as asexual interchangeable parts." In the hearing, Vincent reported, "Only the Marine Corps representative refused to dance around the unmentionable. On behalf of the only service which maintains gender-segregated basic training, Lieutenant General Paul Van Riper said: '. . . In gender-segregated recruit training, the strong positive role of the drill instructor provides impressionable young men and women appropriate role models without the distracting undercurrent of sexual attraction. In short, gender-segregated training provides an environment free from latent or overt sexual pressures.' No other service representative responded to General Van Riper's comment. For his breach of decorum he sat in silence for most of the remainder of the hearings, being asked no questions in two separate rounds of inquiry."

Part of the total denial syndrome is good, important, a feature of the military's attitude of accept your orders, no whining allowed, talk-about-what-you-want-to-achieve—no, what-you're-*going*-to-achieve, gosh darn it! People who've stayed in the "New Military" generally get with the program and decide that the order must be right. I once asked one of the *Stennis*'s chief petty officers how he thought gender integration was working on the carriers. "Just great," he said, beaming. "So what about subs?" I asked. "They may be next, right?" For a moment he looked very weary, his spine sagged, and his eyes looked inward. It lasted half a second; he recovered his poised-for-action stance, fixed me again with a gimlet gaze, and said evenly, "We can do anything we choose to do."

Modern social science, which has lately favored the view that perception and thus historical accounts can't be trusted, is a big help in the we-can-do-anything project. In 1977, for instance, when there were still generals and admirals who needed to be convinced of the need to integrate women, the DOD hired Martin Binkin, then at the Brookings Institution, and assigned Shirley Bach, a Navy officer, to study feasibility. Their report—"Uses of Women in the Military"—stated that "precious little is known about the effects of combining men and women" and dismissed problems like strength disparities by repeatedly using such phrases as "virtually no information is available," "evidence is far from conclusive," and "inadequately researched and poorly understood." The same stance was apparent at a conference held to discuss gender integration outside the United States when a representative for the Canadian military—which had been charged by its Human Rights Council to achieve "proportional representation" in its military, was asked about bonding issues and responded darkly, "We don't know about that yet. We're still studying it. We want to make sure we deal with what we know rather than what we"—here he shifted to a pointed, somewhat jeering tone—"*think* we know."

Overall, "the very presence of sexual desire and tension appears not to exist as a variable" for military leadership, but when it does, Vincent pointed out, there is an odd "institutionalized denial" of consensuality, "a refusal to recognize sexuality that exists outside the confines of abuse and harassment." In other words, the brass seem unable or unwilling to see sex as anything other than a thing that men (men are always the initiators) *initiate against* women in an attempt to weaken, dominate, degrade, and humiliate. In the last stages of the Tailhook investigations, for instance, one of the investigators remarked with surprise to author Jean Zimmerman that "if you read through the statements, you can find they described approximately fifty women who went through the gauntlet. . . . But [when the Navy started its Tailhook investigation] they weren't lined up coming in to report the assaults." He seemed unable to consider that women there enjoyed the gauntlet, and that women might invite the touch of men.

Once again, as at Tailhook, military leadership was content to see adult women, women who they also deemed ready to be soldiers, as passive, near-automatons who cooperate with their rape, even make elaborate preparations for it, because they are powerless to resist their instructors' will. ("I felt like a puppet . . ." one testified in court). Certainly there must never be even consensual sex between an instructor and a trainee, and Simpson deserved to be kicked out of the service, but given the testimony in the Aberdeen trials, the twenty-five-year sentence (albeit with parole) was only possible because the Army refused to admit the mitigating factor of adult female consent and participation.

It is difficult for the more thoughtful flag officers to live with such forms of justice, so many have coped with the gender-integration headaches of the nineties by clinging to the notion that training (the right kind, the right amount, combined with new technology) can right this listing ship.

We can see the training-as-panacea mind-set in a 1996 memo written by former army chief of staff Dennis J. Reimer.

"There is no doubt in my mind that the human aspect of change is the most difficult to manage," he writes in a veiled reference to the Aberdeen sex scandals. Nevertheless, he continues:

> I think you all know the game plan. We've introduced our chain teaching packet and we're making three points in that packet. First, I want everyone to know our definition of sexual

harassment. Secondly, I think it important that everyone know the proper conduct in case of sexual harassment. . . . We've reaffirmed our policy of zero tolerance for sexual harassment. Some say this is a goal that is impossible to achieve. I can't think of any other way to express our commitment to eradicating this cancer. . . . I look at the chain teaching packet as the first step in bringing this under control. We intend to follow up the chain teaching packet with a Consideration for Others program which will be introduced to TRADOC [Training and Doctrine Command] Commandants and Division Commanders at our conference in April. Our long-term sustainment program will be in the Character Development XXI training program to be introduced later this year. Basically, we intend to solve this problem the way we have solved other problems in the past: embed it in our doctrine and train to standards. Fundamentally, we have to reemphasize one of our core values—respect for others. We must treat soldiers, regardless of race or gender, with the dignity they deserve. . . . I think it important that we stress three rules. First we need to desexualize the environment. This is both a male and female responsibility. Things like flirting, posters on the wall, jody calls, etc., need to be looked at from the standpoint of "Are they offensive to others?" Our objective must be to create a team concept where soldiers are willing to die for each other, if necessary, not harass or abuse each other.

Training and Doctrine Command chief Gen. William Hartzog responded to the Aberdeen news in much the same way: "We're just about halfway through redoing the entire bevy of personal relations training that we use to put it in that form," he told reporters on May 28, 1997. "Is that going to be effective? Yeah, I think so."

In 1998, the skipper and executive officer of the destroyer *The Sullivans* (named in honor of five brothers killed in World War II while serving on the same ship) wrote an extraordinarily frank article—"A View from the Gender Fault Line"—for the Naval Institute's magazine *Proceedings*.

Many of their experiences with their recent gender-integrated crews had been excellent. However, they wrote,

The questions that should have been asked during the gender integration debates are: Are we mature enough as a society to have gender-integrated combatants? Do our young people have the self-discipline to serve together in a close, stressful environment without behaving in a way destined to have a profound impact on combat readiness? Our answer to the first question is no, not yet. To the second question it is frequently no.

Young American men and women often do not have the self-discipline or maturity to work together in this close environment without establishing unduly familiar and inappropriate relationships. . . . The amount of time, effort, and administrative elbow grease expended on these cases far outweighed their significance to the Navy.

What saved these men from exile to, say, the Navy's deck-swabbing corps was their conclusion asserting that "when command climate is established correctly, male and female sailors consider themselves shipmates first—the gender distinction tends to fade and the protection issue becomes moot." In other words, if we just keep tinkering . . .

Meanwhile, waiting for the right training blend to materialize, they comply with competing policies by swinging back and forth in what Army recruit Catherine Aspy called "a schizophrenic atmosphere":

On the one hand, they'd be telling us we have to treat each other exactly the same and there's no difference between us; on the other hand, they'd take all us girls apart and the drill sergeant would tell us stuff like "Don't lick your lips," "Don't look at a guy for very long," "Don't tell jokes so anybody can hear." There was this doublethink with women being BOTH excellent warriors, ready to kill the enemy, AND delicate wallflowers who will fall apart at a joke and had to have gender-normed grading and different PT tests with less push-ups. And so on down the barfy road.

"They tell us time and time again to work as a team," said Charlotte Eschbach, a nineteen-year-old at a gender-integrated camp at Fort Jackson, "but when they see us talking to guys, they get on our case for fraternizing. They don't even let us hold each other's feet when we do sit-ups."

In 1996, the Army sent investigators from its Inspector General's office to conduct "a special inspection of initial entry training equal opportunity sexual harassment policy and procedures." When the IG made its report in 1997, it noted various factors "that may cause recruits to be susceptible to sexual abuse or misconduct"—now acronymed as SA/SM.

The report mentioned that recruits might be less susceptible to SA/SM if the halls of their barracks weren't plunged into darkness every night at nine, and they recommended that bases "install night-lights in barracks hallways." On the other hand, a few paragraphs later, it noted that lights had been turned out in the first place because "many trainees' sleeping areas have had doors removed to help prevent SH [sexual harassment]/SM in the barracks" and bright lights in the hallways were keeping the kids awake.

The report noted that perhaps "adequate oversight in the barracks" might reduce "trainee-trainee consensual sex." On the other hand, it mused, "many units have removed their drill sergeants from the billets by 2100 (9 P.M.) to reduce the risk of cadre-trainee abuse. . . .

"[T]he chain of command believes that sexual activity between trainees is an area of indiscipline requiring constant attention," the report noted glumly.

On June 27, 1997, Secretary of Defense William S. Cohen announced the appointment of the Federal Advisory Committee on Gender-Integrated Training and Related Issues, an independent panel comprised of eleven private citizens and chaired by former senator Nancy Kassebaum Baker. Their goal: "To determine how best to train our gender-integrated, all-volunteer force to ensure that they are disciplined, effective and ready."

The report came back wrestling with the housing conflict:

> The committee observed that integrated housing is contributing to a higher rate of disciplinary problems. Both recruits and their trainers, consequently, are distracted from their training objectives, which must be accomplished in a short period of time in basic training. . . . Under the current gender-integrated basic training structure, the Army, Navy, and Air Force attempt to

house female recruits on separate floors or separate wings of barracks occupied by male recruits, though sometimes the separation between "wings" is nothing more than a piece of tacked-up Sheetrock. The reason for this policy is that basic training is an intense, 24-hour-a-day program of instruction. In order to achieve the goals, particularly of team-building, unit cohesion and discipline, the operational training units must remain together day and night. . . .

In the Army, for example, some drill sergeants complained about the inordinate amount of time spent investigating or disciplining male/female misconduct. The committee observed that the problem is exacerbated in mixed-gender housing units, particularly where male and female recruits live on the same floor. It is difficult for trainers in these units to know who should or should not be in the barracks. The committee recommends that female and male recruits be housed in separate barracks. . . . The committee has reviewed the layout and surge numbers at the training installations, and believes this change can be accomplished at marginal cost, if any.

The Kassebaum report was not a popular document; the services did not take up this recommendation and Secretary Cohen promptly commissioned another panel to restudy the situation. Still continuing its pattern of tacking back and forth, in May 1998, the Army launched the "safe and secure barracks program," and a sort of recruit's bill of rights guaranteeing that "each gender has an independent sleeping area; each gender has its own latrine; entrances to sleeping areas are locked at night or monitored by fire guards, door alarms installed, fire-safe barriers placed between the genders on the same floors." The intent: to "maintain to the maximum extent feasible company integrity within a barracks"—without encouraging SH, SA, or SM.

In spring 1999, ostensibly to increase "recruit safety" the Army added surveillance cameras to mixed-sex barracks. This is not Big Brother, Army reps pointed out, as the cameras would be trained only on hallways near entrances, not "in the latrine area," and it told recruits that they were now supposed to change clothes in a changing room adjacent to their bed area, instead of, say, on their bed or anywhere else where they might be startled by the entrance of someone of "the other gender."

Meanwhile, the services' war with SH seems to be helping neither unit cohesion nor company integrity. Fear of creating an appearance of the wrong kind of cohesion was so prevalent at Great Lakes Naval Training Base that a Navy trainee told the *New York Times* that "if a female recruit fell down in the snow in front of him, he would not help her until being granted permission by a commander." "They drum it into us—that sex doesn't matter, that that's just a sailor standing in front of you," a young private said in the same article.

All of this has created a pervasive condition called "fem fear," as Charlotte "Charlie" Crouch, then a Marine sergeant, wrote in an opinion piece for the *Navy Times*: "They get 'Sexual Responsibilities of the Male Marine' classes in boot camp, enough sexual harassment training to stifle Einstein, and annual sensitivity training on women in the workplace. It isn't as if they aren't trained in the textbook methods. So today if a Marine sees a woman, he crosses to the opposite side of the road to ensure she isn't offended because he invaded her space. If he has a woman in his unit, he's afraid to speak to her. . . . I think it's fair to say the atmosphere in today's corps is one of fem fear."

Fem fear hung over the *Stennis* like smog. I got the sense that something was a little "off" most vividly the first time I walked down the central passageway that runs from stern to bow. Unfailingly the men that streamed past me in the narrow tunnel-like passageway kept their eyes glued at about the level of my forehead, necks stiff and chins artificially high, as if they were wearing neck braces. Every time I approached a "kneeknocker" (the raised metal frame where a watertight hatch door locks into place) at the same time as a man, there was an awkward tango over correct protocol ("You first"; "No, it's OK, you were here first"; "Why don't you go first") and since there was a kneeknocker every fifty feet or thereabouts, this happened tiresomely often. The glazed-looking men were unfailingly polite, of course— "'Scuse me, ma'am"; "Morning, ma'am"—but always there was that peculiar Stepford Wife–like rigidity. "Robot eyes," I began to call this affliction.

Debra Maxey knew "robot eyes." "I know men on the ship who don't want to have anything to do with women, who don't want to talk to them because they're afraid that something's gonna happen and they're afraid of harassment charges. It's just there's such a scare tactic going on, they just think it's safest to stay away. The squadrons are told before they even get here not to have anything to do with women on the ship. 'Stay away from them totally. Professionally, yes, you gotta talk to them, talk as necessary, but other than that . . . don't.' We have sexual harassment training four times a year. They're afraid if anybody sees them or if you are offended by anything they do . . . they're busted. I know," she said, looking at me intently, "that Security is watching the couples on the ship; they're writing down their names when they see them together, how often they see them together." (Steve Gifford, legalman first class in the *Stennis*'s JAG office, confirmed that, yes, the ship had stepped up patrols because they'd been finding more people in nooks and crannies but said they weren't writing down names of people merely talking to each other.)

"I think [the command] needs to learn to lighten up on this because we're going to have to learn to work together unless we go back to an all-man ship. But I think men and women can work together if they're allowed to," Maxey said. "A lot of the people on the ship [of officer and senior enlisted rank] won't even allow a man and a woman to be in a room alone for fear of what they might do. If I was working in the main office and a guy walked in and was asking me questions, I would have to open the doors. It makes it harder to do your job."

Steve Miller, a twenty-three-year-old enlisted man, streaked with oil and dust from his shift hitching planes to the catapult, told me that "women are dangerous": "There's always somebody watching you, watching your eyes, and if you focus on some part of her body that's not her eyes, you could get in trouble for fraternizing. If you say the wrong thing, it could be sexual harassment. The girls know there's no fraternizing allowed, but they insist on wearing the tightest dungarees and flirting with you, but if someone looked at you [while this was going on], they would think you're the one who started it and you'd get in trouble. And nine times out of ten it's the guy who gets in trouble. They're trying to make it like all five thousand people are controlled like robots. It's not the way a ship is supposed to be. I'm just glad I'm married. I can't wait to get home."

Things got really confused under the last captain, who unequivocally announced that dating was forbidden but never clarified what "dating" was. As Narda Looney, a tall, carefully coiffed petty officer told the story, one day the captain made his policy a little bit clearer:

"The captain liked to rise early and jog around the Hangar Bay," Looney explained. "One morning he spied a guy and girl talking in a corner. He watched them for twenty-nine minutes as he jogged and when the clock hit the thirty, he decided that was it—a thirty-minute conversation is dating—and sent them to Captain's Mast."

There is an odd generational split over sex-in-the-ranks. The youngest ones who know no other way, the ones who have chosen the military as a job, for the college money, or, as one recruit put it, for "the job security," tend to shrug and wonder why their superiors are in such a tizzy. Young men and women who have followed a father into the services, who have an image of what "the military is supposed to be like," are outraged, as are most of the older generation, from lieutenant colonels in their forties up to the generals and admirals, the so-called dinosaurs of the "Old Military."

What is most intolerable to them is that it tends to create an environment that is just *so* unmilitary. The idea of men and women having sex on a military ship at sea or in tents mesmerized the press because there was so much incongruity. The military stood for rigidity, lines, pristine uniforms, snappy "Yes sir" 's, and brotherly comradery and that contrasted most oddly with the image of the havoc and buffoonish humor that comes with courting and sex. The let's-achieve-gender-parity project only got under way because the brass pinned their hopes on what the lower ranks call "Star Trek"—a vision of sleek button-pushers, quiet professionalism, and quiet control. There was some precedent for this; many officers have had much better, more professional experiences with, say, mixed-sex officer training school (OTS). But OTS is a relatively short period of time, and again, officers make up only about 30 percent of the military. They are the brains; enlisteds are the muscle. And to understand why officers and officers in training tend to act more professional—at least when they are just starting out—you have to understand that it's a bit like comparing graduate and undergraduate students. Graduate students are older; they've already proved that they have a fair amount of self-discipline by completing four years of college. Trained for the responsibility of leadership, they are usually more self-conscious, more aware that eyes are on them, and eager to live up to the role. Often they have already plotted out a military career, while often the eighteen-year-old enlisted kid signed up on a whim—because he got fired from one mall job and found the recruiter's booth just down the hall, or because he wants to save for college. There is a "disjuncture between female officers and female enlisted," observes sociologist Charles Moskos. After a long stint on an overseas Army base, he observed that "the same is true for male officers and enlisted, but not to the same degree. The two female groups had different career agendas and different attitudes toward their positions in the Army. Female officers often expressed resentment, sometimes even anger, at emerging career constraints within the military. Enlisted women saw their time in the Army as a stepping-stone from an unsatisfactory premilitary existence to a better postmilitary life."

Feminist attitudes, the idea that they are there to accomplish something larger than themselves, are common in the officer corps and nearly nil (except in the most superficial way) among enlisteds. Moskos has written, "Female officers tended to deemphasize physiological and emotional differences between men and women while enlisted women were much more likely to acknowledge distinctions between the sexes."

Of course, one uses a crude knife to make large general statements; there are always exceptions. There are, for instance, still many young men and women who sign up with a fervent desire to serve their country. Sometimes people with college educations end up in the enlisted corps for one reason or other. Still, overwhelming experience and the numbers bear out officer/enlisted generalizations.

Officer types—and that includes career NCOs—may be better at keeping their love life "to themselves," but the very young enlisteds are terrible at it, which is why the term *high school* keeps popping up when people talk about the "New Military." Way back in 1992, seaman Elizabeth Rugh said the newly integrated USS *Samuel Gompers* reminded her of "a big high school. You get every type you had in high school with the difference that we're living together. . . . People fall in love on the ship. . . . How do you control that?"

Brian Roou commanded a mixed-sex supply unit in Saudi Arabia during the Gulf War:

Our battalion came over in January. After being with this unit for a few days, I was absolutely astounded at all the little cliques that were formed—e.g., these two girls liked these two guys and they hung around together, but didn't like these other people; this female didn't want to work with that guy because they had gone out and broken up; that guy hated another guy because he had gotten in the pants of a female he liked, etc., etc. Point is, it was like a damn high school! I remember pulling up to a perimeter—not ours—at night, and there were three soldiers "guarding" the perimeter. They did not even notice me until I walked up to them, because the two guys both had their attentions fixed on a cute little female private.

The term kept popping up quite spontaneously on the *Stennis*. A twenty-four-year-old ordnance handler (the people who accompany the bombs and missiles up to the flight deck and then heft them off their cart and load them into aircraft), a married man from South Carolina with two children, sighed and said, "It's more like high school now than anything. There's always all this gossip, hearsay about who's going with who."

"That's it, really," agreed twenty-one-year-old Niki Smith from Memphis, the only woman in the ordnance handling unit. "If you put people of the opposite sex together with hormones raging, you're going to see people pairing off. It's hard on the men 'cause they're aren't enough women to go around." She'd never seen "a physical fight," but said, "There will be animosities among men over women," and she had seen "women getting into confrontations over the men. Even though there's so many, they'll both want the same one. Generally there's a few everybody wants."

Obviously, all the services are worried about the embarrassment and logistical headaches of pregnancy. In the early seventies, the penalty for getting pregnant was leaving the service. That harsh policy was phased out. But after the spate of mediagenic Love Boat incidents and the need to keep recruiting and retaining women, Navy Secretary John Dalton cooperated with the inevitable and launched a new, more family-friendly policy, one that normalized pregnancy by drawing it into the roster of day-to-day, unremarkable events. "Pregnancy and parent-hood are compatible with a naval career," Secretary of the Navy Dalton declared in 1995. "Pregnancy is a natural event that can occur in the lives of Navy servicewomen and is not a presumption of medical inca-pacity." The Army has followed suit, stating that "pregnancy does not normally adversely affect the career of a soldier." The problem with this policy was that it was a bit too female-friendly, and tremendous resent-ment soon developed over the fact that a woman who became pregnant was immediately shipped home from whatever hell tour she was on, had her baby, took her maternity leave on the payroll, and then often elected to take a voluntary discharge. In effect, you could sign up, dis-cover pregnancy soon after, have expenses paid for, and then leave.

Pregnancy was a big problem in the Gulf deployment. Again, men were resentful about the appearance of favoritism.

In a war college monograph, a Lt. Col. Donald E. Fowler, Jr., described his experiences deploying for the Gulf:

> The battalion, one quarter to one third female population, usually had five or six soldiers pregnant at any given time. After rumors of deployment circulated, the battalion's pregnant popu-lation jumped to twenty-six. Even once the battalion arrived in SWA [Southwest Asia], several soldiers tested positive for preg-nancy and had to be immediately returned to the rear detach-ment in Germany. . . . .

The Presidential Commission of 1992 asked DOD personnel department to pull out their numbers, and the commission found that women were four times less "deployable" than men because of preg-nancy. If you removed pregnancy numbers, women were actually more deployable than men—less prone to sports injuries, less prone to "dis-ciplinary problems."

Like someone with a burst appendix or any other malady that would send a soldier or sailor to a hospital, a woman who leaves a ship for pregnancy is, as Debra Maxey explains, "an unplanned loss and unplanned losses don't get replaced right away. It puts a strain on the rest of the crew because the men or whoever in that department have to pull the weight of that girl. They don't replace that girl because she's assumed to be out temporarily." Many military women, both enlisteds and officers, will tell you that a significant number of women use pregnancy that way. "When the going gets tough," says a popular slogan, "the tough get pregnant."

Don't men have ways of getting out as well? "Men have to go to more drastic measures; metaphorically they do have to shoot themselves in the foot," Maxey says. "But whatever they're going to do—act like they've gone crazy, for instance—is going to have a bigger impact on what they do after the services."

Some sound just like Cmdr. Stephen F. Davis, Jr., who said in a 1998 letter to the *Navy Times* that "pregnancy while assigned to sea duty is a problem. It happens more frequently than we would like, but not significantly more often than the loss of male sailors due to knee and back injuries on the basketball court or football field. It was, in retrospect, no more or no less a challenge than the myriad other challenges we faced in preparing the ship for prompt and sustained combat."

Others talk like Senior Chief Damage Controlman Suzanne Pike of the *Comstock*, an amphibious craft, who said, "When we deploy, females have a tendency to get pregnant and walk off the ship. It's still a constant battle."

Actually, both are right about pregnancy. By the numbers, pregnancy is not a huge problem; out of the total number of unplanned ship losses, pregnancy accounts for only 6 percent. Disciplinary problems account for 39 percent, and here men lead. On the other hand, according to the Center for Naval Analysis, which published the study "Women at Sea: Unplanned Losses and Accession Planning in 1999," "The rate of unplanned losses is 2.5 times greater for women than for men. . . . That is, a quarter of women and a tenth of men are lost from ships every year for unplanned reasons." Pregnancy makes up only 11 percent of the unplanned-loss rate for women; the other causes*— family care, medical, disciplinary, honorable discharge—fill out the rest. The rates of unplanned loss for both sexes has increased in recent years, but the gender ratio remains the same.

Of course, horror stories about pregnancies still abound: Navy

---

*My research assistant spent nearly three months making phone calls to naval public affairs trying to get figures for unplanned losses for those oft-cited other causes. By September 1999 (and the final due date for this manuscript), she had received many assurances that staffers were working on her request, but no figures.

ensign Ricky Cura told me he was on a carrier on its way to the Gulf (not a war-related cruise) and had to backtrack for the nearest shore because a pregnant woman had developed complications and they were too far out to remove her by helicopter.

A naval officer I interviewed was overseeing a crew of mechanics who tended F-14 fighter jets. The person who supervised the maintenance of the fighter jets' ejection seats was a single mother who got pregnant with a second out-of-wedlock child while on this officer's watch. She was an excellent mechanic, but because she was pregnant, she was no longer allowed to be around engines, and the officer wasn't allowed a replacement because pregnancy is classified as a "temporary disability." So, this most "critical billet" went unfilled while the young woman did paperwork in another department, and when the officer needed to make sure an ejection seat, the piece of equipment in a fighter plane that is most crucial to a pilot's survival, had been repaired properly, he had to call on "lesser qualified guys" in the unit or finagle some pro bono help from buddies at Miramar.

Pregnancy stats are flattened out somewhat by the fact that they cover all military women—including postmenopausal women and female officers, who have a low rate. Most of the pregnancies occur among junior enlisteds. "The rate of losses for E-1 to E-4 sailors is at least 2.5 times greater than for E-5 to E-9 sailors," reports the Center for Naval Analyses.

Whatever way you shake out the numbers, the real problem is this: Women at sea become unplanned losses at twice the rate as men. Also, pregnancy is not really "just like appendicitis." For most women it is more like the portal to a new life, a whole new developmental stage. And a lot of the time, pregnancy and children are the reason women leave the services. Unlike writing and teaching and design and consulting, a job in the military doesn't combine well with raising young children. As Ellen McKinnon, an A-10 jet pilot who left the services after she became pregnant with her first child, put it, "Yeah, I *could* have stayed in the Air Force, but I wouldn't have been doing either very well."

The services worry about pregnancy because they don't want temporary "unplanned losses"; they're also really worried about female attrition—women leaving the services for good. In 1994, the last year for which there are complete statistics, 34.4 percent of men in the

Marines left a first-term enlistment before it was over, compared to 46.1 percent of Marine women. In the Army, women also attrit at a higher rate, especially, for some reason, Caucasian women. Fifty-four percent of white women leave before their first enlistment is completed. Hispanic women come next: 36 percent do not finish. Black women stay the longest: 35 percent leave their first enlistment before the time is up. For black men the rate is 32 percent. (Not uncoincidentally, black women also file far fewer sexual harassment complaints. "Black women tend to be more savvy about dealing with men," explained University of Texas sociologist John Sibley Butler (who is black and coauthor with sociologist Charles Moskos on books about the military). "There is a tradition of being out there longer, of working around men. If a man makes a sexual comment they know how to shut him down. The black women [interviewed for Butler-Moskos surveys] generally felt the white women weren't as good at taking care of themselves.")

The people most likely to be unable to deploy—because of child-care problems—are single parents and, in the military just as in the civilian world, women tend more often to be single parents. News articles in the military press have cited single mothers who thanked the military for rescuing them from a probable life on welfare. I often theorize, though, in its rush to fill female quotas, the services are a little too ready to consummate an all-too-natural marriage—between a huge institution offering room, board, and cradle-to-grave benefits and financially vulnerable women looking for shelter from the storm. If the military does not make the demands on single parents that it needs to make on all of its soldiers (and often it makes too many excuses for single parents, male and female), it becomes something like welfare.

In fact, it needs less parenthood of any type. The military is creaking under the weight of its proliferating children, all entitled to day care and health care and schooling at on-base schools. (In 1993, a fed-up Gen. Carl Mundy, then commandant of the Marines Corps, signed an order requiring single Marines to get command permission to marry and barred new recruits who were married. He was forced to rescind the order.) Still, in the late nineties, the family-friendly military became so desperate for warm bodies that it was loath to seem discouraging in any way: "Women should not have to choose between their families and their [military] careers," Secretary of the Army Louis Caldera told a cheering DACOWITS audience in 1998, "and nobody should make these choices for them." Secretary of the Navy Richard Danzig recently said that the Navy "need[s] to be more accommodating to single mothers."

The other big reason that pregnancy remains "a huge problem," as one female Army medic puts it, is that, justly or not, the presence of pregnant women and the ways the services now accommodate them—"wellness classes" on the lawn of an Army base for pregnant or post-birth soldiers, maternity uniforms, and so on—is devastating morale like no other "New Military" fact of life. In 1998, Lt. Mark Smythe, who since this writing has left the Army, complained:

> I am a company executive officer in the Army. My supply room, which I run, is nicknamed by the male soldiers in my unit as the "Maternity Ward." This is extremely demoralizing for a young first lieutenant like myself. I entered the Army to be a warrior not a baby-sitter. Both of my 92Y (supply specialists) are female. Both are pregnant. . . . Neither of them can fulfill their duties (lifting supplies, driving military vehicles, conduct refueling operations, conduct maintenance on their vehicles). Instead, other males suffer, thereby working longer hours to pick up the slack and being forced to divert their attention from their assigned duties, thus reducing the entire readiness of the company.
>
> To compound my difficulties even further I cannot lobby to get replacement 92Ys who can do the job because they are being counted against my unit manning roster. In addition, they can only work eight-hour days, while the male soldiers work until the daily mission requirements are complete. Then, after the pregnancy, they receive maternity (recovery-time leave for sixty days, I believe).
>
> But, no, my problems are not solved yet: I have to allow them "bonding time" with their child. One of my accounting specialist 92As was breast-feeding her child. We made her come to the field with us and a flash message came over the command radio net

from our rear detachment sergeant in charge: "Private X needs to come in from the field. Her husband is complaining that the child is crying and will not go to sleep. Request her presence immediately to breast-feed the child." This, of course, was after the mandatory bonding-time requirement. Therefore, my commander said emphatically, "Negative, over. . . ." By order of our battalion commander we had to send her to the rear to fulfill her duties as a mother. Male soldiers felt resentment because they now had to pull an extra shift to pick up her slack. It also took away two hours of my first sergeant's night getting her to the rear when instead he could have been worrying about the perimeter security of my support area.

I entered the Army as a combat arms officer in the Armor Branch. I was then detailed to the Ordnance Corps, which I volunteered for during my officer assessment process. I envy my peers that I have left behind.

The military's gender problems are heightened by the fact that training, drilling, and commanding soldiers is a rough process. It needs to be—you are, after all, preparing a person to accept an order that could end his life. Hazing is much maligned these days, and now forbidden in the services, but it is a key part of that rough culture, and the services drive it out at their peril. Young men challenge each other. That's the way they are. They thrive on competition and that is useful for an army. Doing something like jamming metal wing pins into one another's naked chests is, among other things, a response to conditions of the battlefield. It's a way a unit tests its own strength, a way to identify weak links and to ensure that one's buddies can be trusted.

But when the new gender-integrated military tries to mimic the cold, spartan military discipline, it runs right up against the SH problem once again. As C. J. Chivers puts it: The "institutional intimidation" of military life can often appear to "kind of overlap with sexual harassment." There has always been an objectification in military life— that state modern women are trained to resist body and soul. But about three quarters of the military experience is all about objectification— about turning oneself into a faceless, identical soldier, part of what Air Force pilot Kelly Flynn called a "seamless unit," a gear in a mighty machine, a dark hangar filled with rows and rows and rows of men sitting on what appear to be shelves, numbered below them, like tools waiting to be taken down off a shelf, like chickens sitting passively in a darkened hatchery. There is no room for emotion in this process, no room for histrionics, no room for negotiation, no room for consensus; it is inexorable; it is the essence of war. Being a soldier is an inherently invasive process: The Army takes your life; it takes your body; it makes you its chattel. Paratroopers on a plane line up and shuffle toward the open door; the pace must move steadily and they must jump at precisely the second they are told to jump. A well-trained group of paratroopers looks, in fact, like a line of bottles on an assembly line, moving at nice, regularly spaced intervals, then off, off, off, into a bin. Nothing about this process takes notice of the individual; in times of war, "refusing" a jump, and therefore throwing off troop placement when the unit is reassembled on the ground, is a court-martialable offense.

Much of the way military elders have handled and spoken with their troops is an arrogant tone of ownership. "What are you little runts doing on MY bus!! If you're going to put your sad little asses on MY BUS, you follow MY RULES," roars the first drill instructor the new Marine recruit encounters when he gets off the bus at Parris Island. The Marines particularly—the service that has best retained the old traditions—still hew to the politically incorrect, invasive, concept of training as transformation. They even had a recruiting slogan about it: "The Marines build men—body, mind, spirit."

But when an older male commander grabs one of "his men" by the scruff of the neck, it has one meaning—fury, rough affection, everything mixed together. If he does the same to a young woman of eighteen or nineteen who is considerably shorter, and lighter, it feels like a different act. Suddenly it is freighted with meanings, none of them good, some abhorrent. When a man physically dominates a woman, there are connotations that are worrying to both the discipliner and the disciplinee.

Dress inspection, where the drill sergeant walks down the line of soldiers standing at attention, used to be a *demonstration* of the ownership and of the recruit's acceptance of his status as chattel. The drill sergeant would grab a belt buckle to see if the private had stenciled his name inside. He would yank a shirt that wasn't tucked into the pants properly. The same thing done to women becomes a kind of invasion, and the new obsession with "hands off" training policies coincides with the large influx of women trainees in the nineties.

No one feels the contradictions between military exigencies and the military's women policies more acutely than the country's drill sergeants. The drill sergeant is the biggest person in the recruit's life while he is in training, and today's DSs have a hell of a time finding the right degree of intimacy with their female charges—particularly at a time when the kinder, gentler military is exhorting instructors about the importance of "mentoring," and groups like DACOWITS are complaining that female soldiers don't get "mentored" enough to climb the career ladder. Says one active-duty command sergeant major who did not want to be identified:

> My first platoon as a drill sergeant was a female platoon. It's an understatement to say I was uncomfortable with that. A male drill sergeant instructing a male trainee how to prepare his wall locker right down to how he has to fold his underdrawers is a simple matter. It's not so simple for a male drill sergeant to explain to a female trainee how to fold her panties and to put the left bra cup inside the right when they are put in the drawer, but it has to be done. You see, learning to precisely follow instructions and pay attention to minute detail builds the foundation soldiers need to carry to the rest of their training and lives as soldiers.
>
> When a male drill sergeant walks into a male squad room or platoon bay, he doesn't have to send a point person in to make sure everyone is dressed. When a male trainee's load-bearing equipment needs an adjustment, the drill sergeant reaches out and makes it. He can't just reach out and touch a female trainee's anything. Counseling male trainees one-on-one in his office where their personal problems remain theirs and private is standard—not so for female trainees. He counsels them with a female trainee leader or a female drill sergeant if he's fortunate enough to have one around—with the door open. It's demeaning for her to share her personal problems with whoever passes by the door, but he cannot put himself in a potential career-losing, compromising situation. It's unfortunate, but male drill sergeants training females

spend as much time, or maybe more, thinking about protecting themselves as they do in developing and training soldiers.

So often well-meaning middle management end up between a rock and a hard place.

There was one event in the last decade in which the various strains of the conflict stand out particularly starkly. It involved a young woman named Elizabeth Saum, a cadet at the Air Force Academy, who ended up suing the Air Force for sexual harassment incurred in routine training—training that she said had destroyed her "education, career, and self-esteem."

Saum would have been a recruiter's prize in any era, not just in one with gender quotas. She was only five feet three, which might have made for problems down the road, but she was thin as a greyhound and athletic, and smart. To top it off, she was the daughter of a military man (a major predictor of success, the military has found), had a great high school record, and had been a champion of her school's swim team. When they got wind of this "Air Force brat" in their zone, the recruiters in her area went into overdrive. Saum was given the full-court press: told about the education package (the Air Force values it at about $250,000) and assured that normal application deadlines could be missed.

And thus was Cadet Saum set upon the military fast track—what probably would have become a pilot track. Planes didn't figure into the picture immediately, however, and Cadet Saum's academy days were relatively uneventful—until she was assigned to the SERE component of her training.

SERE stands for Survival, Evasion, Resistance and Escape and is designed to prepare a downed flier (or captured infantryman or sailor) to be a prisoner of war. Since being a prisoner of war is a painful, humiliating, scary experience, SERE training is painful, humiliating, and scary, too—it is a simulation, and the military constantly simulates training at all stages of a serviceman's career. The deal was that cadets were starved for days, screamed at by trainers playing enemy inter-rogators, paraded in front of other "prisoners" in humiliating and degrading ways, isolated in mock tiger cages, and if they were women, subjected to simulated rape.

Why would the military attempt such a potentially explosive simulation? In hindsight it must seem foolish, but rape is usually the fate of civilian women under the control of enemy soldiers. Most men have a deep, visceral reaction to the sight of a woman being tortured and can often be convinced to do the most extraordinary things to get her tormentors to stop, and there is a deeply held fear that female POWs could be used as a sort of lever to unhinge their male cohorts. When combat planes were opened to women, male servicemen started getting SERE training designed to "desensitize" them to the cries of female fellow POWs, so in addition to standard doses of starvation, isolation, filth, and battering noise, women got rape, or as the Air Force called it, "the rape scenario."

For Saum, the rape scenario meant being taken out to a field where two brawny trainers tossed her on the ground, knelt between her (still-trousered) legs, and hissed threats like "You want it, bitch? You're going to get it." They gave her a stick that they called her "masturbating stick," then locked her in an isolation shack with a sign reading, "The Bitch Likes to Be Beat." Except for these sexualized elements, the rest of Saum's SERE training was standard issue, gender neutrally miserable.

But after SERE training Saum began to unravel. She developed anorexia, and its attendant compulsion to purge the flesh with exercise. When her weight dropped below her already delicate one hundred pounds, she was put on medical leave. Sometime during that recuperation period she decided (or was convinced) that her trauma met the legal criteria for sexual harassment and she decided the commanders who had allowed it should be punished. Her suit for punitive and actual damages has been settled (for terms the Air Force will not disclose), but Saum has not returned to military life.

Saum's Air Force commanders claimed that they were just "trying to prepare people for a very difficult, very unpleasant, painful experience." Of course, it's possible that her young male trainers got too into their jobs; that they tapped sexually sadistic parts of themselves; that they used the scenario to say, in effect, "So you want to be a soldier, little girl?" that the "scenario" suddenly felt "too real" to Saum as she lay there on the field.

The bottom line here, what is most significant about the Saum case, is that once again—as at Aberdeen, as at Tailhook, as at so many places in the "New Military" era—military commanders found themselves coping with a public relations catastrophe and dodging charges that they "systematically" encourage a brutal, woman-hating culture. It found them reevaluating the way they train and the way they manage; it found them mired in confusion about how to go about this dicey gender-integration business, and, of course, this being the nineties, it found them litigating.

Part of the reason there have been so many sparks is that what we are actually attempting to do is create a "mixed monastery," something, historian Edward Luttwak points out, "even the Franciscans couldn't achieve."

This is a more natural comparison than it may seem at first. Both traditions use many of the same emotional dynamics to create bonding and instill discipline, and sex separation is a central ingredient in the creation of those dynamics. Discipline—mental and physical—and fervor are required to live outside regular society, to live a life of relative hardship and privation. In the military, as in the church, the life of renunciation—of hair, of clothing, of freedom, of sex (if only for temporary stretches)—was a reminder that you had set yourself apart, that you had been admitted to a special community, and that you had endured and earned the right to place yourself above ordinary folks who were too weak (morally and/or physically) to do what you do. Both the monk and the soldier (in his ideal state, anyway) choose a life of duty; both are fervent about a life of *service*—to God, country, freedom, the American way, democracy, whatever.

What the modern feel-good Army doesn't understand is the intense, near-erotic pleasures of service and privation if it is part of that service. If a system is founded around privation and it has been given *meaning*, there can be tremendous rewards: In an era of automation, central heating, sedentary jobs, and remote control, privation, challenge, pain, can become its own kind of tangible pleasure. (Why else are all those rich people paying thousands of dollars to do "extreme sports" or take tours of the Antarctic?) What the modern military has forgotten is that people crave a life of meaning, of struggle, of risk and deep sensation (which they often equate with a life of meaning)—not just bland comfort and limitless freedom. A world of polarities—hard, soft, right, wrong—is exciting, as Fay Weldon reminds us in her novel about a middle-aged woman assessing her youth in the androgynous, unjudgmental sixties. For the military recruit or new convert, search-ing, as youth so often is, for a new world, a new start, a new role to try on, the sheer physical starkness of military and monastical life was what set it apart—empty, undecorated halls; narrow pallets; long com-munal eating tables; unvarying uniforms—and was exactly what sig-naled, "This is a new place; we do things differently here." And, of course, a life of collective renunciation, of shared miseries, cements a group's bonds—"We few, we happy few, we band of brothers; / For he today that sheds his blood with me / Shall be my brother," were the words Shakespeare's King Henry V used to rally his troops in the hours before a battle.

Over centuries men have expressed their fears about, awe of, and vulnerability to the female sex with stories about consorting with women and losing strength. See Samson and Delilah, for instance, or the football coach who tells his team not to have sex the night before a game. The legends come out of the simple universal truth that men who are besotted are depleted and distracted—and weakened. Armies (here I use the word in a generic sense for any group of warriors—on ships, in planes, or pounding the ground) in combat, whether occupy-ing, invading, or defending, are fueled by the formidable energy of the young male—often amplified, as anthropologist Lionel Tiger points out, by the presence of other young males.

Over the centuries battles have been won because the normally self-ish and survival-oriented human animal has been convinced to "make the ultimate sacrifice." Told to take that hill or die trying (a hill! just a *hill*, mind you!), that normally selfish and self-protective human ani-mal has taken those hills, often dying in the effort, and hill by hill, pop-ulations have been saved. Virtually every person who's been in a battle or studied battle will tell you that this remarkable feat of leadership and service has been accomplished largely because of a phenomenon that military folk—lapsing into the dry, military techno-speak they prefer—call unit cohesion. Grizzled, veteran officers choke up when they talk about unit cohesion, because what they are really talking about is love—in its deepest, most selfless, Christ-washing-the-feet-of-the-lepers sense, love in which sex is irrelevant, love that means you are willing to die for another person. Unit cohesion refers to the deep love and protectiveness troops begin to feel for their unit mates, the feeling that "Goddamnit, I'm not going to run away now because I've got to back up John or Joe or Greg."

The problem is that male/female love tends to work differently from single-sex group bonding. The love that grows up between males and females does generally not exist in the platonic, selfless phase for long. It tends to be more selective, to be more exclusive. It tends to evolve far more quickly into pairing—and "pairing off" at that. In other words, once we have found "our mate," an I-got-you-babe/You-and-me-against-the-world/We-two-form-a-multitude mentality sets in. Men and women are hardwired to "cohere," all right, but it's a very different kind of cohesion.

Women in Infantry?

"Biology is not destiny, but it's good statistical probability."
—Lionel Tiger, author of *Men in Groups*

"A human being is not an animal."
—Capt. Rosemary Mariner, U.S. Navy (Ret.)

"You can't deny a woman who has killer instinct the
opportunity to tryto express it."
—Young male F-14 pilot giving a reporter his views on the
women-in-combat question, 1998

There is something James Bond–like about visiting the Army Research Institute of Environmental Medicine. You have to get to a nondescript little Massachusetts town called Natick, find a gravelly road that takes you to the top of a forested hill, present your bona fides to the soldier in the guardhouse, and follow his directions to what turns out to be a disappointingly ordinary compound of flat-topped, standard-issue, U.S. government buildings surrounded by pine trees.

One can only conclude that the bucolic appearance is part of a clever ploy to fool all those enemy planes on recon missions. This is, after all, one of the places where the military fine-tunes the American soldier—making him stronger, faster, more disease resistant, even happier, and so the world inside the compound turns out to be surreal in a mad scientist–ish kind of way. Fey, New Agey scientist-types in Reeboks and blue jeans pad around, mixing with uniformed military staff who also turn out to be on the more laid-back end of the military temperament scale. Experiments are always in progress: One day a typical specimen of U.S. GI, his skull pasted all over with electrodes, is pedaling on a stationary bike bolted to a mechanized platform above a large tank of water into which he is lowered at intervals.

You can go to the Climate Control Centers, to the Arctic Simulation Chamber, or the Tropical Simulator where more soldiers, fully loaded with gear, slog away on treadmills while being pelted with manufactured rain and humidity. You might take a peek through the port-hole-shaped windows of the Hypobaric Living Chamber to see how the human subjects locked within what looks like a fifties-style silver Airstream trailer are functioning under zero pressure.

For decades, the research done in centers like this—places like Walter Reed in Washington, D.C., or Armstrong Laboratory at Wright-Patterson Air Force Base—was all about the male soldier. Then 1994 arrived: Men and women started going through basic training side by side; women were assigned to fighter jet squadrons; and Representative Patricia Schroeder shepherded a bill through Congress that created the Defense Women's Health Research Program (DWHRP), which was empowered to spend $40 million a year building a bigger, stronger, more disease-resistant female soldier.

When I visited in 1995, there were many DWHRP-funded studies under way at "Natick Labs," as it is nicknamed, and the civilian scientists, even the military researchers, seemed fairly oblivious to the political context of their work. They weren't troubled by questions like whether it "was a problem" to ask women to assume what were now called "male norms" when they joined the military. This, after all, was that stratum of humanity called "scientist," imbued with a temperament as well as a calling. Scientists have a greater gift for single focus. The new research subject matter was thus only another blob of protoplasm whose concrete qualities had to be explored and documented. They approached the loaded subject of women and war with their usual childlike clarity. They had been given problems and were simply burrowing toward a solution. In such a politicized world, at the top of their hill, surrounded by pine forest, they seemed strangely untouched. It was grounding to come here, after the antimatter world of Congress and official offices. The characteristics of physical reality—for the hard sciences are all about what is demonstrable—were respected currency here.

At that point, the first time such a large amount of research on the female soldier had been attempted, research could go in a number of ways: toward converting the woman to her new world, or changing the world itself to be more welcoming to her. There was a lot to do if one was going to change the environment. A DWHRP-authored "Profile of Military Women" stated that "women face all the challenges men do along with clothing, equipment, even rations that, more often than not, were designed for and tested almost exclusively on men. . . . Equipment such as backpacks, tools, helicopter cockpit displays/controls and protective gear for biological warfare agents which are not easily amenable to the statures and physical attributes of women may pose serious safety hazards and warrant further study." The DWHRP required that the proposed studies be unique to women and that they tackle a significant problem documented in previous research.

This seemed pretty great! All along media and legislators had seemed to have this odd habit of not looking below the neck (in so many ways). Maybe because civilians are increasingly disconnected from the concrete details of soldiering, there was little in the media or from the legislators that recognized what I called the squish factor— some recognition that impediments to full integration did not come from attitudes alone. A lot of the problems had to do with the fact that we were dropping a softer, weaker, shorter, lighter-boned creature into a world scaled for the male body. When butts drop onto seats, and feet grope for foot pedals, and girls of five feet one (not an uncommon height in the ranks) put on great bowl-like Kevlar helmets over a full head of long hair done up in a French braid, there are problems of fit— and those picayune fit problems ripple outward, eventually affecting performance, morale, and readiness.

The problem was that the approved model for gender integration was the military's experience with racial integration. But racial integration, which took the military about a century to achieve (quite successfully in the end), involved differences that are only skin deep. An effective fighting force in the field depends on a steady supply of known quantities; it needs "units" made up of interchangeable elements called soldiers, and once one got over skin color, racial integration was still about integrating the same body. Men certainly have their physical idiosyncrasies, but military equipment and tasks have had centuries to adapt to those bodies. Basic sex differences that are masked by technology in the civilian world stand out in high relief in the elemental, physical-labor-intensive world of the soldier.

The average woman is about five inches shorter than the average man, she has 55 to 60 percent less upper body strength, a lower center of gravity, a higher fat-to-muscle ratio, lighter bones that are more subject to fracture, a heart that can't move oxygen to the muscles as fast as a man's (i.e., 20 percent less aerobic capacity), and a rather more complicated lower abdomen full of reproductive equipment.

The female triathletes, marathoners, and swim team captains tend to gravitate to or get scooped up by the officer corps. Athleticism is often part of the officer "syndrome"—the cluster of characteristics that includes a competitive nature, a love of physical challenge and the outdoors, the preference for the company of men and men's harder ways. Feminist lobbyists tried to downplay structural sex differences (a typical argument was that women were weaker physically because they grew up in a culture that didn't encourage them to be physically active and "go out for sports" like boys). But in part, because the military had virtually abandoned stringent entrance and general fitness standards in the nineties, and, aside from preexisting structural differences, one did find a particularly female body in the enlisted corps—round, soft, bottom-heavy, and a center of gravity that is already low (centered around the abdomen) made even lower because of excess body fat. The boys often had a head start because of jobs in construction or loading, and because they played more after-school sports. It was not unusual for enlisted women to say that they'd "never been really physical" or "never exercised much," but by the late nineties, when recruiters nationwide were averaging one recruit a month, one began to see an increase in heavier, softer, unathletic young men as well.

In 1995, the second year of DWHRP largesse, all the female soldier's nooks and crannies were being probed. Studies under way included "Evaluation of the Performance Impact and Treatment of Exercise-Induced Urinary Incontinence among Female Soldiers"— spurred by pilot research indicating that 12 percent of women in Airborne School (parachute jump training) drop out because of incontinence developed during the program; "The Effect of Menstrual Cycle Phase on Physical Work Performance during Exposure to High Terrestrial Altitude"; "The Effects of Inadvertent Exposure of

Mefloquine Chemprophylaxis on Pregnancy Outcomes and Infants of U.S. Army Servicewomen Returning from Somalia"; "Vulnerability of Female Produced Speech in Operational Environments"; "Protocol for the Identification of Reproductive Toxins Which May Affect Servicewomen." There was even a study titled "Lady J and Freshette Complete System: A Field Trial for the Active Duty Woman," based on research that showed that women were prone to urinary infections and/or dehydration because they were reluctant to urinate in the field. (Some would not drink enough water so they wouldn't have to face the embarrassing problem.) The "Lady J" study was an attempt to find a way to allow women to relieve themselves standing up. Ironically, when Newt Gingrich made his infamous statement about "females who [would] have biological problems staying in a ditch for thirty days because they get infections" as compared to men ("little piglets") who can be dropped in a ditch and just "roll around in it," he was reacting to a study he'd just seen about the high incidence of urinary infection among women soldiers in the field.

You would think that the side of the press that had adored "the Love Boat" and the "Coed Army" would have had a ball with the "Freshette Complete System," but, no, they made hardly a peep and the funnel-like device never became a standard piece of field gear.

One study, however, did ignite press interest. Civilian physiologist Everett Harman never expected that "Effects of a Specifically Designed Physical Conditioning Program on the Load Carriage and Lifting Performance of Female Soldiers," an "experiment [involving] the most intense, extended, and specifically designed resistance training program ever carried out for the purpose of improving heavy work performance of women," would generate calls from news outlets around the world.

Harman, a Natick labs staffer, proposed a sixteen-week physical training program, using women between eighteen and thirty-five who met "the normal physical requirements for entry into the Army, including the height/weight standards." A 1997 study reported that women had two—in one study three—times the rate of overall injury and twice the incidence of stress fractures in military training environments. The Natick scientists said that, with the increase in women soldiers, reports were beginning to pour in from the field about new recruits who simply could not handle the physical demands of their

jobs and needed help to complete tasks like loading a truck and changing a tire. When one asked the scientists what motivated the many
studies on women and strength, the scientists would respond in their
guileless, stark, and precise way with answers like "The problem is the
women; they can't do their jobs because they don't have the upper
body strength." Of course, they didn't mean all women or all jobs, but
they were the problem fixers and this was the problem that had been
presented. Part of "the problem," they explained, was that many of the
MOSs that required heavy lifting were also the ones that came with a
signing bonus, and no recruiter would dare discourage a woman from
selecting one of these MOSs, or any MOS for that matter.

Why was the press so fascinated with something as dull-sounding as
"Effects of a Specifically Designed Physical Conditioning Program . . ."?
The TV producers were probably interested because this study had
better visual potential than, say, the experiment on urine retention. With
the strength study you could have that always-desirable mix of sex and
high-mindedness—young women running in shorts in an experiment
to destroy the myth (as some scriptwriter would be sure to put it) that
they are "the weaker sex." But print media loved the story as well.
Some news outlets worked the woman-as-hero-in-a-sexist-world angle;
the more conservative publications went for "Scary": women trying to
become men, modern science paired with government to turn women
into men (see Communist-bloc swimmers pumped up on government-
supplied steroids), the march of androgyny, and so on.

"U.S. Army Builds Female Rambos," cried a German newspaper,
with a photo of Linda Hamilton muscled-up for her role in *Terminator 2*.
"U.S. Army Is Creating the Bionic Woman in a Lab and Pump[ing]
40 Civilian Women Up to Man-Size Proportions!" it continued in a
subhead.

Under the headline "Why Can't a Woman Be More Like a Man,"
the *Washington Times* accused the Army of trying to "turn the average
woman into the average man—strengthwise." *Heterodoxy*, a California-
based magazine founded by student-radical-turned-conservative David
Horowitz, accused the Army of wanting to "trump nature and create
the female cyborg soldier."

Harman, a most unideological kind of head-buried-in-a-book guy,
said he was merely addressing problems that TRADOC was concerned about. In his initial research proposal Harman wrote that

TRADOC had "indicated that many soldiers are not physically capable of meeting the demands of their military occupational specialties (MOSs)." "Unfortunately," Harman continued, "women fall disproportionately into this category." In 1982–83, tests given to 970 graduates of advanced soldier skill training showed that, while all men in heavy lifting MOSs qualified for their jobs, fewer than 15 percent of females qualified. Yet many women currently serve in "very heavy" and "heavy" MOSs, including Food Service Specialist, Motor Transport Operator, and Unit Supply Specialist. Not surprisingly, "attrition of women in [those] MOSs is high." Harman also noted that "retraining and reassigning a soldier [who has been assigned to the wrong job] has been estimated to cost about $16,000."

The physiologist proposed to take eighty Army women and train them for sixty to ninety minutes a day, five days a week, for fourteen weeks, to "determine if women can be trained to perform heavy work tasks typically performed by men." Training would include a weekly run of two and a half miles with a pack that would get heavier over the weeks so that the subjects would end up being able to run with an eighty-pound rucksack—a standard weight for a pack loaded with necessities for the field.

Reporters began to call immediately after the study was announced. But the Army press division, whose job it is to get film crews out to film promising developments, suddenly balked—perhaps they were reluctant to have anything to do with a study that could develop a politically incorrect spin; perhaps they were afraid of visuals they could not stage-manage. What if the women dropped out or didn't improve? (How long, for instance, did the infamous videotape of female firefighters attempting to climb over an obstacle-course-type wall circulate around television stations?) Army public affairs put Harman's project on hold. When CNN anchors asked a spokesman about the study on air, they were told it was "being reevaluated."

"The Pentagon is extremely sensitive," Harman said, "and I told them I don't think that's a good attitude. If they're doing something, they should be able to defend it rather than go into the shell. But they shut us completely off; we weren't allowed to talk to the press for several months and they almost cut the study." After weeks of limbo, Harman and the Olympic-trial-qualified decathlete who was going to work with the women *did* go ahead with a study, but it was smaller than they'd hoped. They got roughly half of everything they'd requested: half the funds, half the human subjects, half the time. Lack of money dictated that they could not use military women (because it would be too costly to fly them to Natick and put them up), so Harman had to advertise (using an inducement of $500 upon study completion) for civilian volunteers who were within the age, height, and weight limits the Army sets for its recruits.

Once the female test subjects got used to their daily ninety-minute strength-training workouts, they and the training staff were champing to show their stuff on outlets like NBC's *Dateline*—one of the shows that had requested a visit.

Still, the Army continued its no-visiting-reporters policy. Finally, two more harmless-seeming print reporters were allowed to "observe"; a young woman from the local *Middlesex News*—who actually went through the whole cycle as a trainee to supply personal dispatches for her paper and me, and then only for the last day of the experiment when the girls were cleaning out their lockers and saying their good-byes.

So what mysterious activities was the blackout shielding? When finally admitted to the cyborg sanctum, I found friendly, not strikingly muscular young women from all walks of life—waitresses, beauticians, bartenders, teachers, a landscape architect. Most had joined not out of any passionate feminist sentiment, but, as one put it, because going through the program "was cheaper than a health club."

And they had gotten what they were looking for. All of the volunteers lost about six pounds of fat and gained two pounds of muscle. They increased their speed running with a rucksack by 33 percent. Chest circumferences increased an average of 12 percent because of new muscle. At the beginning of the study only 24 percent could lift a hundred pounds; at the end, 78 percent could. They were, in other words, now as strong as the army's weakest males.

The press responded approvingly, with headlines like "Army Study: Women Can Pull Weight in Combat" and lead paragraphs such as "G.I. Jill, get ready to take a load off G.I. Joe."

Apparently, however, the Army didn't think Harman's research was a solution to their problems in the field. His next grant proposal—suggesting further research on remedial strength training for women—was turned down. Harman still works at Natick Labs, but has since moved on to gender-neutral subjects like making a better sole for Army boots and designing a lighter rucksack. The Modular Light-weight Load Carrying Equipment (MOLLE), made to eventually replace the old-standard All Purpose Lightweight Individual Carrying Equipment (ALICE), is a recent project of Harman's gang at Natick Labs.

Harman said he thought his idea had fallen out of favor "because a couple of key women in positions of power nixed the funding. At the highest level they feel that we would be doing more service if we light-ened all jobs rather than trying to say that they can get stronger. . . . I think they feel that if we show that women can get stronger, then the onus would be on the women to get stronger, but [their opinion is that] the jobs should be made easier."

Harman doubted that many jobs could be made much easier, espe-cially in a downsizing military that would eventually find great "sav-ings" in the R&D area. "A shell casing is always gonna weigh ninety pounds; there's nothing we can do about that," he grumbled as he walked around the project's warehouse-turned-gymnasium.

Some branches would find it easier. The Air Force, for instance, which has tended to boast that it is the most female-friendly of the ser-vices, was claiming great success in this area. But, Harman explained,

> in the Air Force it's easier to automate. Let's say you have a plane sitting on the runway and you have to load it with supplies, bombs, whatever. You can have machines that you drive out there, that raise the stuff on a little elevator, but when you're out in the woods and the fields, a lot's done by hand. Most Army jobs are in the "heavy" and "very heavy" category. "Heavy" means you have to lift between eighty and a hundred pounds occasionally. For "very heavy" the weight is one hundred pounds. Whether you're a mechanic, in the infantry, if you're changing a tire on a truck, even in the kitchen, where you have to pick up big pots, it's a major technological challenge to make a piece of equipment lighter. You're talking about reengineering the whole thing; there are certain jobs, for instance, where you have to carry a toolbox

that might weigh a few hundred pounds and put it up on the wing of a plane. . . .

Three years later, when I called Natick to check on some things that had been said, the sense of islandlike insulation seemed to have disappeared. People who'd chatted quite comfortably now sounded frightened; their voices were tight and distant, they answered with yeses or nos only, there were long tense pauses, and when asked about specific conversations, they denied having them and suddenly remembered an urgent appointment requiring their immediate attention somewhere else in the compound.

It was sad to see this politics-free zone fall under the bulldozers. The pursuit for a remedy for the strength mismatch problem had been a twenty-year crusade for scientists at Natick and at military research centers around the country, and their proposed remedy was developing skill tests for every Army MOS. In other words, if you wanted to be a tank crewman, the guy who drops seventy-pound shells out of the turret onto the ammunition rack every three minutes, you'd take a test simulating the demands of the job at its peak and if you couldn't pass it, you couldn't get the job.

Dr. James Vogel, head of the occupational health and performance directorate at the Research Institute of Environmental Medicine at Natick, was there from the beginning, at the helm of each of the three proposals the scientific community made to the Pentagon in a span of about fifteen years.

The first time around, he recalled, they were nudged into action by a 1973 study by the GAO that stated that "a large number" of women in the military "were assigned to specialties that were too physically demanding." Accordingly, scientists at Natick and other research centers began dissecting MOSs, asking how much strength was required at periods of peak demand and for how long. "That didn't go anywhere," Vogel says. ". . . There were a number of problems. There was a concern that if standards were imposed, too many women would be prevented from filling jobs that they were really needed for, as far as quotas, to meet accession and recruitment standards."

Two years later, essentially the same complaint came from another entity, and a military department at that, not outside auditors like the

GAO. The project was revived. Vogel and others categorized all Army jobs as light, heavy, or very heavy, and then devised standard physical requirements—expressed as low, medium, high—with which to separate applicants for a particular MOS. They then conducted preliminary tests to see if soldiers in the field, already out there in assigned jobs, were matched with an appropriate MOS.

"The results," as the *Army Times* put it, "did not bode well for women." "While most men exceeded the high and medium standards for aerobic capacity," the paper reported, "no woman met the high standard and very few the medium. In other words, by the proposed test's standards, all of the men were qualified for their jobs in heavy-lifting specialties but fewer than 15 percent of the women."

Sounds of protest began to emanate from Congress. A member of DACOWITS charged, for instance, that there were "inherent biases in such a standard." "The Army is a male-oriented institution and officials are resistant to changes that will allow women to be fully utilized," she said. "Those [strength] standards reeked of that resistance."

Uncertain of what to do with this controversial issue, the Army turned the data over to a panel calling itself Women in the Army Policy Review Group. It studied the test dilemma and decided to hand the hot potato off, not to basic training camps where trainees request and are assigned to an MOS, but to recruiting centers, who were then supposed to use the test as a way to assess upper body strength in incoming recruits and recommend an appropriate MOS. The test got an official name—the Military Enlistment Physical Strength Capacity Test—and an official acronym: MEPSCAT. Still, the MEPSCAT could not seem to work its way into the hearts of Army bureaucrats, and officials at the Training Command began referring to MEPSCAT as merely an optional "counseling tool." By 1990, the test (even with that zippy acronym for a name) had disappeared altogether.

In 1995, "TRADOC again asked us to revive our work," Vogel remembered. A Maj. Gen. Carl Ernst (TRADOC's deputy chief of staff for training) had come back from field duty and had seen first-hand what he had begun to get reports about: A lot of women and some men had been put in jobs they didn't have the muscles to handle, and he felt it reduced unit effectiveness.

The *Army Times* got wind of the effort to resurrect strength standards, and ran a cover story headlined "New Strength Standards

Could Cost You a Job!" with a lead paragraph that warned: "The Army is quietly working on a project to establish physical requirement standards for every enlisted specialty. . . . Once in place, the new standards could bar female soldiers from some combat-support jobs, many of which have only recently been opened to women."

For a third time, the idea of testing soldiers to see if they could qualify for the job to which they'd been assigned was dropped. Vogel's last postmortem was essentially the same as the first two: "I have a feeling that when TRADOC and the personnel people at the Pentagon began to really look at the numbers, they were also concerned—theoretically they wanted to do this—because they didn't know how to cope with the results," Vogel continued, "and by that I mean preventing a significant number of women from taking the most demanding kinds of jobs and how they would fill those, because in '95— and it has continued—recruiting is a big problem. . . . When we were asked to do the research, we saw it rather purely as a physiological situation matching a person's capability with what the job demands. That was pretty straightforward, but then you go to implement it and it gets pretty messy."

The upshot is that throughout the nineties the Army was beset with strength-related problems—starting in boot camp, continuing in advanced individual training (AIT), and on at duty stations. A study of the rate of stress fractures in women recruits in Army boot camp, commissioned by DOD and executed by the Institute of Medicine, a subdivision of the National Academy of Sciences, published data showing that women got stress fractures at more than twice the rate of men and that the kinds of fractures they got—in the upper leg and pelvis—heal more slowly than those of the lower leg more common to men. Their report said that "both men and women will benefit and have a lower incidence of stress fractures if they are required to meet an appropriate level of fitness before entering basic training."

"I worked at the VA during the eighties, when women had to do most of what the men had to do," one older soldier told the readers of David Hackworth's on-line newsletter, "The Voice of the Grunt."

My position on where, when and how women serve in the military is this: Either do the job as it was designed or get the hell out. Cornered, women could be some bad-ass fighters, but they

don't have the physical build to haul all that crap around. I executed many claims for women who were chaptered out of the
Army because physical evaluation boards said they were too
injured to do their jobs. I recollect that almost 80 percent of the
injuries were lower extremity damage, broken or cracked fibula
or tibia bones, stress cracks, etc. Many, many claims for foot
injuries too. That told me that women don't have the LEGS to
do what soldiers do, haul ass over hilltops, diddy thru jungles,
carrying ammo and radios, and shooting the shit out of pursuers.

Studies on strength continued: Another Army research division
reported in 1997 that "females [in advanced training—that is, those
who have completed boot camp] accounted for more than half of all
cases [of stress fracture]. The hospitalization rate among females was
more than tenfold than among males. The rate among white, nonhis-
panic, junior enlisted female soldiers was more than 15 times higher
than that of the Army overall." (This may help explain the strikingly
higher rate of attrition among white women.) Another study indicated
that women's rate of injury dropped if their AIT immediately followed
BCT, which suggests that training can help. The injury rate of men
stayed about the same—in BCT, if AIT followed BCT, and even if
there was a year off between AIT and BCT—which seems to confirm
that today's boot camp is a challenge for many women but not for most
men.

Since remedial strength training to keep up with "Old Army" pace
and rigor appears to be out, gender-integrated boot camps (other than
those like Fort Benning, which ready all-male classes for the combat
arms) have handled the injury threat by gender-norming skill tests (by
allowing women to pass with a lower grade). They've created dual
obstacle courses, the easier one for the women, and many have shifted
emphasis to more cerebral skills like map-reading, first aid, and
putting on protective gear.

Many official regulations describing standard tasks have been rewrit-
ten to compensate for weaker soldiers and to avoid the spectacle of
female failure—a woman attempting to do a task the way it is described
in a training manual and failing. Take stretcher carrying: Evacuating a
wounded sailor from a deck and carrying him or her to a safer area

means putting that sailor (weight range approximately 130 to 180 pounds) on a standard-issue stretcher (30 pounds) and carrying him or her across decks the size of football fields and up spindly metal ladders. Faced with the influx of female recruits, the task of stretcher carrying has quietly "evolved," as a doctor testifying before the Presidential Commission put it, from a task that is expected to be performed by two people into a task that is generally performed by "teams" of four, five, or "however many it takes to get the job done." The problem is, a mob of people can't carry a stretcher up a ship's ladder together; eventually those and the narrow passageways on ships will force you back to the one-at-the-head/one-at-the-tail configuration.

Getting around strength discrepancies is mostly what's behind the "New Military"'s new romance with the concept of teamwork. Teamwork is one way to avoid daily comparisons of male and female physical abilities. Why do we need each person to be strong, the "New Military" argues, when teams of men and women, or women and women, can accomplish anything two fit men used to do? But as ex–Air Force lieutenant Karen Dahlby can report, the more-the-merrier tactic doesn't always work. On one base:

> we had a generator, but we didn't have the right equipment to put it into place [to lift it to the level of the plane's engine]. We did have a couple of weight-lifter guys who were able to get it up there. If you go by the Air Force standards about how many people are supposed to lift a thing, we couldn't have gotten that many people around a generator. It's a small hunk of pretty hard metal. If you don't have the equipment, you just need some pretty strong people to lift it.

With this new enthusiasm about doing everything in teams, one often sees a flock of trainees clustered around a stretcher, with several just sort of touching the frame in a token way, as if they're trying to communicate team solidarity.

A unit's morale begins to crumble when there are too many soldiers (and in the past they have usually been junior enlisted females) who can't pull their weight. One officer talked about his experience in Saudi Arabia during the Gulf War:

When we set up tents in our units, women simply could not lift some of the poles. Officers will lend a hand and jump in to do whatever's needed to get a mission done, but when we had to jump in there and do it because they physically weren't able, then it takes away from your planning and whatever you have to do. An example of that is this lieutenant and I had four females who worked for us in the desert. They had their own separate tent, and we had our own tent. We were called to get out of there pretty quickly and they simply couldn't lift this tent, when it was broken down, onto the back of a truck. So the lieutenant and I told them to just step aside and we lifted it and threw it on the truck. Here was an example of two guys who didn't have any problem lifting, and four females who were basically trying to drag it along the ground and struggling to get it up on the truck.

During the Gulf War, Army captain Mary Roou, then twenty-five, had to cope with trucks full of boxes of medical supplies that had to be unloaded, parceled out to places in the field, and then loaded back on trucks again. Since it had to be done fast, she usually tried to find one of the men in the unit she ran. "I'd obviously want the males because they could pick up the boxes and carry more, load trucks better," Roou says.

Women could lift the boxes, but there's no way they're going to lift as many boxes as a guy, as fast. I don't think I'd want my daughter to be an infantry soldier; I'm not saying she couldn't do it, but I think there's a natural tendency for other soldiers—I guess by that I mean men—to take care of them, to stop what they're doing and make sure you're okay. And there's no way that women can dig foxholes or as many as may be required, as men. There's no way! Unless you had that one woman that maybe is different, you know, lifts three hundred pounds, it just doesn't happen. Unfortunately, when you're in basic training and stuff like that, those foxholes are already dug.

The strength/job mismatch adds a kind of "gender mathematics" to the chore of assigning soldiers. As one Army CO put it, "You need somebody to drive a truck and then you gotta think, 'Wait, I can't use so-and-so, because if it gets a flat, she won't be able to change the seventy-pound tires."

Another matter of simmering resentment is the softer PT and weight standards. Every soldier has to take a PT test every year. They get another chance if they fail, and then another, but failing three times puts you in separation country. There is much back and forth about the need for PT tests. One side in the debate argues that they are supposed to ensure a certain basic level of fitness and competency, something that armies or squadrons or ships' crews should have to inspire confidence. The resentment over PT standards comes out of the fact that a perfect score on your twice-yearly PT adds points counting toward promotion and men get mad because it seems that women have a head start. "The physical standards are insanely higher for men," says Army captain Jalesia Griffin, an army captain who left the service in the fall of 1999 to start law school.

For example, for the eighteen to twenty-one age group, women only have to do eighteen push-ups; men have to do forty-two—that's a big, big difference. So it's like when you enter the military as a woman, you almost have to overcompensate and prove yourself because the system is not set up for you to have that respect when you come in. People look at you and say, "What are you doing here?" because you have to meet different standards than they do, and the Army's very physical. So when I first came in—I can do about fifty to sixty push-ups—but I wasn't like that always; it just takes practice. It's just that women accept the lower standard because that's all they have to do, and it does a disservice to women in general, but it's in everything—it's in every aspect of the military—women are given special treatment because they're women and I think that's crazy.

Weight standards are also required to ensure that soldiers look soldierly. And that's not a superficial concern. The most basic form of intelligence gathering is simply eyeballing soldiers on the other side of the barricades—do they look fat and out-of-shape, thin and worn-out, has the enemy been forced to draft boys of twelve or men of sixty? Whole tides of battle have shifted because a new force entered and simply looked more intimidating than everybody else on the board.

But over the last decade, with a military that started the decade fighting to meet its gender quotas and acutely conscious that if women dropped out en masse, they might be accused of misogyny, women's weight standards have inched upward. What happens, of course, is if one group is allowed to slip, everybody else starts hollering, "Why not me, too?" Thus we've ended up with a military force with a big weight problem. (By the end of the nineties, the services were trying to hang on to every body they could—male or female.)

Griffin had two overweight soldiers in her command, one a man, one a woman, both very overweight, both failing their PT tests. She wanted both of them out, but Griffin's commander decided to attribute the overweight woman's weight gain to pregnancy, thereby keeping her in the service. "I went in and argued with them and said, 'Look, he doesn't have that option; it just seems unfair.' People are so on edge with women that they will just let them do what they want to do. I think if the Army is going to have a standard, then it has to be an equal standard," says Griffin.

Unequal fitness standards have been causing morale trouble for years. Fitness grades become part of one's personnel file and they are considered at promotion time. Obviously, it looks good in your personnel file if you continually "max" your PT test, but with female scoring significantly dumbed down, men complain about having to work much harder for something many women can now accomplish easily.

And it's not just men that get mad: "My fifty-one-year-old command sergeant major father has to run faster and do more push-ups than I do to max/pass the APFT [annual personal fitness test]," Capt. Maryann D'Alessandro-Belanger wrote in the *Army Times.* "As a thirty-two-year-old female I will continue to max my APFT, but it is very discouraging to see that the lame female in my age group still is allowed to virtually walk the two-mile run and still pass the test."

After many letters of this sort, in 1999, the Army announced with much fanfare that it was going to make the female PT tougher. Once more, this third-rail (i.e., "gender-related") topic became an occasion for bureaucratic delays, cryptic official statements, and a long, long wait as promised deadlines for the tougher standards passed. Finally, the new PT tests were unveiled . . . and they weren't much different from the old standards.

"The new standard to me is moving toward equality. I won't say it was too easy for women, but I will say there was a very large gap between what men and women of the same age were expected to do," Spec. Richard South hesitantly told the *Army Times*. The *Army Times* posted two charts, the new compared with the old, and the only category that had gotten harder was sit-ups, an exercise that has always been easier for women because of their different center of gravity. In many categories, "maxing" had actually gotten easier. The number of push-ups—the exercise that actually has real bearing on military job performance—required to max actually decreased across all age groups. In the seventeen- to twenty-one-year-old age range, a woman can score a hundred by doing forty-two push-ups, while a man of the same age must do seventy-one. A woman between the ages of twenty-two and twenty-six must do forty-six for a winning score. A man of the same age must do seventy-five; and so on. Still, the *Army Times* was ready to celebrate the new age. Reporter Jane McHugh quoted experts who told her that "the old standards were based on physical training test results from small groups of male soldiers in similar Military Occupational Specialties [and] the soldiers were not representative of the Army's diversity."

The real innovation in the revamped PT standards was finally made clear by Col. Stephen Cellucci, commandant of the U.S. Army Physical Fitness School at Fort Benning: "The new standards are, overall, tougher for both men and women; we had to establish equity for men and women of all age groups." Where was the equity if men and women were still tested to different standards? "Now you have equal points for equal effort," Cellucci declared.

Proponents of women-in-infantry put their faith in the any-day-now high-tech future that will make the strength discrepancy irrelevant. But that day has not yet arrived. As the *Army Times* put it: "Hundreds of years of technological and tactical advancements haven't made a dent in lightening the load that is the bane of every infantryman's existence. Like Roman foot soldiers 2,000 years before them, American infantrymen hump about 80 pounds of gear. . . . Today's soldier has to be a pack mule with computer skills."

In fact, high tech has actually been adding weight by giving soldiers new tools—night-vision goggles, for example—to haul around.

Besides, reducing the weight of the rucksack itself and the standard rifle just means that you have room for more ammunition—and everybody wants more ammunition.

The brass wax poetic on the subject of "future war." "[T]echnology will transform the way our forces fight," rhapsodized Secretary of Defense Cohen in the introduction to a recent address. "The key to success is an integrated 'system of systems' that will give [troops] superior battlespace awareness, permitting them to dramatically reduce the fog of war."

Well, there may be better electronic gizmos, but nearly everyone who studies the military agrees it will still be plenty down and dirty because we will fight more crucial battles in the heart of cities—à la Mogadishu. (The subtitle to Mark Bowden's book *Black Hawk Down* is, fittingly, "A story of modern war.")

"No army will lay itself out on the desert for us to come get them again," thundered former Marine commandant Gen. Charles C. Krulak during an address to military techies at an annual technology fair in San Diego. "Iraq has learned and the rest of the world was watching and has learned."

Krulak, a much-admired, fire-and-brimstone-style leader, started his address with images of knights and dragons and dark forests, and when he got to the part about "urban warfare," he painted a picture of a "murky, chaotic," lawless, frontier-town world. (The *Mad Max* movies come to mind.) "And it is into this maelstrom," he roared, "that the Marine Corps will deploy!"

"Ultimately," he boomed, "the key will be the individual Marine warrior, that soul of the warrior. Battle has always been a clash of wills, not just a clash of weapons and organizations."

Krulak forecasted "the growth of the nonstate," and its product, the "three-block war." "They will not attempt to match us tank for tank," Krulak warned. Instead, spake this Jeremiah, leaders like Saddam or leaders of sects, as in Somalia, will burrow into cities, effectively making the entire city their civilian shield. Instead of piles of weaponry, their advantage will be the element of surprise—guerrilla warfare often staged for the ubiquitous cameras of CNN and based on the assumption that, with that all-seeing eye watching, the United States would never dare create piles of dead civilians.

For recent glimpses of "future war," see Saddam Hussein, winter 1998; Slobodan Milosevic, spring 1999; and our recent adventure in Somalia, which ended with the battle of Mogadishu. The Marine Corps is a small, lean, ornery service and they have taken to the idea of the three-block war with particular relish because it seems likely that much of "future war" strategy will not be based on the force of hordes of soldiers and the power of numbers, but on individual cunning and cohesion of small, elite groups.

Because civilians are expected to play an increasing role in street-by-street warfare, the Marines are experimenting with nonlethal weapons for crowd control, but they are "still in their infancy," according to the Marine Corps Warfighting Lab in Quantico, Virginia.

Too bad we didn't have any in Mogadishu. At one point in *Black Hawk Down*, Bowden describes a Somali gunman seizing a live woman, sticking his stiff, outstretched arms (which held pistols) under her armpits, and then "walking" her limp body forward into fire while he used her body as a shield.

To become the service that's ready for future war, the Marines spent the last years of the nineties with future war scenarios and newly developed weapons. A Marine initiative titled Advanced Warfare Experiment (AWE) was about taking war-gaming to real cities, among real obstacles like civilians—the stubborn cabdriver, and the like. In the summer of 1997, for instance, a squad of Marines fast-roped onto the roof of New York City's hulking Port Authority building and spread out, running down halls and crawling through ventilation systems.

Will the urban warrior need upper-body strength? "We're finding out in these exercises," replied the commandant. "So far it looks like they'll need quite a bit."

On the other hand, urban warfare would seem to create special opportunities for a Special Forces cadre of elite women. When Israel sent a squad of its Ranger-equivalents into Beirut to kill leaders of the Palestine Liberation Organization, Ehud Barak, now Israel's prime minister, was forced to don a blond wig and a dress so he could attempt to pass as one half of an ordinary married couple just out for an evening stroll (one hopes the sun was setting). Compared to the challenge of passing Ehud Barak off as a woman—a blonde yet!—having a company of *real* women who were fit enough to hump the gear and penetrate enemy circles would seem to be a real advantage.

* * *

If we want to know whether women can hack it on the front lines or in the trenches with the rest of the ground-pounders, we should look at the countries that have been putting women on the front lines for decades, right? And the obvious example would be Israel, right? Not so. Actually, "women are something of an afterthought in the IDF [Israel Defense Force]—odd, given the amount of press they receive in foreign media," said Shoshana Bryen, who studies the IDF at the Jewish Institute for National Security Affairs. In fact, its women are far less equal than ours. Israeli women serve in a separate division named CHEN (the acronym means "grace" in Hebrew). They train separately from men and with female instructors. They enjoy a shorter period of conscription and are eligible for many waivers from service that men are not. And they have been kept much farther from the front lines. Up until the midnineties, they were only allowed in support roles—as clerks, medics, in communications. The widespread misimpression that Israeli women hole up in front-line trenches with men probably started with the fact that Israel is the only country in the world that drafts women—meaning that tourists see the bronzed women in uniform everywhere. Civilians, who tend not to realize that there are a whole lot of military jobs that don't involve shooting at all (our ratio is 30 percent combat to 70 percent support), tend to assume that every woman Israeli soldier is GI Jane. (I can't count the number of times nonmilitary people have smugly produced the "Well, what about Israel?" card when I said I was skeptical about gender-integrating the combat arms in this country or any other.)

The myth also probably comes out of the fact that the Haganah, the underground defense force that grew up to become the IDF, *did* put women in combat units—in keeping with the early socialist philosophy that animated the communal farms in the territory then called Palestine. In Palestine's kibbutzim, as they were called in Hebrew, no major personal possessions were allowed, children were raised outside the home in large nurseries, and anyone was eligible for any kibbutz job—though in practice, people tended to gravitate. The *metaplot*, for example, the people who cared for the babies and young children, were nearly always female. In keeping with this spirit of comradeship, the Palmach, the most elite, strike force of the Haganah, was gender-integrated as well, though in practice, says Martin Van Creveld, a military historian, women were relegated to support and defense positions once again—holding extra ammunition, acting as communication liaisons. Women would take up rifles on the front line if a position was being attacked, but raids on Arab positions relied mostly on men. Gruesome mutilation of enemy corpses and POWs had been common in the early wars against Arab troops. "One of the things our CO told us," recalls a former Palmach-nik, "was 'Do anything you can, but don't let them take you alive.' We were told to keep a bullet or a grenade for ourselves." After a battle in the Negev, which left the ground strewn with bodies, a number of them female and, true to form, mutilated in unspeakable ways, Palmach leadership ended the policy of assigning women to combat.

But Israel has changed since the forties. Egypt and Jordan are restrained by peace agreements. Iran, Iraq, Lebanon, Libya, and Syria, all Israel's enemies at one time or another, are preoccupied with their own tottering economies and with developing weapons of mass destruction.

In other words, there is less sense of imminent danger. As one recent visitor put it, "There isn't that feeling of claustrophobia, of being surrounded by three hostile fronts and the ocean." Able to take a bit of a break, Israel has been able to catch up to other developed countries by acquiring what Van Creveld calls the "peacetime luxuries" of a litigation industry and an influential feminist movement. In 1995, the supreme court overturned an army policy barring women in combat, though Israeli president Ezer Weizman said he disagreed with the decision. In 1997, the same court ordered the Israeli Air Force to accept women in its training pipeline, and in 1998, one Israeli woman earned her "wings." Nevertheless, sexual harassment cases are now filed regularly and top generals are beginning to find themselves in Aberdeenesque career-ruining scandals.

No, if one is looking for case studies of women in infantry, it is more instructive to look at Canada, which has actively been attempting to recruit women for its front lines (such as they are) since the early nineties. It all started when Canada's Human Rights Commission, set up to oversee Canadian citizens' equal rights, was challenged by "various individuals and rights organizations" about the inequity of combat exclusion. According to Maj. Kelly Farley, director of land personnel, the commission then said in effect, " 'You are hereby ordered to open all your occupations to women with the exception of submarine service.' They gave us a ten-year deadline to fully integrate [a term that was never defined] women. That deadline was February '99." The Canadian Army (the entire force is about the size of New York City's fire-fighting department) duly recruited one hundred women for its combat arms training program. Unlike the United States, they put the one hundred volunteers into unadapted, standard infantry training along with male recruits. No adaptions for strength or any other kinds of differences were made. Only one woman graduated: twenty-two-year-old Heather Erxleben, a former timber hauler and construction worker.

But the Canadian forces seemed undaunted. When I met Maj. Howard Michitsch, who was then the head of the Canadian military's gender-integration program and is now retired from the military, at a DACOWITS conference, he was still upbeat about gender-integrating combat arms. "We didn't do it right," he said. "This time we're going to try to attract women who are more athletic; we have to go where they are."

Even if they attracted recruits, he mused, there was still the problem with attrition they'd been observing in the female support community. "We can't seem to keep them beyond eight years," he said. "It's like they hit twenty-six and there's this wall there; that's when they drop out." He maintained that they needed to find out what that wall was all about.

In 1997, still resolute after the military's first failed attempt to recruit women for combat and unfazed by the 42 percent dropout rate they were experiencing among female soldiers in noncombat MOSs, the Human Rights Commission continued to press the Canadian forces to achieve the goal. There had been some ugly sexual harassment cases in the ranks, and most procombat activists believed that women had been "scared off."

But Cmdr. Deborah Wilson, an official in the military's gender-integration program, readily accepted the marching orders, saying, "We see it as the way the future is going to go. We've never really made a conscious effort to get the word out to women that opportunities exist, that they will be made welcome."

As for previous recruiting attempts, she said, "We have to phrase the messages differently. Teamwork is more attractive to women than driving a big piece of equipment. Women are more inclined to want to make a difference."

"We got about one to two million in advertising alone—a lot for Canada," said Michitsch, who was put in charge of the recruiting campaign.

We hired a company in Toronto to come up with a nationwide advertising campaign, TV ads, the works. The campaign was presented to the minister of defense, the equivalent of the U.S. secretary of defense, but the women on the staff said the ads were "too warlike" and that we should show women in more nurturing positions We told them that we've got plenty of female medics and nurses and ads showing [them] helping babies, but still our campaign had to change.

We then ran major recruiting efforts in all of the major cities. Toronto, for instance. There was an advertising blitz in the city in everything from women's magazines to all-girls' schools. We found all the women in the combat arms that we could—a total of about six, both regular and reservists—and we brought them in so they could talk to the women. We put together demonstrations. We'd bring in tanks, armored vehicles, artillery pieces, rucksacks, weapon systems. The people [we'd contracted with] were in the concert business, so there were big screens showing flashing lights and rock music. This was *big*. We'd never done anything like this before. We had a lot showing up, but they were not looking for combat arms; they were looking at being in communications and computers and signal equipment. Most of 'em tried to pick up a rucksack and would say, "Whoa, nonstarter!" . . . or pick up a fifty-caliber sniper rifle and go, "I don't think so." . . . We had simulators where they could actually be in the armored vehicles and experience the noise and whatever, and it was "No, we don't think so."

Assessing the big recruiting drive, Kelly Farley said, "We had four hundred applications to the combat arms by women, a great increase over the previous year—so the advertising seemed to have worked. Of those applicants, the [number that] showed up for training was just less than a hundred—or about one in four. After training, we ended up with about fifty who went on to units."

At the ten-year deadline for "full integration," the commission called the military's attempts a "total failure."

"We told [the commission that] we've removed all systemic barriers to women that we've identified; we've opened all occupations to women; there's nothing barring them from a systemic point of view, but the numbers just aren't there," Farley said. "They are coming in in dribs and drabs and ones and twos, but they certainly aren't represented to their proportion in society."

All of this raises another uncomfortable issue: As we push closer and closer to opening infantry and artillery to women, are they really champing to go?

What we do know is that women are not rushing to fill many of the new more-combat-related jobs now open to them. As one surveys the most junior enlisted women and commissioned and noncommissioned junior officers, it becomes more and more clear that the clamor is mostly generated by a relatively small group of commissioned officers, most of them retired and/or too old to serve as foot soldiers. The voting is done with the feet. Since 1994, 19,971 new jobs and units—air and ground—have been opened to women, but as the *Army Times* wrote recently, "Of those potential positions, 1,367 are actually held by women."

"Many of the jobs recently opened still stand open," noted the Associated Press. "In aviation programs women are opting for their now-traditional role flying helicopters [instead of learning to fly fighter jets]." Women were allowed to join fighter plane squadrons in 1994. But since 1998, "more than half of all female Navy and Marine aviators who entered primary training chose helicopters over fixed-wing aircraft, which includes jets and propeller-driven planes. The numbers are just the opposite for men."

The *Army Times* has observed a similar pattern among aviators:

When Capt. Cindy Doane completed Army flight school in 1995, she would have been among the first women eligible to fly Apache attack helicopters. But she declined invitations to transfer from utility helicopters—not once but three times. . . . Doane, who commands a Black Hawk helicopter company [Black Hawks transport troops—and thus can be exposed to ground fire—but Apaches are made to pursue and kill tanks] at Fort Bragg, N.C., said, "I guess I just didn't want to blaze that trail. The attack role just didn't turn me on at the time. The mission of the aircraft just wasn't something that appealed to me. I liked the diversity of roles that utility helicopters have."

In an interview accompanying the article, Lt. Gen. David H. Ohle, the deputy chief of staff for Army personnel, was asked to explain the continuing dearth of women flying fighter planes and why women are generally not taking MOSs that would put them closer to the "action."

"It would not be productive in a volunteer army to force someone into a job," he starts. But, he says, sending the kind of mixed message so typical of leaders at that level, "clearly we have understood that we have some things to do, in terms of doing a better job in adjusting our culture to accept everybody." When people are assigning others to jobs, there is a "human tendency to find someone that more closely resembles you," but he will attempt to counter this by urging his officers to "work at it." The new dictates for "gender parity" are a change, he tells the reporter, "and the way that we can effect change is to make sure that the leadership understands what they need to do."

So it seems even with all the effort and the inducements and the cajoling, sex differences exert themselves. Karen Dahlby didn't protest when the early nineties downsizing downsized her out of her job as a maintenance officer in the Air Force. She took a job as a technical writer at the TRW corporation and began a novel (informed by her experience, of course) titled *Placeholder*—which uses two female characters, one middle-aged and totally gung ho, the picture of a "squared-away," by-the-book military officer; the other, younger, a lieutenant, who could have a great career but is increasingly troubled by the feeling that no matter how hard she tries, a man will do the job better, because "women have different priorities and they think differently; men think of themselves and others just as a cog in the machine." A man is a military animal while she is not. Says Dahlby:

I thought about things for a couple of years, and that it would be easier to write a book than to keep explaining to people why I liked the Air Force, but I wasn't particularly recommending that other women go into it. If you don't recommend it to people, people immediately assume that it must be because of all these sexual harassment things they keep hearing about. That's not it at all. I didn't see that as any more of a problem than on any other job I've been in. Probably a lot less than high school. . . . But I was never quite sure that I *was* in the military, though I kept hoping that someone would convince me differently because I liked it so much.

I wondered whether she was just having difficulty being a manager, with telling other people, especially grown men, what to do. Maybe it felt odd to have people salute her. Maybe she was just having the usual problems that come with being an officer in such a hierarchical class-conscious system. I asked her if this wasn't something many women had trouble with, and suggested that maybe her feelings weren't particular to the military at all.

"No," she said. "The military is made for the way men do things, but other jobs are not as strongly that way." Struggling to be more concrete about the differences that seemed to stand out in high relief while she was in the military, she said, "Men and women think about forming teams completely differently. Men think of teams as a bunch of people doing a job, told what to do by someone else; women think of a team as everybody talks about it and decides what to do. One way works in a system organized around the battlefield; the other way doesn't."

Army captain Jalesia Griffin is not as hard-line as Dahlby. She has no problem with women commanding support units, but she doesn't believe the Army is ready to put women in combat MOSs. "Most women do not have what it takes to be in a direct combat situation. Some do, but is it worth the hassle to begin allowing women to serve in a direct combat capacity?" It could be possible if the Army could adhere to absolute, no-kidding standards and not flinch if only a few women could meet those standards, but she doesn't believe that is going to happen anytime soon. "In the smoke jumpers," firefighters who parachute into forest fires, both men and women are required to carry a "one-hundred-pound backpack through the woods to graduate from the course and become a bona fide smoke jumper; the men do not help the women carry their backpacks," she says approvingly. "Either the individual makes the cut or does not."

As Betty Friedan predicted, women do "civilize" military culture. On board the newly integrated USS *Eisenhower*, for instance, men with several cruises under their belts talked about how women seem to have improved the environment on the ship and on port visits. Men shower more, they said. They had cleaned up their language. "It's kind of like a home atmosphere away from home," said Instrumentman Second Class Mike Munroe.

Male sailors and officers credited their female counterparts for helping them find nicer gifts for their wives, and for being better bargain hunters and more skilled at negotiating for better prices.

Risking typecasting the ship's four hundred women, Capt. Leo Enright, the ship's operations boss, declared: "They're much better shoppers than we are. . . . Our wives are happy because they're getting better gifts."

"We'd come back with bags full and show each other what we bought," said Cmdr. Janice Hamby, assistant operations officer.

Unable and unwilling to make women behave more like men, the brass have cooperated with the inevitable and begun to insist that in fact a kinder, gentler soldier is just what's needed in an era in which we are increasingly assigned as peacekeepers. The British Army, for instance, recently began running a television ad directed at the nurturing side of the female prospective recruit. We see a civilian woman shaking with fear in a bombed-out building—the clothes and terrain suggest Kosovo. "At this moment," the voice-over intones, "the last thing she wants to see is another man."

This is some improvement over the take of the early nineties, which suggested that the average GI Jane could kill and fight and jump over the barricades along with the men. Except that now the military seems to be suggesting that *it is just better to be this way*. Period. That we actually have to reformulate how we fight war—with a new man who, as former chief of staff of the army Dennis Reimer put it, is "able to defeat the eighth-largest army in the world in the hundred hours which we did in Desert Storm, but immediately turn to a humanitarian assistance type of mission. It is much more sophisticated than charging that hill."

The question is, How many of these men exist? Enough of them to form even one battalion?

After all the logical arguments about women in infantry have been made—strength discrepancies, effects on unit cohesion—the government will still have to deal with another objection, an instinctive "no"; the recoil of the heart, of the nerves, and of the gut. It's the "argument" that can't be rationalized with logic or at least not with the kind of argument modern politically correct society accepts. I call it the aesthetic argument. I know that I find the prospect of a coed front line depressing somehow—even though I am convinced there are some women who would make excellent front-line soldiers, and that they are so rare that the gender-integrated part of that line would be very short indeed. Something in me craves a restoration of darkness, of risk, of mysteries, and certainly of a world of stark polarities, not bland sameness. I think androgyny is chilling, at the very least deeply boring. And I do not think we could have a capable integrated combat arms without real androgyny, without real suppression of male and female qualities—and I do not think that is possible. At least it would require something like what we are in today except multiplied by a power of ten. If anything, think how expensive a full-fledged battle against human nature would be. SERE training for prisoners of war has added a component to "desensitize" male soldiers to the screams of female unitmates. This is the brave new world that waits for us if we are firmly committed to getting and keeping a gender-integrated combat force. For those sexual differences and sexual interests will out; they will be flushed out by the urgency of war. And knowing that they would—that a man would probably stop to mourn at the body of a woman, any woman, just for the fact of her being a woman—makes me kind of happy.

In a world saturated with tales of domestic violence, rape, abandoned mothers and abandoned children, the last decade brought us the spectacle of generals apologizing for protective feelings toward the female sex. "It's hard for me to explain," said Gen. Merrill A. McPeak, then Air Force chief of staff in a speech to DACOWITS in the early nineties. "I just can't get over this feeling of old men ordering young women into combat. . . . I have a gut-based hang-up there. And it doesn't make a lot of sense in every way. I apologize for it."

This chapter started with quotes from two people, one a proponent of women in combat who says we will prevail in this struggle because human beings are not animals and can control their behavior on a ship or on a battlefield or anywhere else. The other quote comes from Lionel Tiger, an anthropologist, who wrote "there is a biosocial link between males for purpose of work, defense production, politics, for hanging around. It was as evolutionarily important as the link between males and females for reproduction and domestic life." In 1998, he wrote an opinion column addressed to "my fellow primates," in which he said, "We are members of a species unimaginably old and sharing a common inheritance in the millions of years. Your five fingers echo the starfish of the ancient briny deep. Nearly every archaeological excavation or carbon dating or chemical analysis puts us back further in time. . . . We are fascinated by apes, especially the chimps, because we share some 98 percent of our genes with them—more than they share with the monkeys."

I suspect that ultimately one's feelings on the women-in-combat question will come down to temperament and whether you insist you're "not an animal" or are proud to call yourself just another happy primate, a naked ape, species of man, clan of mammal, and family of vertebrate.

It's really about whether one loves the idea of a natural law—whether one experiences it as sort of a grand web in which we are all connected and in which humans are just a small part—or whether one experiences natural law as a restriction, an insulting detail human beings are forced—for now—to acknowledge sometimes. Natural law, the existence of something bigger than ourselves, the existence of something we still fight to conquer but still has its way with us, has always been comforting to me; it is what adds mystery. A future where everything has been tamed—even the male sex—"a land so crossed with light," a land where we all do the same thing in the same proportions, where there is no hate or jealousy, where we march in lockstep, the world the women-in-combat proponents seem to be proffering, is awful. Some of the revulsion to the idea of women in combat comes from very deep hardwiring. Most beings, plant and animal, exist to produce offspring, protect that offspring until it can reproduce itself, and then die. In a very fancy, embroidered-upon way, that is what still orders our lives. Our ultimate marching orders come from the imperative to extend our species, and on some very primitive level we "understand" that eggs are expensive and sperm—that is, men's bodies, which have throughout history been treated like so much matchwood—are cheap. Thus the deep sense of "not rightness," of queasiness, of taboo, at the thought of an organized, government-sanctioned use of women to kill and be killed comes out of hardwired instinct that there is something blasphemous about a bullet shot into a womb. War using the bodies of men (bodies that are designed to be more disposable in the defense of the species) can seem civilized, but a war involving women combatants (on a large scale, that is) seems barbaric. Men even tend to treat their own bodies as if they were expendable, while women tend to hold themselves more closely.

To see the casualties of the male imperative to throw their bodies at the perimeter, go to any rehab unit of any hospital. It will be full of young men in wheelchairs, usually survivors of car accidents. If you want to see whether there are sex differences or not, go and watch people at leisure, when they have chosen what to do. In New York City you will see fleets of boys of around thirteen, careering in and out of traffic, circumnavigating the city, on skateboards and in-line skates patrolling the perimeter.

Ambitious young women see the young men and feel at once competitive, shamed, and guilty. This is partly what the passion to have women in combat—to give one's life for one's country, to have the right to die—is all about. Men have one up on us; in this regard, they own the cherished victim status, the most precious currency of the age.

One of the E-mail conversations I struck up while working on this book was with a female historian of the radical feminist persuasion. In her E-mails she raged about what she saw as omnipresent threats to women from men and the consequent need for the government to put women in combat units so they could be given guns and trained to use them. "Look," I replied, "if you're so eager to use a gun, don't wait for the government to confer one on you. They're easy enough to get. Get some, form a militia with your friends, and train yourselves."

That was not good enough. That was not winning the battle. Government had to put its stamp of validation on her warriorhood. Actually, she didn't really want to fight her enemies; she didn't really want to fight at all in the physical sense. She just wanted government to somehow assuage a nagging sense of inequality.

The armed forces exist to defend us and advance our interests. Bases and battlefields are not supposed to be used as backdrops for soldiers' interior dramas. Certainly the services have played a psychological role in the lives of men, but that wasn't the point. If that happened, they and we were lucky. When they stopped being able to defend the nation, they were out.

There are many ways to get the various benefits of military service. If you want to be patriotic, you have to ask yourself (and the military) where you will do the most good. That is why military service is called service. It may be that many women provide the best service to their country by working in intelligence (where women are said to have a special talent), or in the medical corps, or in administration, or in rare cases in some part of the combat arms.

The bottom line is we cannot have a military unless its first priority is military readiness, and that will mean looking for and keeping warriors. It is likely that most of them will be men. Ultimately, when we are involved again in a real war—not a work-out-the-kinks war against a much weaker force—the law of the jungle will still rule. The fiercer, angrier, most-blood-lusting force will win. Certainly there will be cooler-headed strategists in the background, but even they have to be driven by the desire to follow through, by a killer instinct. "Cry 'Havoc!' and let slip the dogs of war," roared Shakespeare's Marc Antony. Something tells me he (Henry or Marc) wasn't talking about nineteen-year-old girls. "Let the dogs loose," read a piece of locker-room samizdat, observed by writer Kathy Dobie at a coed basic-training program in Florida. Men ache to unleash their dogs of war. Women generally have to be exhorted or trained to act that way, and most could probably manage a semblance for a while. But do we want them to? Can a thirty-five-year-old man be trained not to stay his hand when he needs to send a twenty-year-old girl onto a mortar-strafed field? Can the impulse that still impels men to try to protect women be overridden? Do we want it to be? Won't sex just always have its way? Do we really want it to stop doing that?

Conclusion

"Men would rather vacate the arena [of combat] altogether
than share it with women."
—Amelia Earhart, circa 1930

A melia was right. The nineties have been all about soldiers "vacating the arena." Two years of "quality of life" improvements, bonuses, and revamped ad campaigns have not boosted recruitment or ended "the exodus" of attrition. With Congress now pushing to see a "return" on their "investment" of bonus money, the brass are desperate enough to try new methods. Exit interviews are slated to become more in-depth; outside contractors have been hired to use focus-group data (not a common tool in military research) because the focus group is the only method that stands a chance of drawing out the answers that the rigid yes/no, pick-one-from-column-A questionnaires miss. One prays that the focus-group leaders are able to hear the things people say between the lines and to pursue those leads to their source, and then that the Pentagon will listen to the politically incorrect answers that will emerge.

Actually, if the Pentagon really wanted to know why everybody has been heading for the exits (and I theorize that they do but won't say what they know until "a study" says it for them), the answer is everywhere. In a recent Internet newsletter, for instance, one that the official-types surely read, U.S. Army captain Jeff Church supplied the answer: "It's not just about money. The U.S. military has never made anybody but flag officers wealthy. People used to stay in because they felt like they were warriors, making a difference, with commanders they respected, in units they were proud of. Those feelings don't exist today."

Sure, the cranked-up operations tempo has been unbelievably hard. There is also the issue of inadequate pay coupled with the inherent taunt of a defense budget that seems to have something for every Senator Pork Barrel or anybody else with a good song and dance, but nothing for nuts-and-bolts stuff like pay raises and new parts for basic equipment.

All of this could be borne, the servicemen say, if the U.S. military was still the institution they once joined. But the services made one, single, suicidal mistake at the beginning of the last decade: They threw away the mystique, the one thing that gave them an edge over the civilian economy with which they now find themselves in competition. As ex–naval officer Patrick Vincent put it, the brass "refused to defend their own culture"; they even began to systematically criminalize the warrior spirit as its manifestations (seen through the template of political correctness) were deemed anachronistic, abusive, insensitive, elitist.

Without all those intangibles, without the monastery, stripped of its aggressive "we kill people and break stuff" nature, military service becomes the corporation at its dreary, petty, soul-killing worst, or just another civil service job—a place of low pay, dim lighting, crummy furniture, ugly buildings, piles of paperwork, and a sort of sexless, exhausted male/female rapport. With the loss of the military, as essayist Dave Shifflett put it, "there is no frontier to which a man can escape."

It was once a happy marriage: young men who like to risk their bodies and shoot and blow things up, and a society that was plenty happy to let them do it when it needed to be done. And it served a special social good—besides keeping us free. It was a kind of refining valve. A training ground for many of our best men, it also took in some of the worst and it took that energy roiling around and put it to worthy service.

One of the frightening things about the new recruiting problems—and the new male recruits we are getting—is that the tough guys, including the tough criminal guys, who used to be reformed by the military, are not heading for this socialization crucible because it simply seems too nanny-ish. Many of them are going . . . well, we don't really know where . . . probably into street gangs or the new "militias" or the criminal underground, which offer rites of passage, powerful male mentors (not "bossy" female majors and captains), and a place in a hierarchy of "elites" who fight real blood-stake battles—while our boys in uniform are busy checking to see if a Bosnian grandma has been getting her medicine. A worrisome trend of the nineties has been the services' growing problem with various kinds of extremists—white-power group members, for instance, and unrepentant gang-bangers—who merely take a small sabbatical in the military in order to get next to guns and ammunition, then go AWOL or sneak 'em out to aides-de-camp.

But the brass have responded to their "image problem" by simply pouring gas on the fire. There are very few ads—some aired during the NBA playoffs, for instance—that show a man's world; most are scrupulously gender-balanced. In some of its displays and literature the Army even uses the image of a woman wearing a helmet, BDUs, army boots, carrying a rifle, walking forward, shoulders hunched menacingly. The Army is about 22 percent female and none are "ground-pounders," but the Army still uses a lone female looking very much like an infantryman to represent itself to the world!

So the heart-wrenching question becomes what do we do about the women—so many of whom are brave, devoted, loyal, hardworking, and more warrior-like in spirit, more identified with the "Old Military," than a portion of the "New Military"'s new corporation men!

Because of their superior performance in most of the support MOSs, women became an indispensable part of the U.S. armed forces a long time ago. Except for the new permission to fly combat planes, what we have to take back are the "innovations" of the nineties; what we have to reform is the nineties mind-set driving the integration of women and most of the policies it produced. As we have seen in our "engagements" in Vietnam, Kosovo, and Somalia, morale is everything. "If I had enough colored ribbons," Napoleon Bonaparte once said, "I could rule the world." It's not clear if he was talking about streamers and banners waving in front of marching soldiers, or the medals they were promised at the end for bravery, but clearly he was talking about the elixir of morale.

Right now, morale is at rock bottom. Remedies for the parts problems and the pay problems and the waste and bloat problems will have to be covered in another book. Here are some ways to begin healing the morale wounds left by the bungled gender-integration policies of the last decade:

- Eliminate all recruiting quotas for women and make sure every recruiting office in the country knows this is for real, that the order comes from the top, that it's not some kind of thought-crime spot-check sprung to identify closet sexists.

Restore "back of the neck" recruiting. If gender quotas are removed—and racial quotas, too—recruiters can spend less time frantically trying to fill "recruiting goals" and more time targeting and working on the most likely prospects. To bring in more of the working-class black and Hispanic men who have shown an increasing tendency to avoid the "New Military," we could increase the number of high school dropouts we currently accept. Military studies show that high school dropouts are not a good risk because about half don't complete boot camp or their first tour of duty. I think what may be reflected here is the effect of the racial quotas and the panicked "just get 'em on the plane" mentality. The numbers also mean that there is a 50 percent chance that a dropout will stay and become a good soldier. Freed from quota pressures, a recruiter can concentrate on determining if a particular high school dropout is one of the good risks or one of the poor ones. Dropping out of high school can reflect contempt for authority and apathy, but it can also reflect a surfeit of energy and impatience with book learnin' and the often infantilized life of the student. As a high school dropout myself, I know that a high school diploma does not necessarily certify the ability to learn and to work hard. Recruiters generally have to spend about five times the effort to recruit a woman than to recruit a man, and, with the startlingly higher rates of female attrition, they get far less return. Qualified women will still show up, but our recruiters should be allowed to focus relentlessly on one goal: getting the best people.

• Follow the lead of the Marines and the Israelis and go back to separating the sexes in boot camp. This would allow drill sergeants to restore discipline and standards because they could train the men as hard as they need to, without worrying about injuring the women. And stop the grandma-izing of boot camp. Get used to it. This is training designed to prepare people for the battlefield—whether they end up there or not. There is no way to do it and not risk hurting people's feelings. "In the era of 360-degree combat," says USMC brigadier general Jim Mattis, "everybody has to be ready to be an infantryman." And if some folks are so keen about putting women in combat, they should realize that when a thirty-five-year-old man sends an eighteen-year-old woman into harm's way, you've got the potential for one big mess of hurt feelings. There is a military mind-set, and one of its basic principles can be summarized as "No wimps allowed!" That means stop coddling, stop excusing. Since it is easier for women to be harder on other women, we need more female drill sergeants. One of the problems, according to the Army's personnel division, is that fewer women graduate from drill sergeant school, often because they choose to drop out. (A report published in 1997 said that "the most recent assignment process required 66 nominees to obtain 10 female drill sergeant candidates with only three graduating.") Once again this may just be a sex difference revealing itself, but military surveys have also shown that people prefer training their own sex. That's very plausible. A twenty-five-year-old woman can still feel self-conscious under the cool regard of eighteen-year-old men. Maybe we could keep more women in drill sergeant school if they faced the prospect of drilling platoons of eighteen-year-old women only.

• In boot camp, in advanced individual training, and beyond, restore high and equal standards—physical, moral, and performance-based. The hard, mean, standards that sometimes end up being "not fully inclusive," the kind that occasionally give a young person a temporary loss of self-esteem. The younger generations who command the platoons or march in those platoons seem to be ready for such harsh lines in the sand. "Get used to it," a recent coinage popular with Generation Y, is an expression of the tragic sense, the recognition, that one choice often rules out the others, and you can't always have it all.

There is no real sense of achievement without the possibility of failure. A sense of mastery only comes out of enduring a shock to one's self-esteem but then mastering the task that had clobbered you, shedding the old skin.

• Along those lines, finally, implement MOS-specific qualifying tests. After speaking with hundreds of military personnel and reading considerable material generated by civilians about the military, it seems most of us are ready for a consensus policy to reform gender integration. People express it as "If women can do the job, let them do it"; or "I wouldn't mind women in the infantry, if they could do the job." As Gen. Jeanne Holm (Army, Ret.) once wrote:

"It seems to me we need the highest quality people we can recruit from the young people in our society without artificial barriers or artificial notions about what they can and cannot do . . . [and] they should be able to be classified and utilized based on their individual capabilities, not on some extraneous social issue."

So we should let the scientists have a go. There would not be a great cost. Some MOSs may have changed with technology, but in the main the hard work has already been done; the tests are ready to go. Ultimately there will be a ruckus in congressional hearing rooms—that the tests are not realistic, that they are weighted to favor men. Too bad. The military world does favor men, though that doesn't mean there aren't women who can work in the old jobs and many of the new ones. Trust the scientists. They live in an unforgiving world where if you're wrong, the stuff blows up in your face.

• Restore openness. The move by Secretary Cohen to do away with "the zero defect mentality" was a good one. Now he should extend that attitude to the "third rail" subject of "gender." Just because someone says he is "having problems with the women in his platoon" doesn't necessarily mean he is a "sexist." Never again should a member of the leadership elite call all drill sergeants on a base together, announce dicey new policies about gender-integrated training, and then quash the inevitable clamor of comments, complaints, suggestions, that followed by saying, in effect, "Too bad, that's what we're going to do."

• It is not overly dramatic to say that the memory of Tailhook is like a great festering toxic waste dump in the middle of the military consciousness. That the stench of the "Witchhook" lowered morale and has driven people out of the forces. If Commander in Chief Clinton could find it in himself to hold a very public ceremony pardoning Civil War soldiers who were, it is now believed, unfairly court-martialed, he should be able to do something along those lines for men who are still living. The commander in chief and the joint chiefs of staff (since we're fantasizing, let's throw them in, too) should hold a televised ceremony apolo-

gizing to all the men (and in this case it is exclusively men) who
were treated like common criminals and/or unfairly separated
and/or held back from promotion because they attended, had
friends who attended, or commanded someone else who attended
the Tailhook symposium and convention of 1991. The Tailhook
Association should also receive an official apology. Paula Coughlin has received some restorative balm in the form of $5 million
from the Hilton Corporation; the Navy has been tortured for a
decade; after a ceremony of absolution, this thing should be
buried.

• If the United States continues to play social worker to the
world, it is time to create a separate branch to dispense medicine,
deliver bags of disposable diapers, show third-world mothers
how to use them, inoculate animals, et cetera. In other words, it's
time to beef up the Peace Corps or something like it. The Peace
Corps was extremely popular throughout the sixties, even
groovy. There was no shortage of applicants, and the government
had the luxury of doing exhaustive screening for mental and
physical fitness. It still exists, though with a lower profile, and if
we intend it to be the "alternative service" to the U.S. military,
some changes need to be made. First of all, enlistment has to
come with a salary and the GI bill—in other words, everything a
regular military enlisted would get, including a fixed term of service with penalties if you break your contract. This shouldn't cost
more money, because we would simply convert a lot of military
billets to Peace Corps billets and shift a proportional amount of
recruiting resources as well. It is the right time to open a peacekeeping branch of the armed forces. There is strong evidence
(increasing enrollments in schools of social work and education)
showing that young people in America are searching for challenge and meaning. Warriors and peacekeepers are two very different kinds of animals. This would relieve the military of trying
to "soldierize" people who won't be or can't be; and we could stop
torturing the aggressive, risk-craving, edge-courting soldiers
who rage, "I didn't sign up to be a social worker."

Sure, these peacekeepers would need to be protected, so have
them protected with military police who aren't restrained by
simultaneously having to attend to the next crying baby. Soldiers

everywhere say that the emotional wrench of psyching up to be the professional killer and then rheostating back down to be the benevolent peacekeeper is literally killing their buddies. There was a rise in military suicide rates after our Somalia adventure—the one where units of Marines crawled onto a Somali beach only to be met by a crowd of reporters and film crews. Many service people say this had something to do with an adrenaline crash, the buildup for expected combat, and then despair at the desultory new world of peacekeeping. In other words, two very different temperaments are involved. The person who can do both equally well is rare. Don't mix it up. There is no other institution charged to do what the military does, so let others "respond to a domestic disturbance" and "rescue cats and dogs" (as one CO described his unit's daytime activities in Kosovo).

• Finally, to paraphrase Mao's little red book: "The Marines: Live like them." There have not been many mentions of the Marines in this book; that's because they are generally doing all right. Though their existence is always in jeopardy, because one or another senator is always trying to defund them, they are the service that has stood its ground best through the politically correct nineties. There have been little tactical, diversionary, give-ups along the way, but mostly they've stayed the course. In the winter of 1999, when the chiefs of the other three services kept chirping to Congress about how the forces were more ready than they'd ever been, only one, Marine commandant Charles Krulak, chose to offer a dissent about real-life attrition, burnout, and parts shortages. "What is it with most Marine generals?" asked David Hackworth in March 1999. "Do they get inoculated with double shots of truth serum in boot camp?" He was referring to Marine general Charles Wilhelm, headman for troops south of the Rio Grande, who told Congress our presence in Haiti wasn't needed anymore and that, in Hackworth's words, it was time to "yank our troops and write off the $6 billion 'meals-on-wheels' mission as a failure." When other service chiefs listened to Kosovo planning and stifled their many criticisms with the strategy, only Commander Krulak asked, "What's the end game?"

The Marines have been applauded by business consulting firms and business magazines as a model for "a corporation" that runs lean and mean. And one reason they have collected less service bloat is that they maintain a democratic "every man is a rifleman" philosophy, and a more open, no BS culture, where people are less afraid to say what they think. It is indicative of this culture that Brig. Gen. Jim Mattis is the highest-ranking officer on active duty who talked for attribution for this book.

Because the Marines have the toughest standards, working-class Hispanics and blacks still tell each other, "Yeah, man, well [if you're looking for something really tough] then you got to go to the Marines," and they are the only service that hasn't had recruiting problems. (August 1999 marked the fiftieth consecutive month in which the Marines "made mission," that is, met their recruitment goal, though they are having junior officer retention problems.) Their continuing popularity has a lot to do with their strong identity—the "maybe you can be one of us," "the few, the proud" message. As think-tanker and former Gulf War combat veteran John Hillen puts it, "The Marines continue to sell themselves not as a place to work, but as a thing to be."

Yes, implementation of all of the above will result in fewer women in the ranks. If we stop waiving any and all standards for women recruits, if we stop pursuing "the numbers," if we stop virtually charging women with butterfly nets, we will probably drop from our present 15 percent to about 6 percent women in the ranks. There will be an outcry about "taking a step back," about discrimination, about lack of opportunity. The only appropriate answer is "Too bad." War, as John Hillen puts it, "is the ultimate shit-happens situation." This is one area where we absolutely have to cleave to a certain bottom line. We have lost the depth on the bench that we once had, and along with it the luxury to have decorative soldiers and reparational billets. In the downsized military everyone must be the real deal. The women we want in the military (in fact, everyone we want in the military) understand this. Our freedom and prosperity is dependent on getting the best people for the job. There are enough women in the pipeline so that sometimes a woman will be that best person. But the best person for the job will usually be a man.

The natural world makes us creatures of different abilities and preferences, but also creatures with the courage to push beyond our own abilities and to explore other people's preferences. We have been given a human kaleidoscope of tribes and clans and castes and bizarre cults, some murderous, some merely hostile, some beneficent—all mixed up. Our world is like a chaotic Indian souk; there are delicate and beautiful saris over here, and a pile of sheep dung over here, very odd dusty jars of pungent spices and pornographically sweet candies attracting flies in the sun. The Indian souk is not always a nice place— there are charlatans who are ready to take your money, and pretty cakes that may give you food poisoning; there are even sexual deviants hovering in the corners who would whisk your children behind the curtains of their little storefronts. But it is this unedited variety and intimation of risk, and the way that risk makes one reach into oneself for cunning and speed, that make the jumbled market so much more exciting and interesting than the blandness, enforced safety, conformity, and censored "diversity" of the world pushed by the current crop of social reformers. Living in the real world is so much more interesting and fun than attempting to live in a politically correct state enforced by threats, fear, constant vigilance, and policing. People will continue to choose real life over utopia. As the Gen Y-ers, the rebellious new generation coming up, would say: Get used to it!

Sources Consulted

Books

Bowden, Mark. *Black Hawk Down: A Story of Modern War.* New York: Atlantic Monthly Press, 1999.

Breuer, William B. *War and American Women: Heroism, Deeds, and Controversy.* Westport, Conn.: Praeger Publishers, 1997.

Dahlby, Karen. "Placeholder" (unpublished novel). 1987.

Erikson, Erik H. *Childhood and Society.* New York: W. W. Norton, 1950.

Flinn, Kelly. *Proud to Be: My Life, the Air Force, the Controversy.* New York: Random House, 1997.

Francke, Linda Bird. *Ground Zero: Gender Wars in the Military.* New York: Simon & Schuster, 1997.

Friedan, Betty. *The Second Stage* (rev. ed.). New York: Summit Books, 1986.

Hackworth, David. *Hazardous Duty.* New York: William Morrow, 1996.

Holm, Jeanne. *Women in the Military: An Unfinished Revolution.* San Francisco: Presidio, 1992.

Jones, James. *WWII.* New York: Ballantine Books, 1975.

Keegan, John. *Six Armies in Normandy.* New York: Viking Penguin, 1982.

———. *The History of Warfare.* New York: Alfred A. Knopf, 1993.

McMichael, William H. *The Mother of All Hooks: The U.S. Navy's Tailhook Scandal.* New Brunswick, N.J.: Transaction Publishers, 1997.

Office of the Inspector General. *The Tailhook Report.* New York: St. Martin's Press, 1993.

O'Hanlon, Michael. *How to Be a Cheap Hawk.* Washington, D.C.: Brookings Institution Press, 1998.

Ricks, Thomas E. *Making the Corps.* New York: Scribner, 1997.

Santoli, Al. *Leading the Way—How Vietnam Veterans Rebuilt the U.S. Military: An Oral History.* New York: Ballantine Books, 1993.

Smith, Kyle. "If I Die While Sipping Tea" (unpublished memoir). 1994.

Spears, Sally. *Call Sign Revlon: The Life and Death of Navy Fighter Pilot Kara Hultgreen.* Annapolis, Md.: Naval Institute Press, 1998.

Terkel, Studs. *"The Good War": An Oral History of World War II.* New York: The New Press, 1984.

Tiger, Lionel. *Men in Groups.* New York: Random House, 1969.

———. *The Decline of Males.* New York: Golden Books, 1999.

Van Creveld, Martin. *The Sword and the Olive.* New York: Public Affairs, 1998.

Vistica, Gregory L. *Fall from Glory: The Men Who Sank the U.S. Navy.* New York: Touchstone, 1997.

Webb, James. *Fields of Fire.* New York: Pocket Books, 1978.

Wolfe, Tom. *The Right Stuff.* New York: Farrar, Straus and Giroux, 1979.

Zimmerman, Jean. *Tail Spin: Women at War in the Wake of Tailhook.* New York: Doubleday, 1975.

Reports, Regulations, Congressional Hearings, and Reference Books

Defense Manpower Data Center. "Youth Attitude Tracking Study, 1996: Propensity and Advertising Report." May 1997.

Department of the Army, Inspector General. "Special Inspection of Initial Entry Training Equal Opportunity/Sexual Harassment Policies and Procedures." 22 July 1997.

Department of the Army Headquarters. "TRADOC Regulation 350-6 Initial Entry Training (IET) Policies and Administration." United States Army Training and Doctrine Command, Fort Monroe, Va., 10 August 1998.

"Department of Defense Dictionary of Military and Associated Terms." Joint Publication 1-02, from the Joint Terminology Master Database as of 10 June 1998.

McCain, John. "Going Hollow: America's Military Returns to the 1970s, an Update." October 1998.

Miller, Laura. "Feminism and the Exclusion of Army Women from Combat." Olin Institute for Strategic Studies, Harvard University (presented to the Presidential Commission on the Assignment of Women in the Armed Forces on 10 September 1992).

Morris, Madeline. "By Force of Arms: Rape, War, and Military Culture." *Duke Law Journal,* February 1996.

Presidential Commission on the Assignment of Women in the Armed Forces. *Report to the President: Women in Combat.* 15 November 1992. Association of the United States Army, 1993.

Secretary of the Army. "Senior Review Panel Report on Sexual Harassment, Volume Two." July 1997.

Index

Index

Index

Index